BUREAU FOR PARANORMAL • RESEARCH AND DEFENSE •

B.P.R.D.: THE DEVIL YOU KNOW
MESSIAH

Created by
MIKE MIGNOLA

The Ogdru Hem stand dead after the defeat of the Ogdru Jahad that came to earth. The B.P.R.D.'s victory cost them the lives of Johann Kraus, Panya, and Kate Corrigan. As the Bureau struggles to rid the world of the remaining monsters, a much larger threat simmers . . .

MIKE MIGNOLA'S

B.P.R.D.

THE DEVIL YOU KNOW

MESSIAH

Story by
MIKE MIGNOLA and **SCOTT ALLIE**

Art by
LAURENCE CAMPBELL

Colors by
DAVE STEWART

Letters by
CLEM ROBINS

Including "BROKEN VESSELS"
art by
TIM SALE

Cover by
LAURENCE CAMPBELL with **DAVE STEWART**

Chapter break art by
DUNCAN FEGREDO

Publisher
MIKE RICHARDSON

Editors
SCOTT ALLIE and **KATII O'BRIEN**

Collection Designer
PATRICK SATTERFIELD

Digital Art Technician
CHRISTINA McKENZIE

DARK HORSE BOOKS

Neil Hankerson EXECUTIVE VICE PRESIDENT • Tom Weddle CHIEF FINANCIAL OFFICER • Randy Stradley VICE PRESIDENT OF PUBLISHING • Nick McWhorter CHIEF BUSINESS DEVELOPMENT OFFICER • Matt Parkinson VICE PRESIDENT OF MARKETING • Dale LaFountain VICE PRESIDENT OF INFORMATION TECHNOLOGY • Cara Niece VICE PRESIDENT OF PRODUCTION AND SCHEDULING • Mark Bernardi VICE PRESIDENT OF BOOK TRADE AND DIGITAL SALES • Ken Lizzi GENERAL COUNSEL • Dave Marshall EDITOR IN CHIEF • Davey Estrada EDITORIAL DIRECTOR • Chris Warner SENIOR BOOKS EDITOR • Cary Grazzini DIRECTOR OF SPECIALTY PROJECTS • Lia Ribacchi ART DIRECTOR • Vanessa Todd DIRECTOR OF PRINT PURCHASING • Matt Dryer DIRECTOR OF DIGITAL ART AND PREPRESS • Michael Gombos DIRECTOR OF INTERNATIONAL PUBLISHING AND LICENSING • Kari Yadro DIRECTOR OF CUSTOM PROGRAMS

DarkHorse.com   Facebook.com/DarkHorseComics   Twitter.com/DarkHorseComics

B.P.R.D. THE DEVIL YOU KNOW VOLUME 1: MESSIAH

This book collects *B.P.R.D.: The Devil You Know* #1–#5 and "Broken Vessels" from the *Hellboy Winter Special* 2016.

Published by Dark Horse Books
A division of Dark Horse Comics, Inc.
10956 SE Main Street
Milwaukie, OR 97222

International Licensing: (503) 905-2377
Comic Shop Locator Service: comicshoplocator.com

First edition: April 2018
ISBN: 978-1-50670-196-7

10 9 8 7 6 5 4 3 2 1
Printed in China

Library of Congress Cataloging-in-Publication Data

Names: Mignola, Michael, author. | Allie, Scott, author. | Campbell,
  Laurence, 1969- artist. | Stewart, Dave, colourist. | Robins, Clem, 1955-
  letterer. | Sale, Tim, artist. | Fegredo, Duncan, artist.
Title: Messiah / story by Mike Mignola and Scott Allie ; art by Laurence
  Campbell ; colors by Dave Stewart ; letters by Clem Robins ; including
  "Broken Vessels" art by Tim Sale ; cover by Laurence Campbell with Dave
  Stewart ; chapter break art by Duncan Fegredo.
Description: First edition. | Milwaukie, OR : Dark Horse Books, April 2018. |
  Series: B.P.R.D. The devil you know ; Volume 1 | "This book collects
  B.P.R.D.: The Devil You Know #1-#5 and "Broken Vessels" from the Hellboy
  Winter Special 2016."
Identifiers: LCCN 2017051680 | ISBN 9781506701967 (paperback)
Subjects: LCSH: Comic books, strips, etc. | BISAC: COMICS & GRAPHIC NOVELS /
  Horror.
Classification: LCC PN6727.M53 M47 2018 | DDC 741.5/973--dc23
LC record available at https://lccn.loc.gov/2017051680

CHAPTER ONE

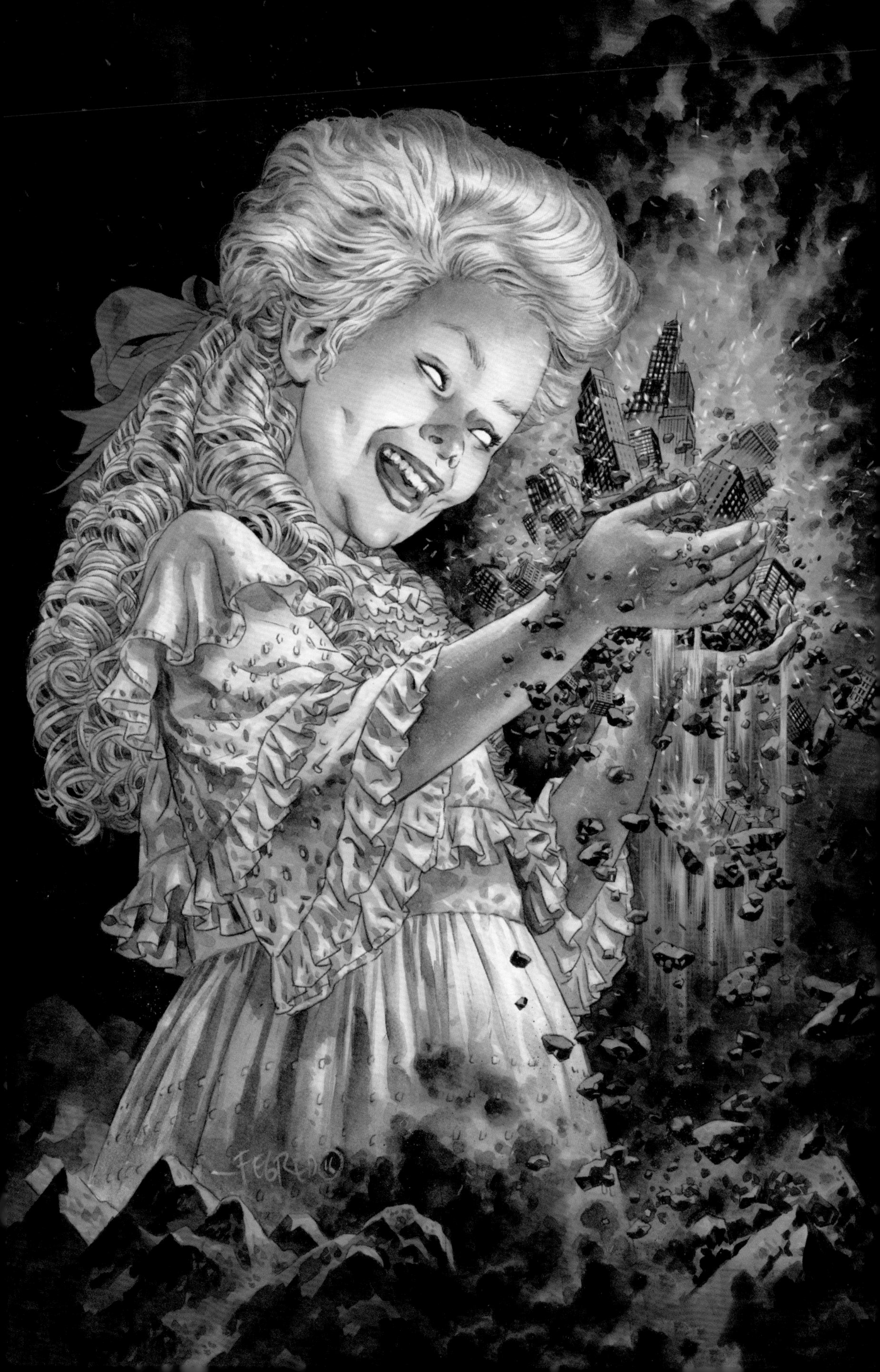

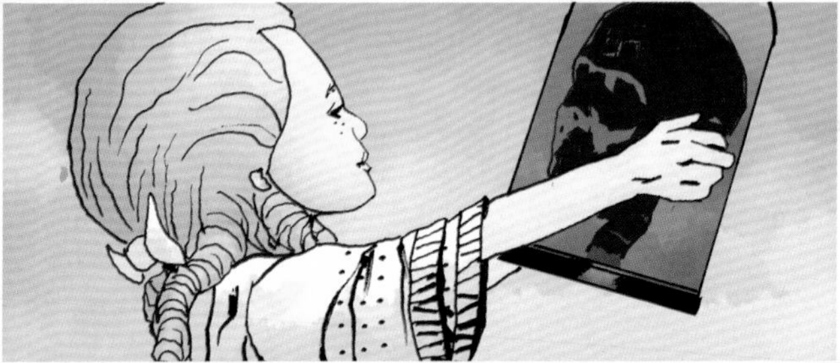

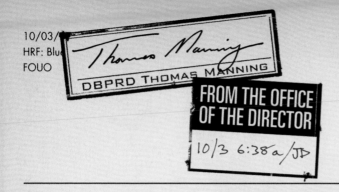

found there and the request to search the area is granted. Primary objective remains the placement of the explosives and documentation by drone of the aftermath--after the search party and all personnel are at a distant remove from the area. Important: be well clear before detonating. DOD and DHS are confident there are no settlers in the area to be placed at risk, an observation your team should confirm in recon.

After Parkinson, domestic cult activity is your top priority. Due to the nature of these cults, no other organization is better equipped to assess than your team, with exceptions: continue to refer revenant groups in the SW and elsewhere to the National Guard directly or through this office, and the president would prefer all Sapien cult activity be handled by DHS to avoid conflicts. Your help is requested in investigating reports of activity centered around an unidentified young woman who has "appeared in dreams" nationwide. Specialists in the DC office confirm these dreams, which direct dreamers toward an unspecified spot on the east coast, possibly the northeast. Currently the largest such group is heading east on I-80 through Nebraska and bear investigating. We suspected a connection to the group led by your former ward, but as Fenix has dispersed that group and is believed to remain in N. Calif., this is unlikely.

An unrelated group in Taos, NM died in a mass suicide--232 total including children. The president appreciates any help we can provide in stopping events like this, which do not bolster his message that conditions are improving.

We might need your vessel, if not your team, in the Red Sea. Some survivors in Eritrea are reluctant to flee. They reached out to Russia, who are exerting their option to temporarily recall the ship, though negotiations continue. FYI, Iran claims President Afwerki gave his blessing for the strike, knowing his country was doomed and that this was the only way to spare the region. CIA confirms. Devastating. Afwerki himself made no attempt to flee. Will he be remembered as a lunatic or a man of unusual courage?

The review of the incident in Wichita Falls is complete: no loss of life could have been prevented through alternative courses of action. However, this cannot be stated emphatically enough: No one in our Bureau except myself or any acting replacement can make a unilateral decision of such magnitude. Agent Sherman has been exonerated, but she's to remain on a probationary status until further instructions. She cannot lead missions into populated areas, but permission is granted for her to lead in Parkinson. Important that the team uses the specified explosives rather than incineration, so that the results can be duplicated in other locations. If Parkinson goes as expected we hope to destroy and remove the remains

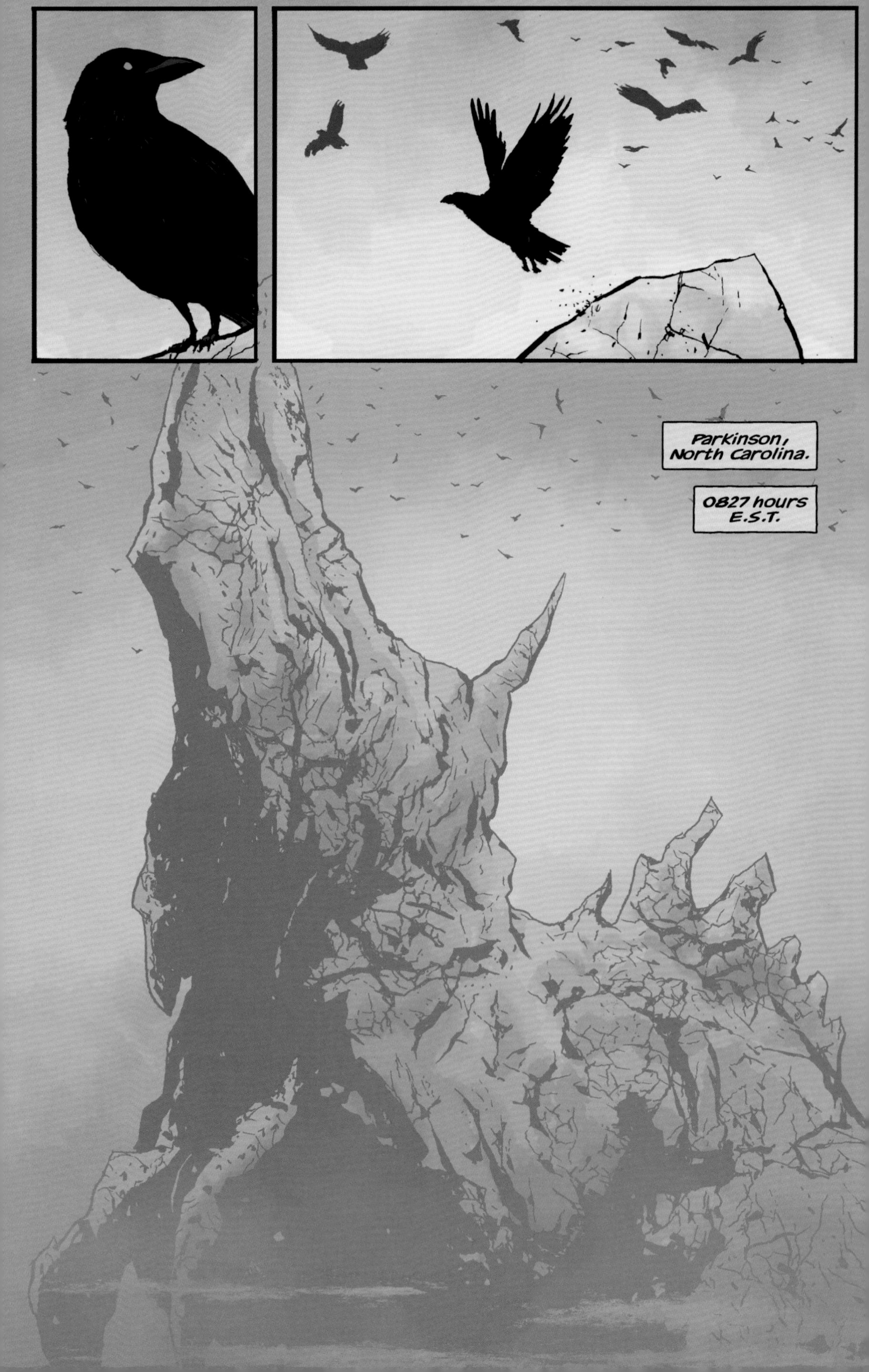

Parkinson, North Carolina.
0827 hours E.S.T.

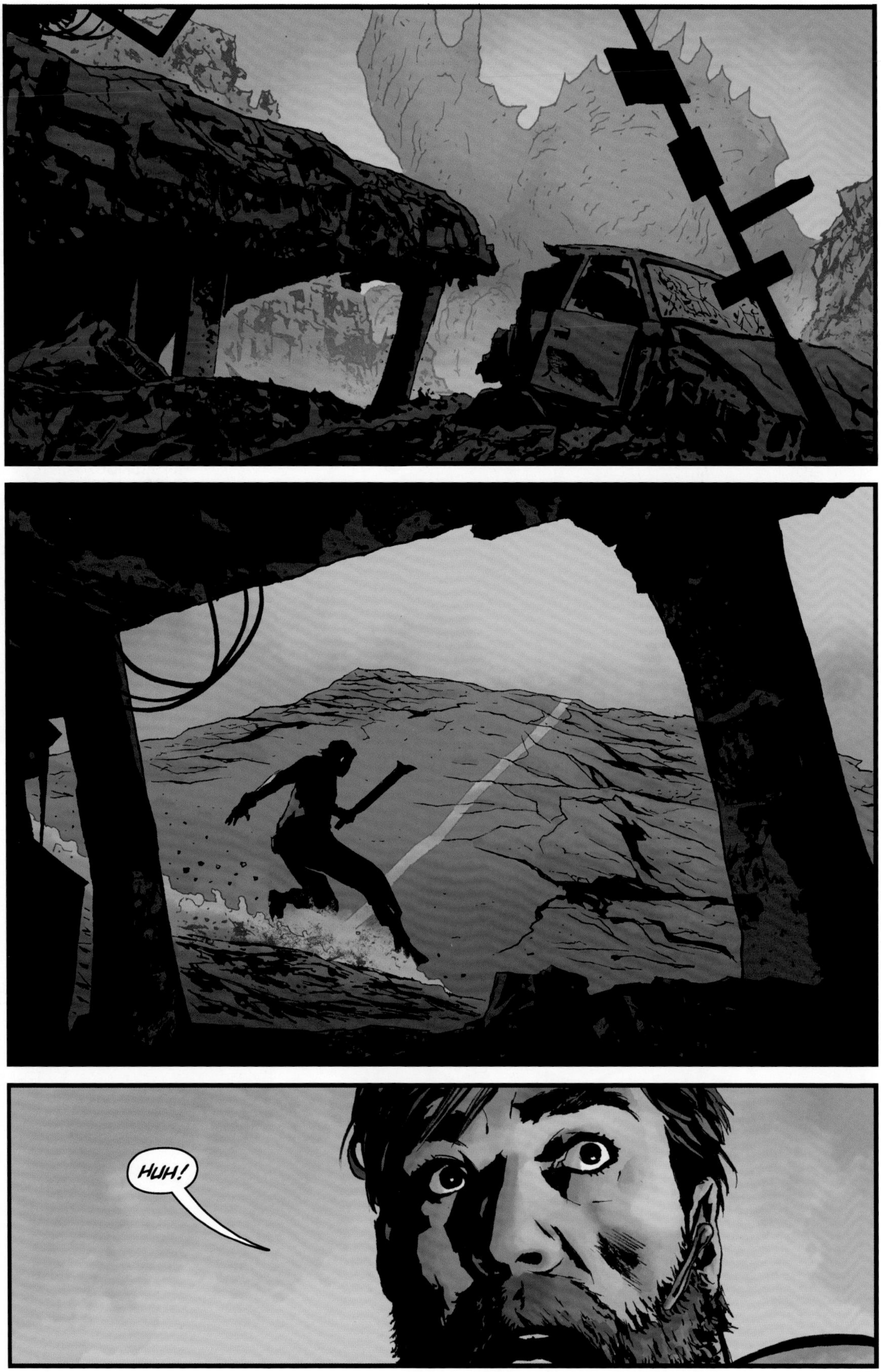
HUH!

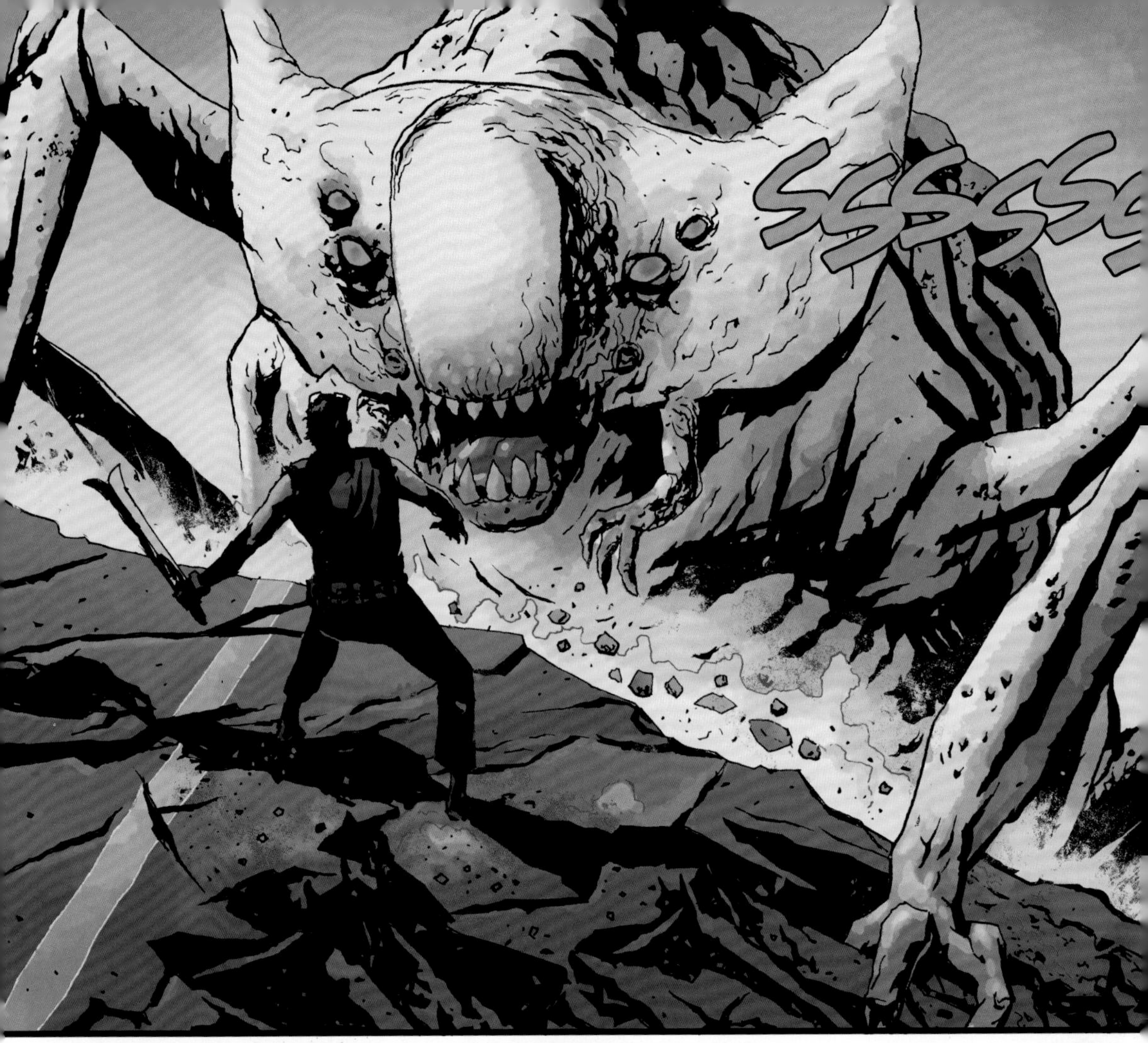
SSSSSS
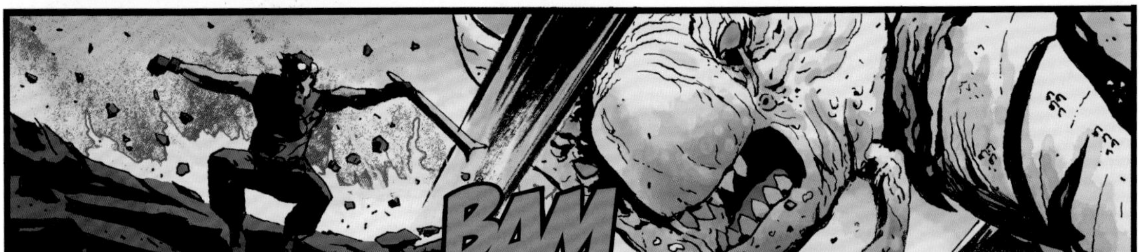
BAM
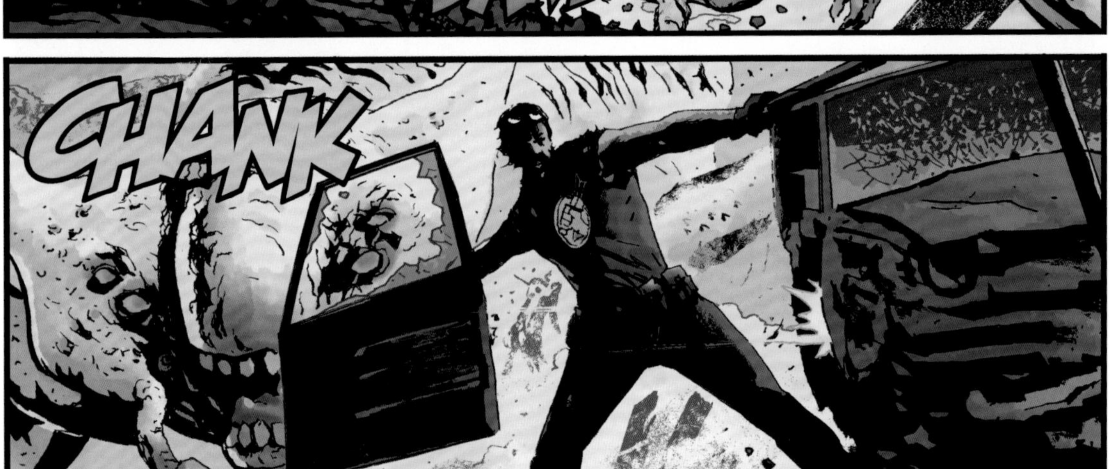
CHANK

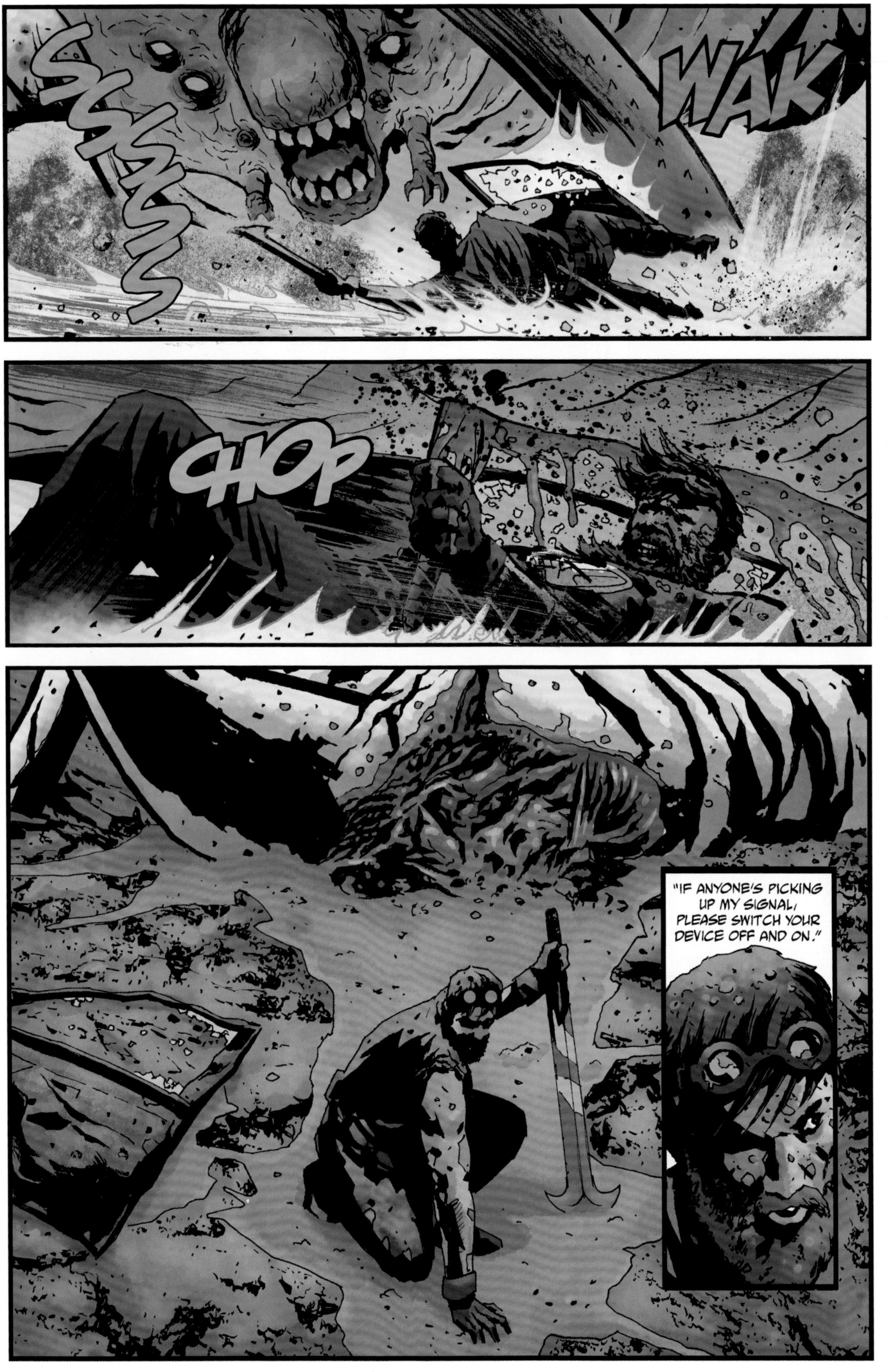
SSSSSSS
WAK
CHOP
"IF ANYONE'S PICKING UP MY SIGNAL, PLEASE SWITCH YOUR DEVICE OFF AND ON."

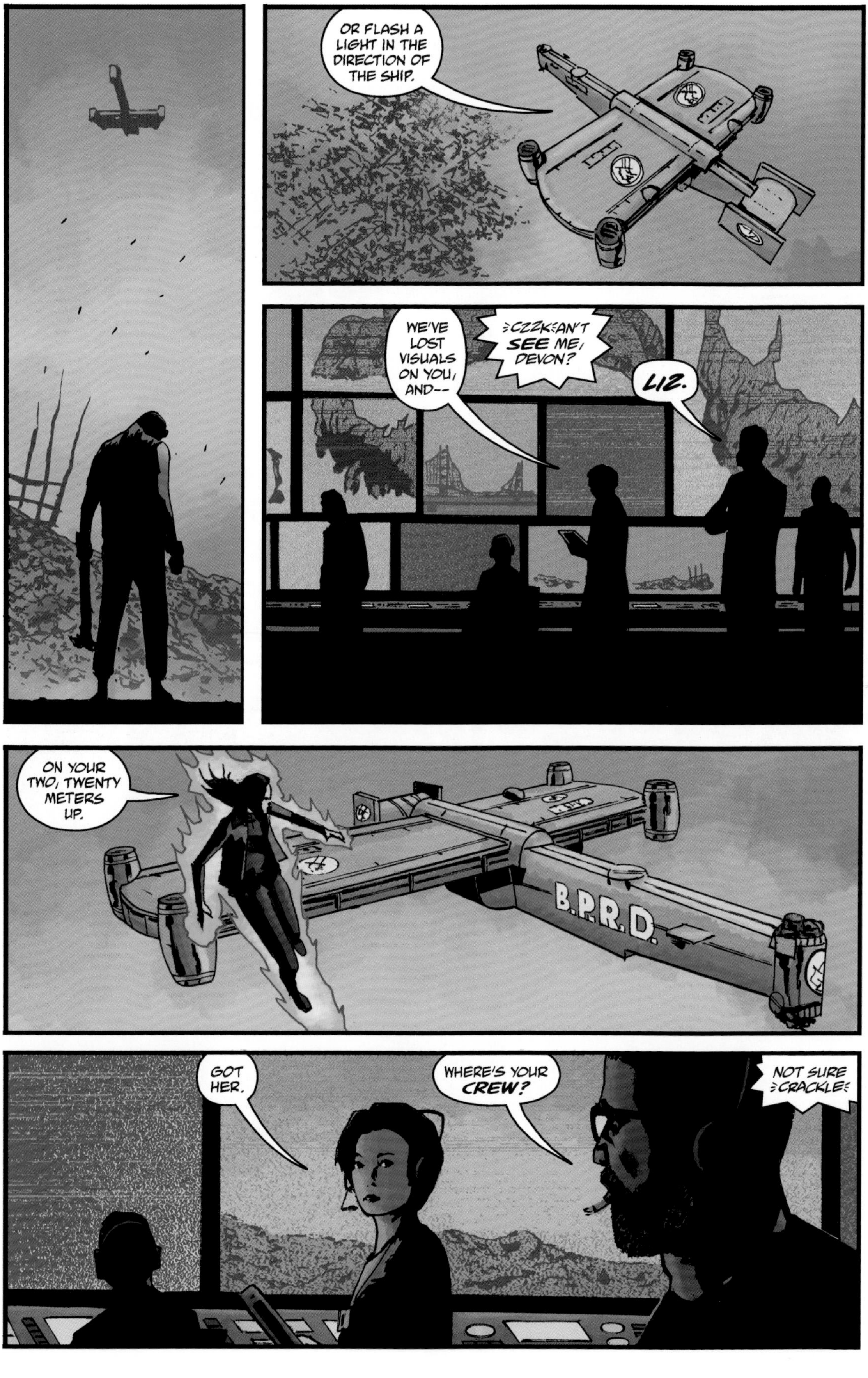
OR FLASH A LIGHT IN THE DIRECTION OF THE SHIP.
WE'VE LOST VISUALS ON YOU, AND--
CZZK AN'T SEE ME, DEVON?
LIZ.
ON YOUR TWO, TWENTY METERS UP.
B.P.R.D.
GOT HER.
WHERE'S YOUR CREW?
NOT SURE CRACKLE

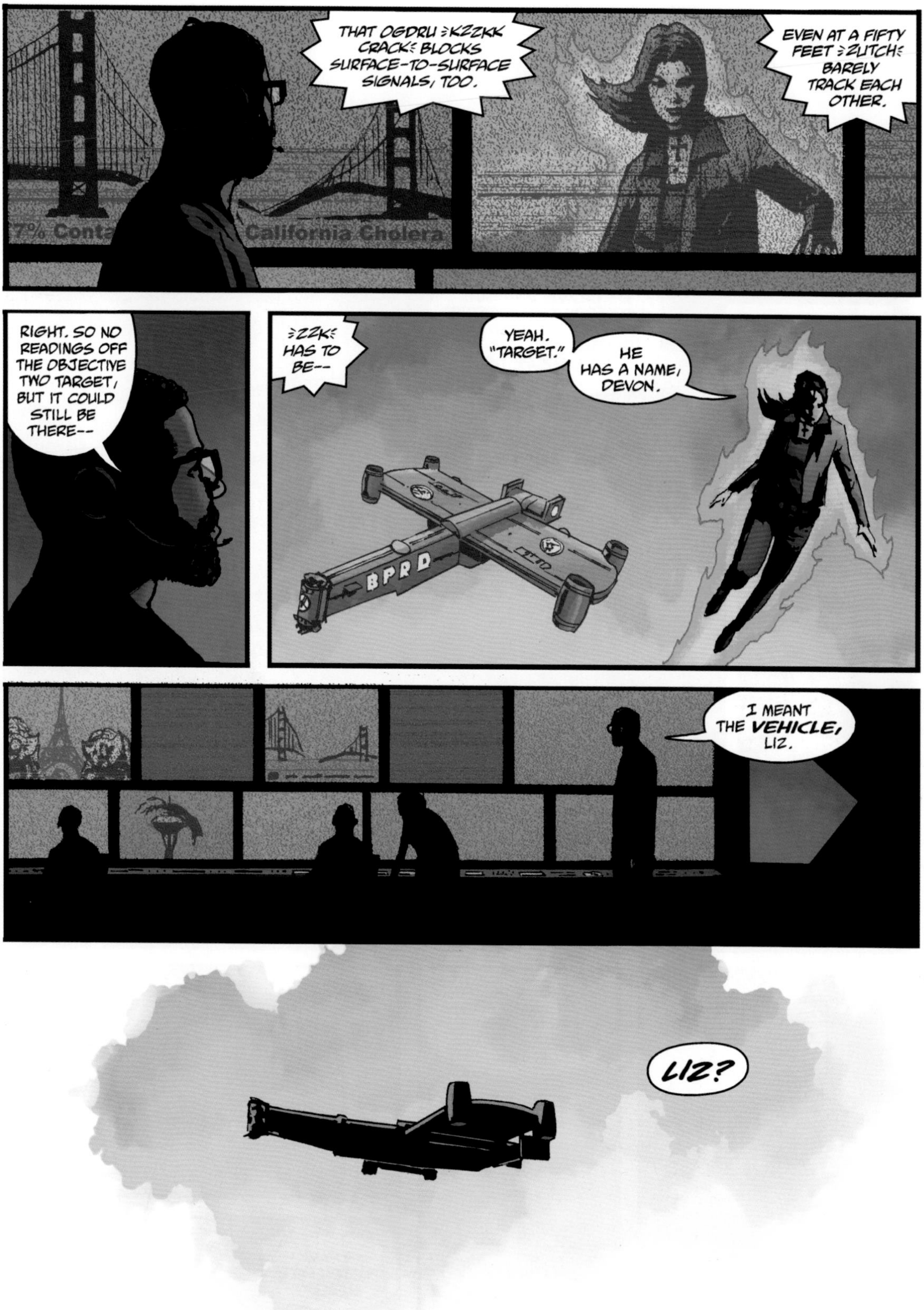
THAT OGDRU ≶KZZKK CRACK≶ BLOCKS SURFACE-TO-SURFACE SIGNALS, TOO.
California Cholera
EVEN AT A FIFTY FEET ≶ZUTCH≶ BARELY TRACK EACH OTHER.
RIGHT. SO NO READINGS OFF THE OBJECTIVE TWO TARGET, BUT IT COULD STILL BE THERE--
≶ZZK≶ HAS TO BE--
YEAH. "TARGET."
HE HAS A NAME, DEVON.
BPRD
I MEANT THE **VEHICLE,** LIZ.
LIZ?

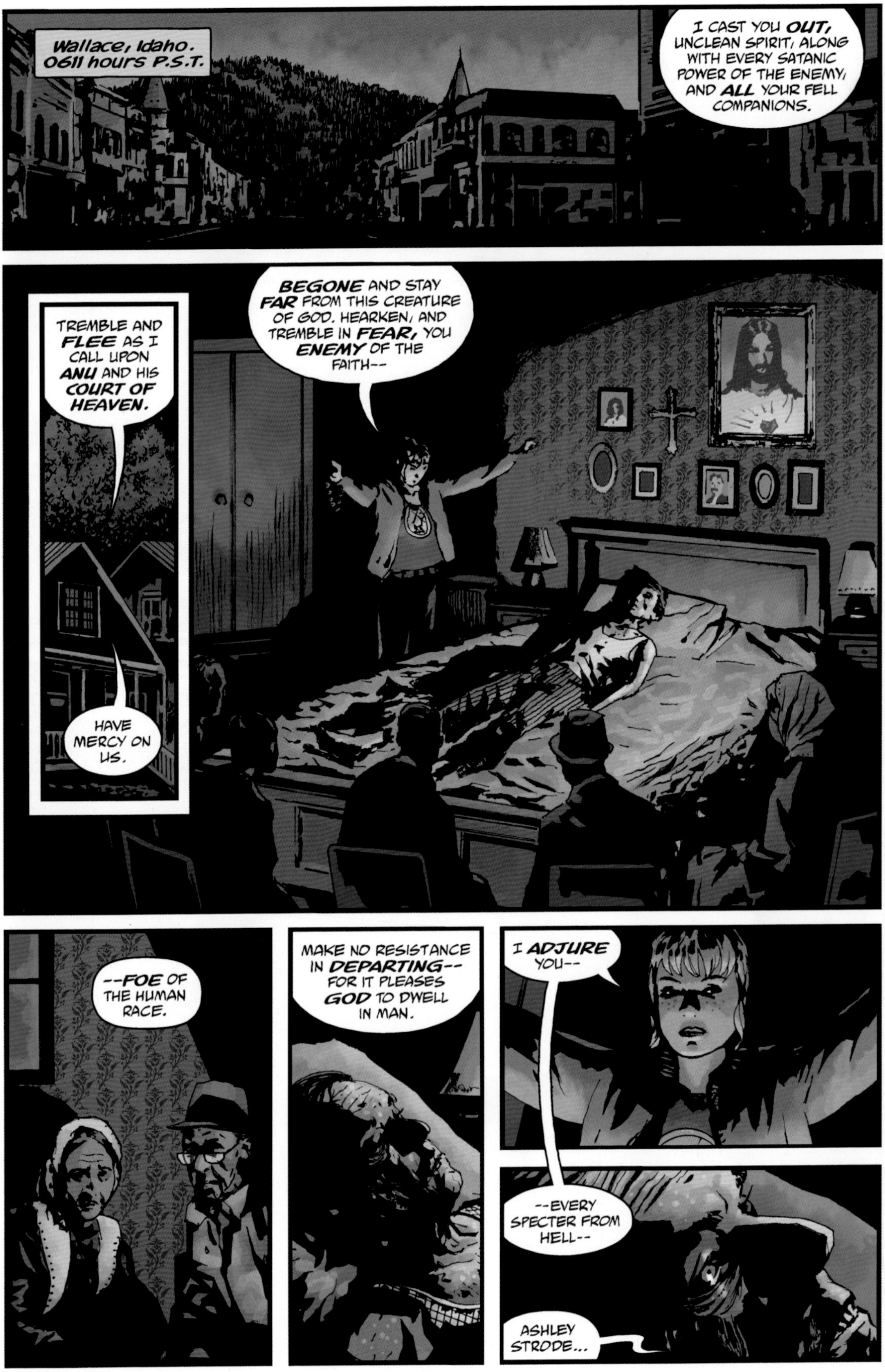
Wallace, Idaho. 0611 hours P.S.T.
I CAST YOU OUT, UNCLEAN SPIRIT, ALONG WITH EVERY SATANIC POWER OF THE ENEMY, AND ALL YOUR FELL COMPANIONS.
TREMBLE AND FLEE AS I CALL UPON ANU AND HIS COURT OF HEAVEN.
BEGONE AND STAY FAR FROM THIS CREATURE OF GOD. HEARKEN, AND TREMBLE IN FEAR, YOU ENEMY OF THE FAITH--
HAVE MERCY ON US.
--FOE OF THE HUMAN RACE.
MAKE NO RESISTANCE IN DEPARTING-- FOR IT PLEASES GOD TO DWELL IN MAN.
I ADJURE YOU--
--EVERY SPECTER FROM HELL--
ASHLEY STRODE...

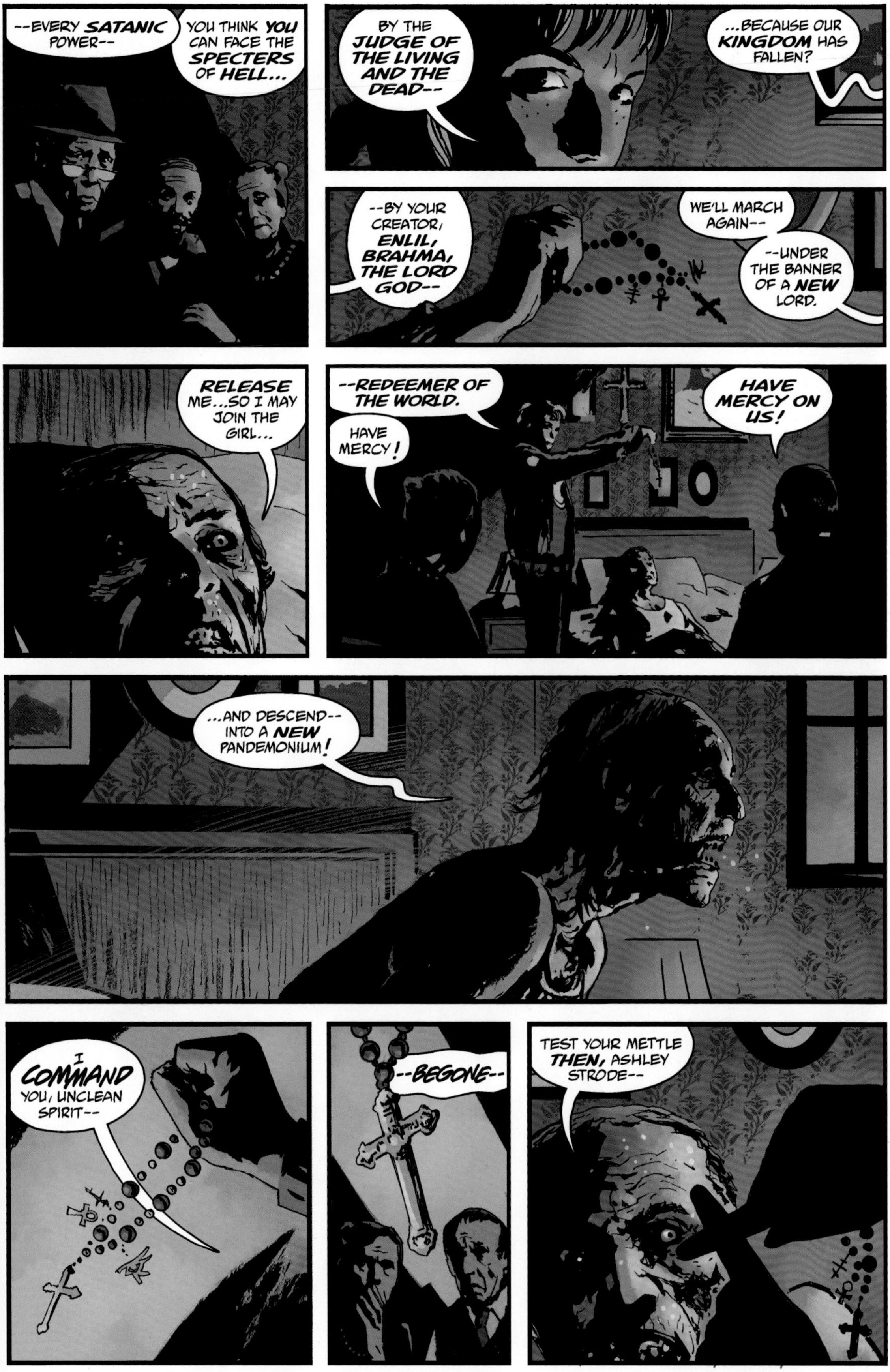
--EVERY SATANIC POWER--
YOU THINK YOU CAN FACE THE SPECTERS OF HELL...
BY THE JUDGE OF THE LIVING AND THE DEAD--
...BECAUSE OUR KINGDOM HAS FALLEN?
--BY YOUR CREATOR, ENLIL, BRAHMA, THE LORD GOD--
WE'LL MARCH AGAIN--
--UNDER THE BANNER OF A NEW LORD.
RELEASE ME...SO I MAY JOIN THE GIRL...
--REDEEMER OF THE WORLD.
HAVE MERCY!
HAVE MERCY ON US!
...AND DESCEND-- INTO A NEW PANDEMONIUM!
I COMMAND YOU, UNCLEAN SPIRIT--
--BEGONE--
TEST YOUR METTLE THEN, ASHLEY STRODE--

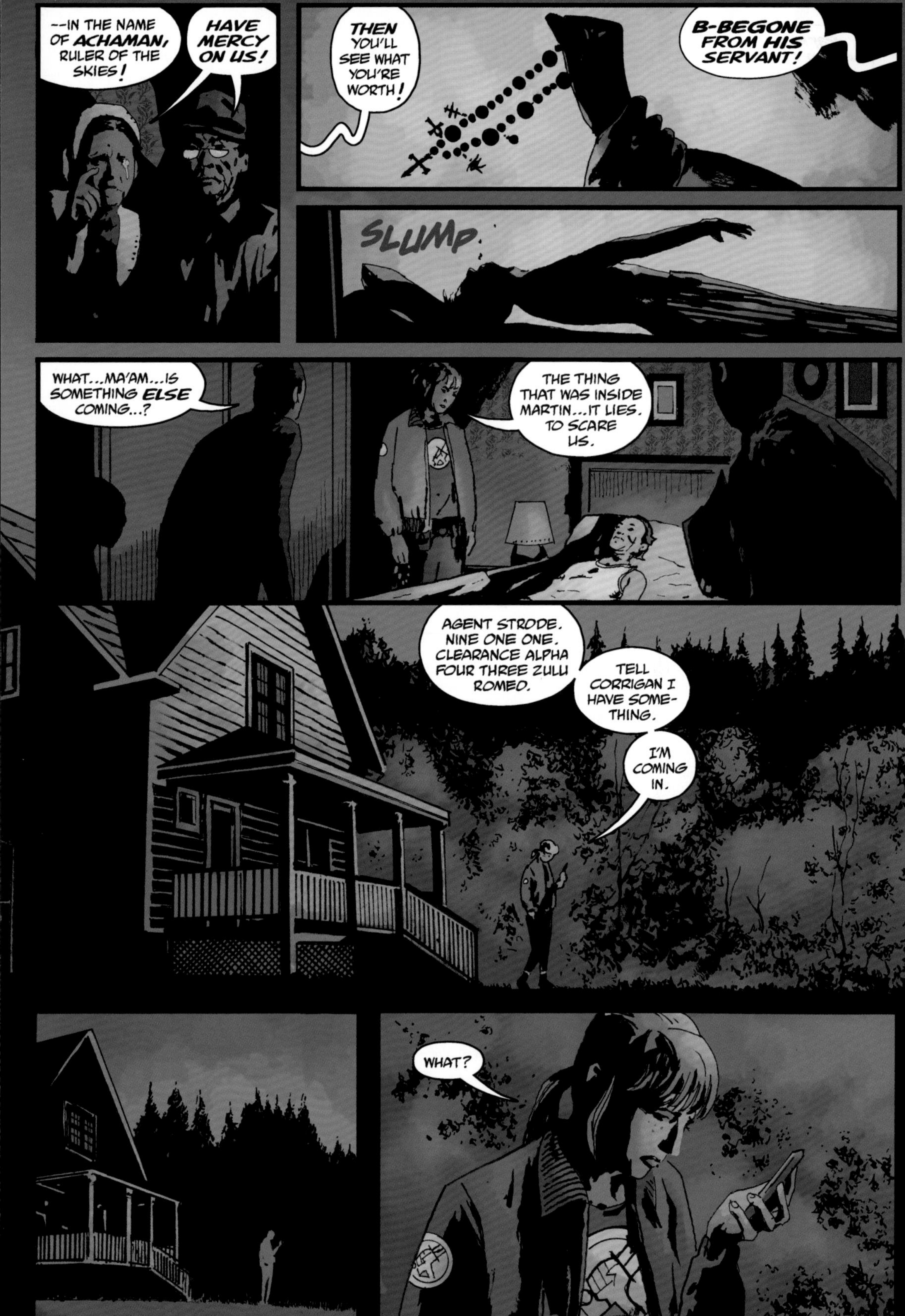
--IN THE NAME OF ACHAMAN, RULER OF THE SKIES!
HAVE MERCY ON US!
THEN YOU'LL SEE WHAT YOU'RE WORTH!
B-BEGONE FROM HIS SERVANT!
SLUMP
WHAT... MA'AM... IS SOMETHING ELSE COMING...?
THE THING THAT WAS INSIDE MARTIN... IT LIES. TO SCARE US.
AGENT STRODE. NINE ONE ONE. CLEARANCE ALPHA FOUR THREE ZULU ROMEO.
TELL CORRIGAN I HAVE SOME-THING.
I'M COMING IN.
WHAT?

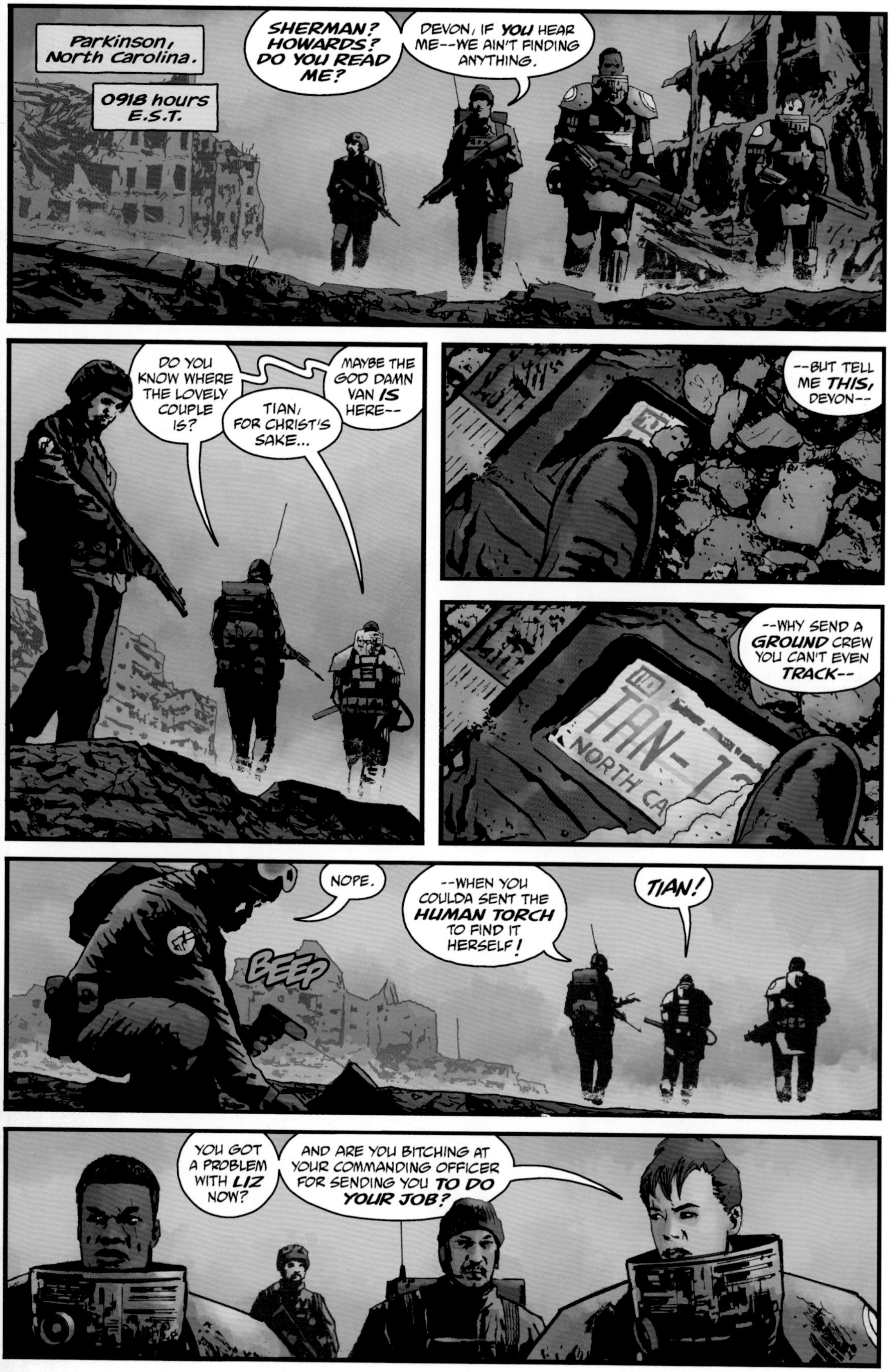
Parkinson, North Carolina.
0918 hours E.S.T.
SHERMAN? HOWARDS? DO YOU READ ME?
DEVON, IF YOU HEAR ME--WE AIN'T FINDING ANYTHING.
DO YOU KNOW WHERE THE LOVELY COUPLE IS?
MAYBE THE GOD DAMN VAN IS HERE--
TIAN, FOR CHRIST'S SAKE...
--BUT TELL ME THIS, DEVON--
--WHY SEND A GROUND CREW YOU CAN'T EVEN TRACK--
NORTH CA
BEEP
NOPE.
--WHEN YOU COULDA SENT THE HUMAN TORCH TO FIND IT HERSELF!
TIAN!
YOU GOT A PROBLEM WITH LIZ NOW?
AND ARE YOU BITCHING AT YOUR COMMANDING OFFICER FOR SENDING YOU TO DO YOUR JOB?

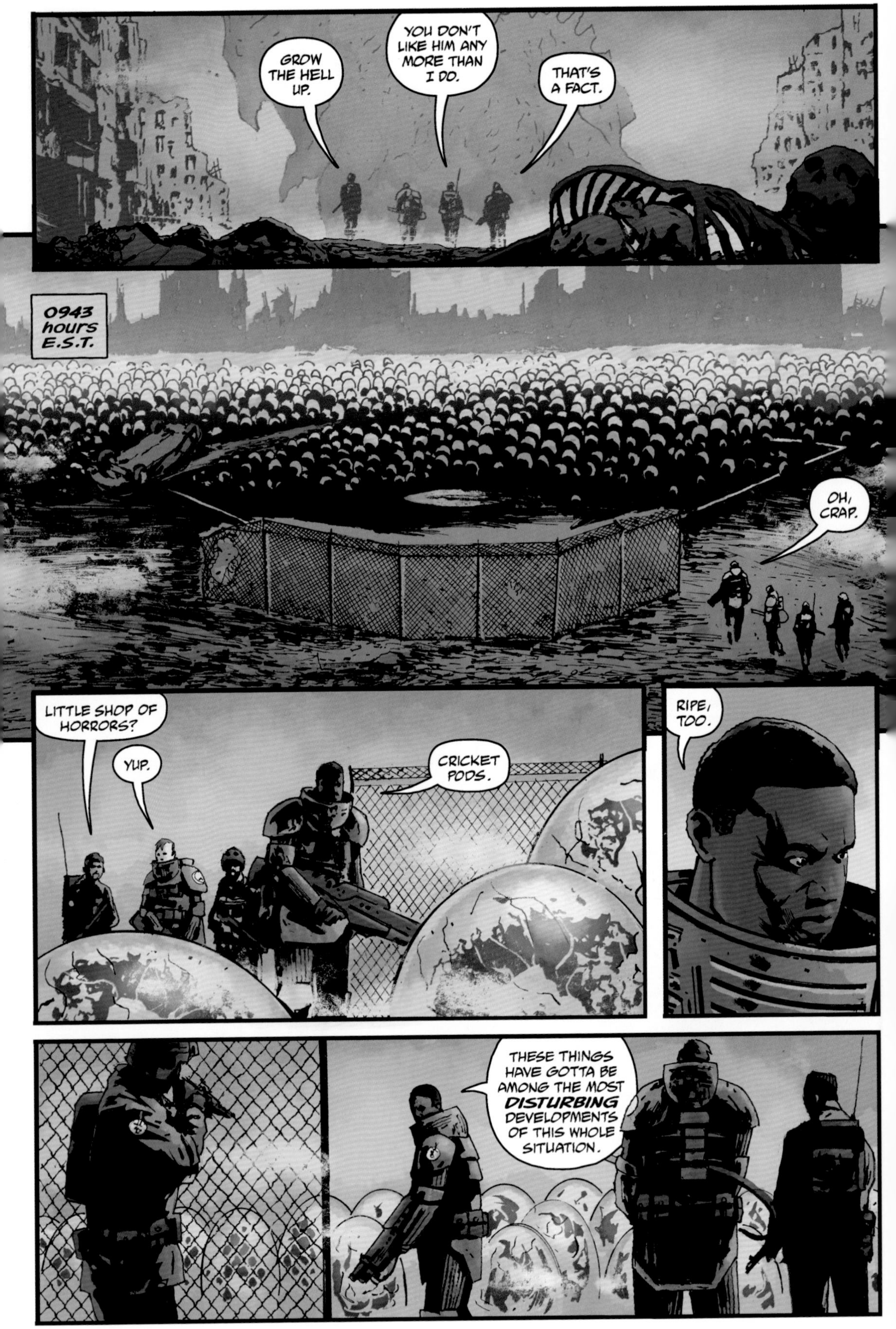
GROW THE HELL UP.
YOU DON'T LIKE HIM ANY MORE THAN I DO.
THAT'S A FACT.
0943 hours E.S.T.
OH, CRAP.
LITTLE SHOP OF HORRORS?
YUP.
CRICKET PODS.
RIPE, TOO.
THESE THINGS HAVE GOTTA BE AMONG THE MOST DISTURBING DEVELOPMENTS OF THIS WHOLE SITUATION.

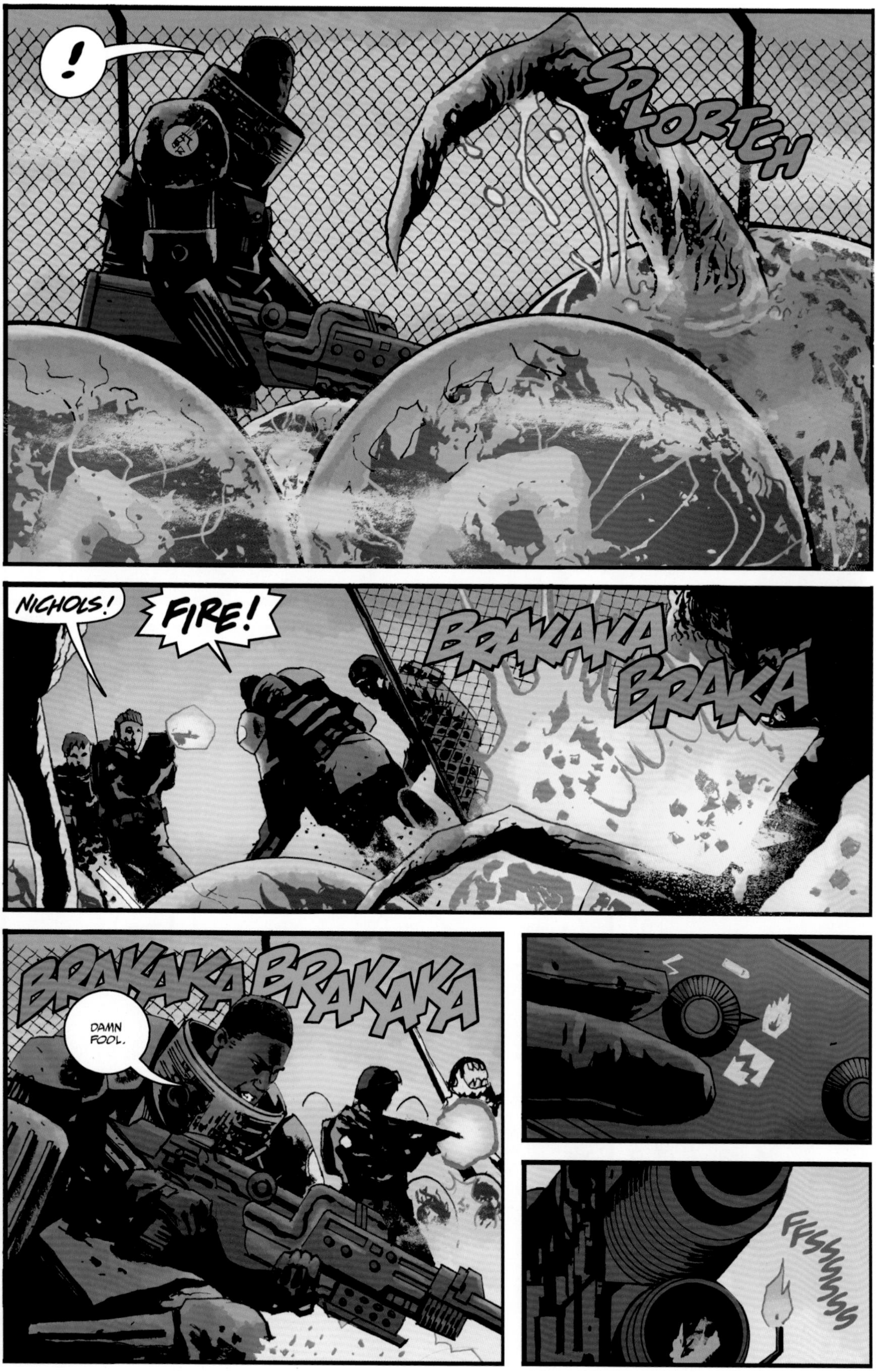
!
SPLORTCH
NICHOLS!
FIRE!
BRAKAKA
BRAKA
BRAKAKA BRAKAKA
DAMN FOOL.
FFSSSSSSS

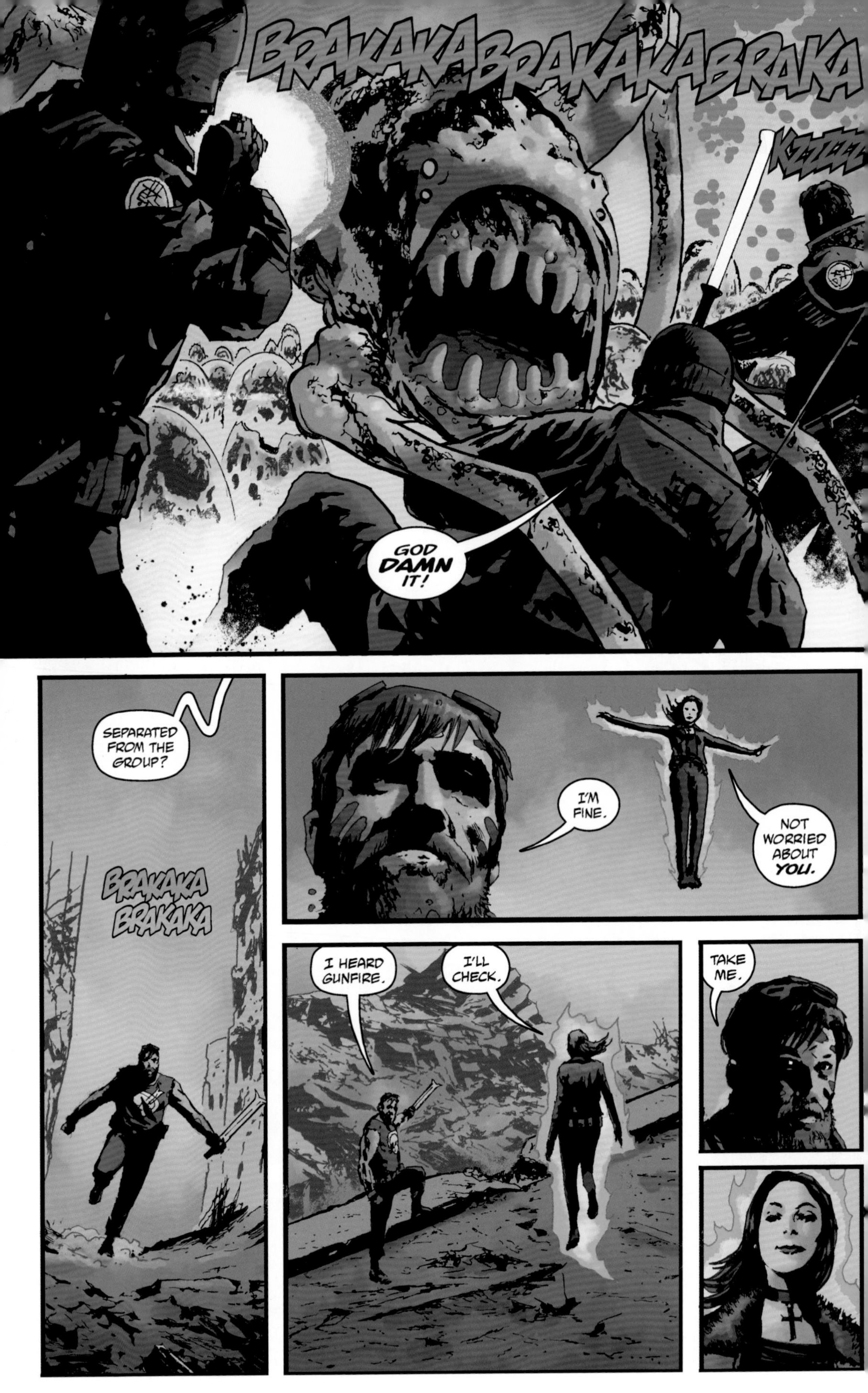

BRAKAKA BRAKAKA BRAKA
KZZZZT
GOD DAMN IT!
SEPARATED FROM THE GROUP?
BRAKAKA BRAKAKA
I'M FINE.
NOT WORRIED ABOUT YOU.
I HEARD GUNFIRE.
I'LL CHECK.
TAKE ME.

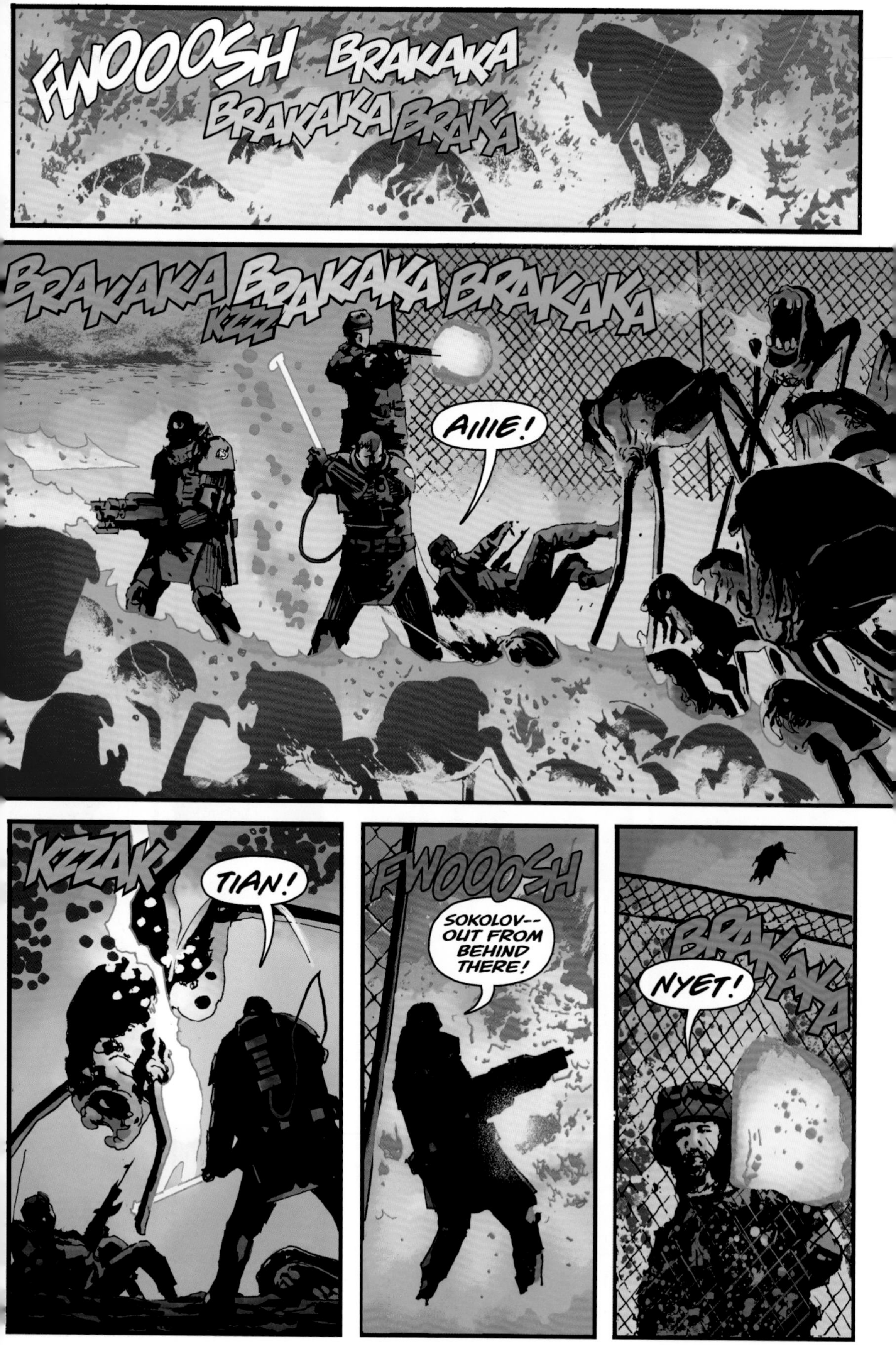
FWOOOSH
BRAKAKA
BRAKAKA BRAKA
BRAKAKA
BRAKAKA
KZZZ
BRAKAKA
AIIIE!
KZZZAK
TIAN!
FWOOOSH
SOKOLOV-- OUT FROM BEHIND THERE!
BRAKAKA
NYET!

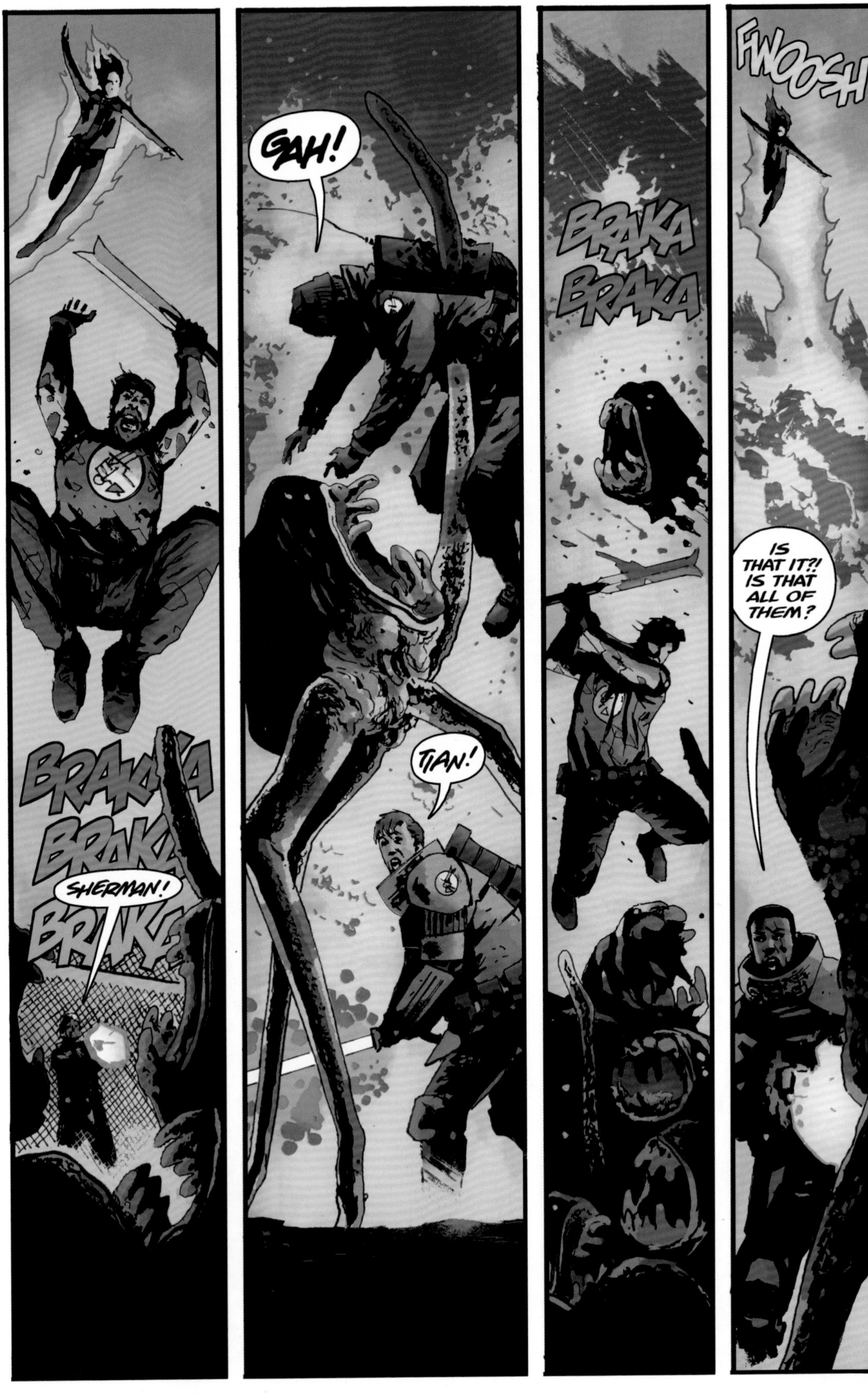
BRAKA
BRAKA
SHERMAN!
BRAKA
GAH!
TIAN!
BRAKA
BRAKA
FWOOSH
IS THAT IT?! IS THAT ALL OF THEM?

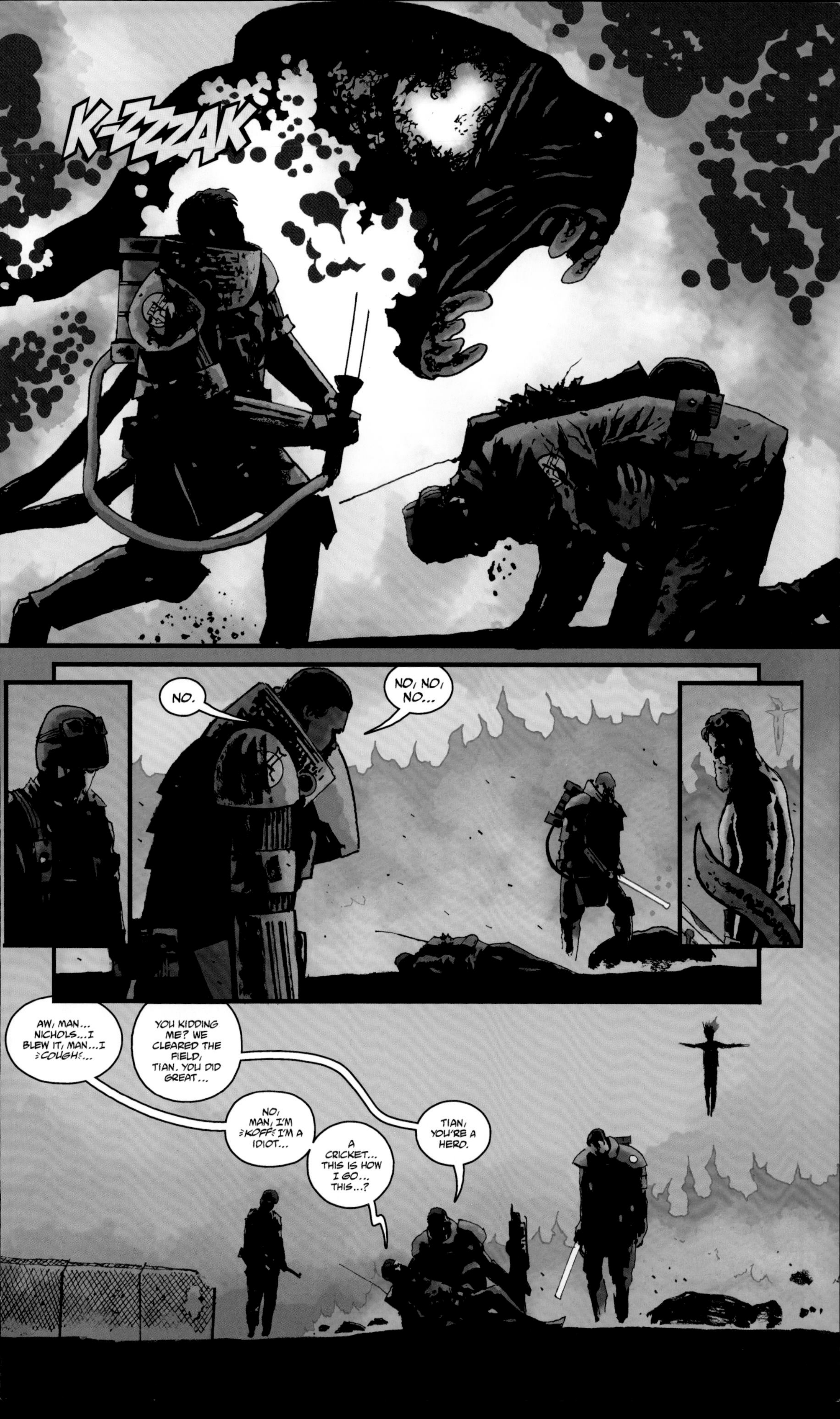
K-ZZZAK
NO.
NO, NO, NO...
AW, MAN... NICHOLS...I BLEW IT, MAN...I *COUGH*...
YOU KIDDING ME? WE CLEARED THE FIELD, TIAN. YOU DID GREAT...
NO, MAN, I'M *KOFF* I'M A IDIOT...
A CRICKET... THIS IS HOW I GO... THIS...?
TIAN, YOU'RE A HERO.

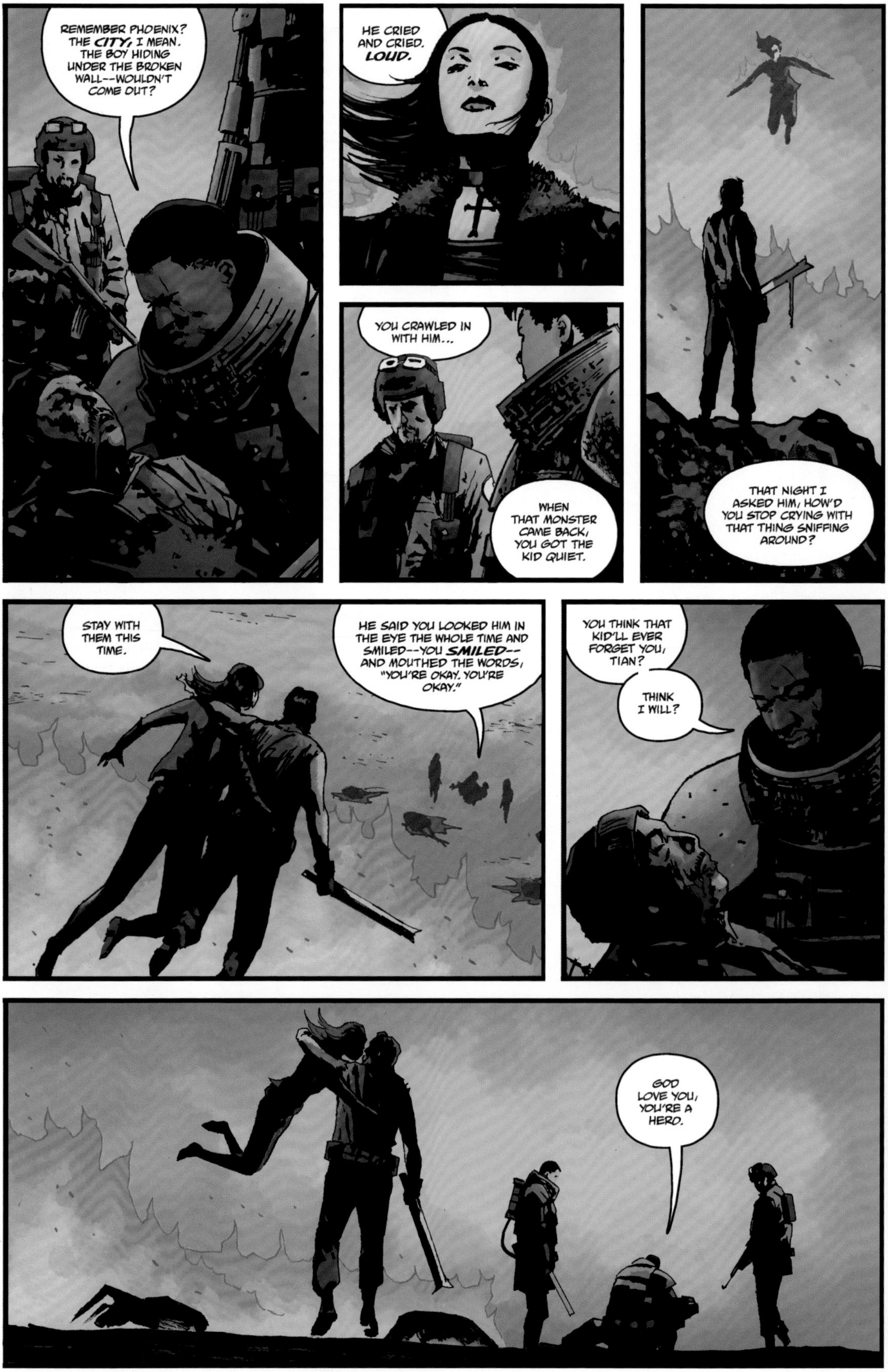
REMEMBER PHOENIX? THE CITY, I MEAN. THE BOY HIDING UNDER THE BROKEN WALL--WOULDN'T COME OUT?
HE CRIED AND CRIED. LOUD.
YOU CRAWLED IN WITH HIM...
WHEN THAT MONSTER CAME BACK, YOU GOT THE KID QUIET.
THAT NIGHT I ASKED HIM, HOW'D YOU STOP CRYING WITH THAT THING SNIFFING AROUND?
STAY WITH THEM THIS TIME.
HE SAID YOU LOOKED HIM IN THE EYE THE WHOLE TIME AND SMILED--YOU SMILED--AND MOUTHED THE WORDS, "YOU'RE OKAY. YOU'RE OKAY."
YOU THINK THAT KID'LL EVER FORGET YOU, TIAN?
THINK I WILL?
GOD LOVE YOU, YOU'RE A HERO.

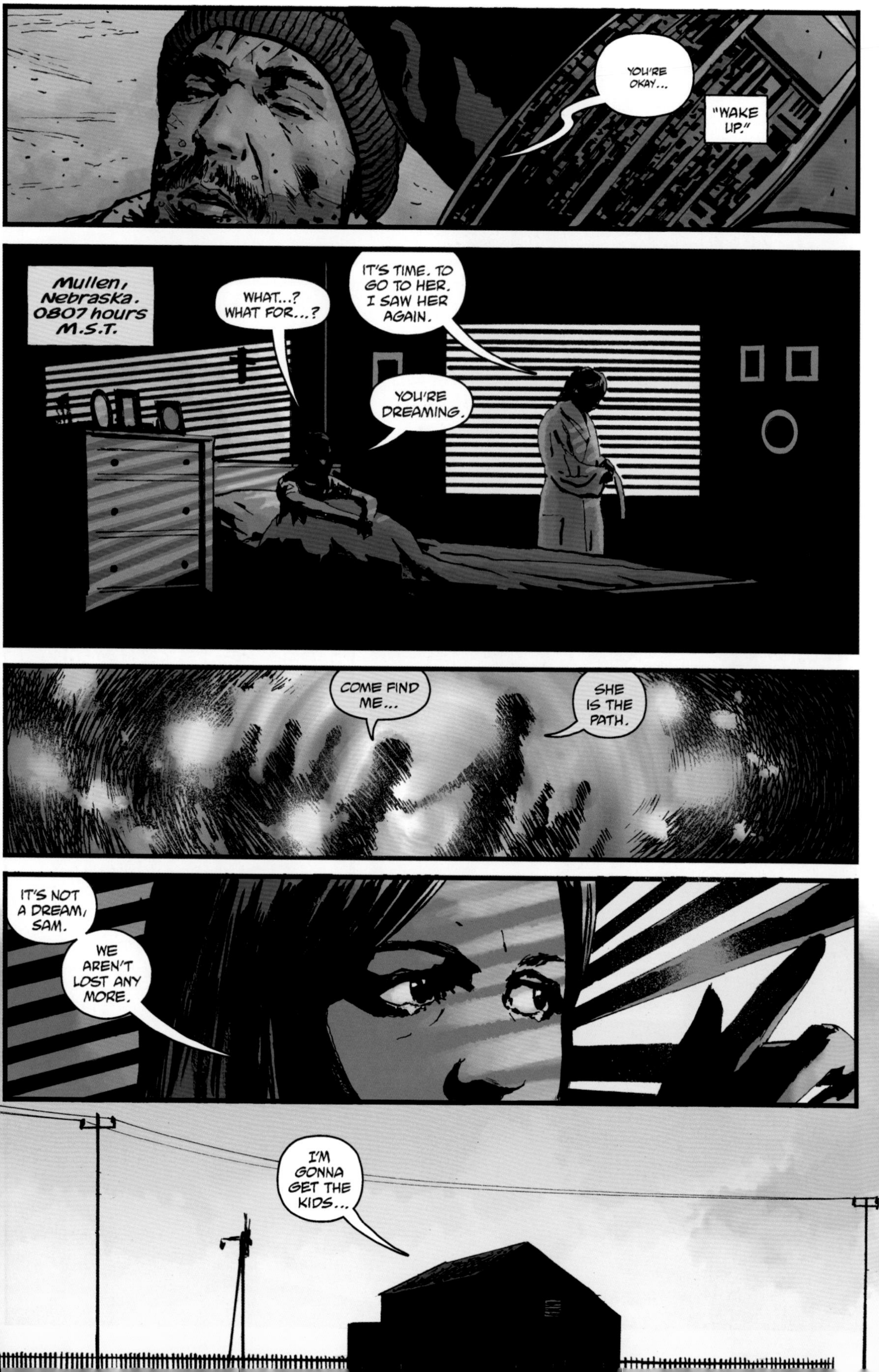
YOU'RE OKAY...
"WAKE UP."
Mullen, Nebraska. 0807 hours M.S.T.
WHAT...? WHAT FOR...?
IT'S TIME. TO GO TO HER. I SAW HER AGAIN.
YOU'RE DREAMING.
COME FIND ME...
SHE IS THE PATH.
IT'S NOT A DREAM, SAM.
WE AREN'T LOST ANY MORE.
I'M GONNA GET THE KIDS...

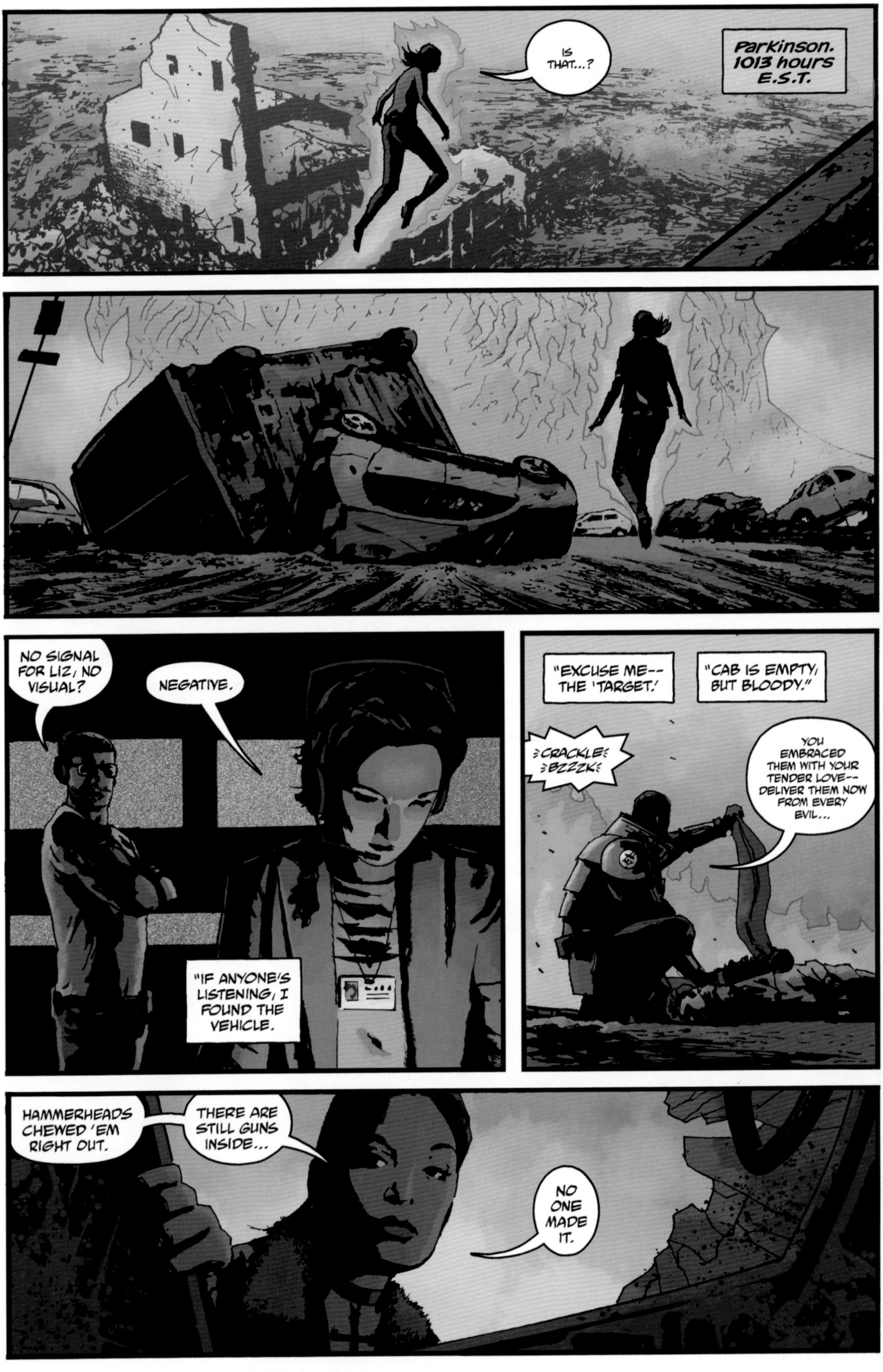
Parkinson. 1013 hours E.S.T.
IS THAT...?
NO SIGNAL FOR LIZ, NO VISUAL?
NEGATIVE.
"IF ANYONE'S LISTENING, I FOUND THE VEHICLE.
"EXCUSE ME-- THE 'TARGET.'
"CAB IS EMPTY, BUT BLOODY."
CRACKLE BZZZK
YOU EMBRACED THEM WITH YOUR TENDER LOVE-- DELIVER THEM NOW FROM EVERY EVIL...
HAMMERHEADS CHEWED 'EM RIGHT OUT.
THERE ARE STILL GUNS INSIDE...
NO ONE MADE IT.

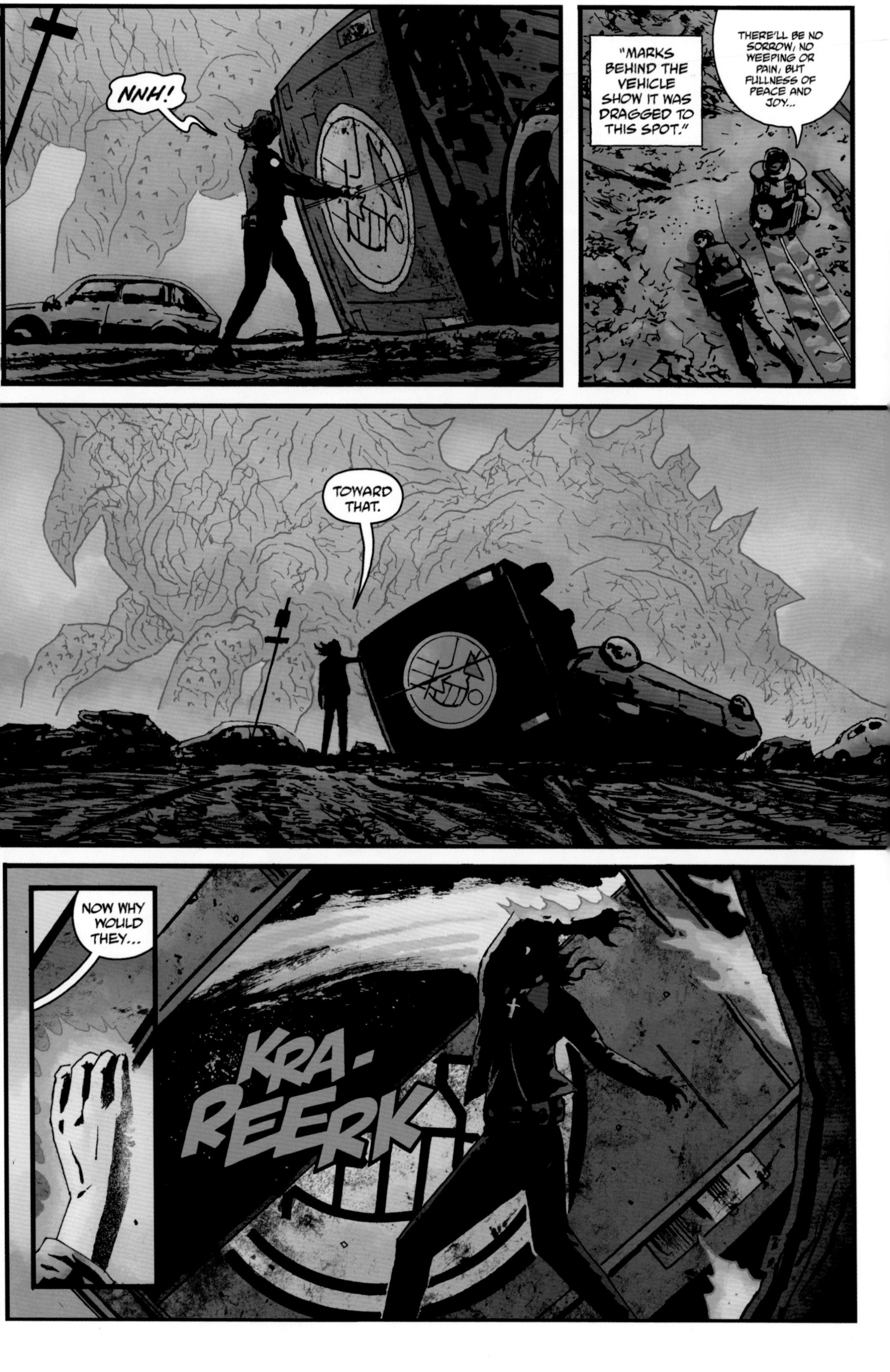
NNH!
"MARKS BEHIND THE VEHICLE SHOW IT WAS DRAGGED TO THIS SPOT."
THERE'LL BE NO SORROW, NO WEEPING OR PAIN, BUT FULLNESS OF PEACE AND JOY...
TOWARD THAT.
NOW WHY WOULD THEY...
KRA-REERK

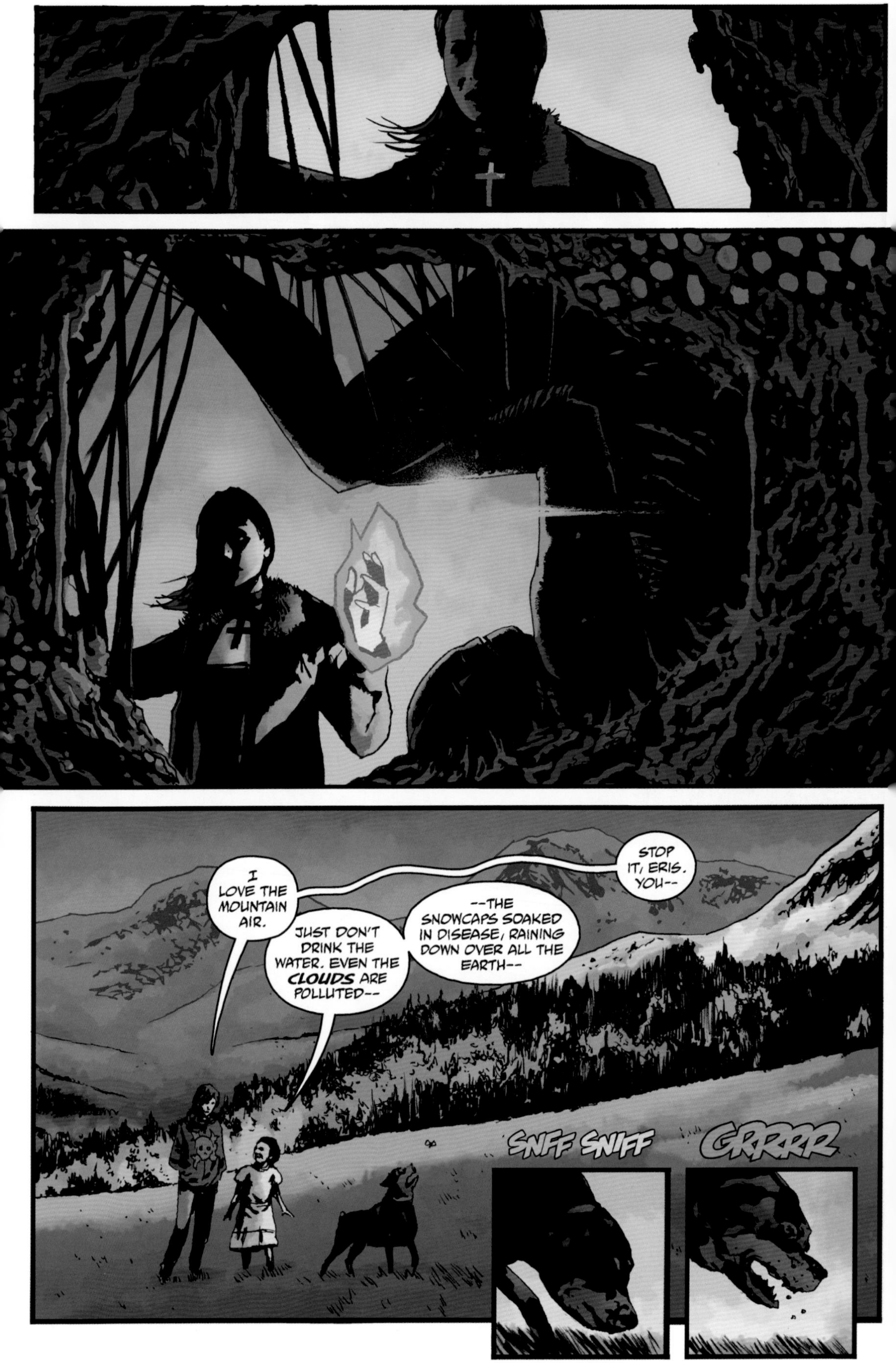
I LOVE THE MOUNTAIN AIR.
STOP IT, ERIS. YOU--
JUST DON'T DRINK THE WATER. EVEN THE **CLOUDS** ARE POLLUTED--
--THE SNOWCAPS SOAKED IN DISEASE, RAINING DOWN OVER ALL THE EARTH--
SNFF SNIFF
GRRRR

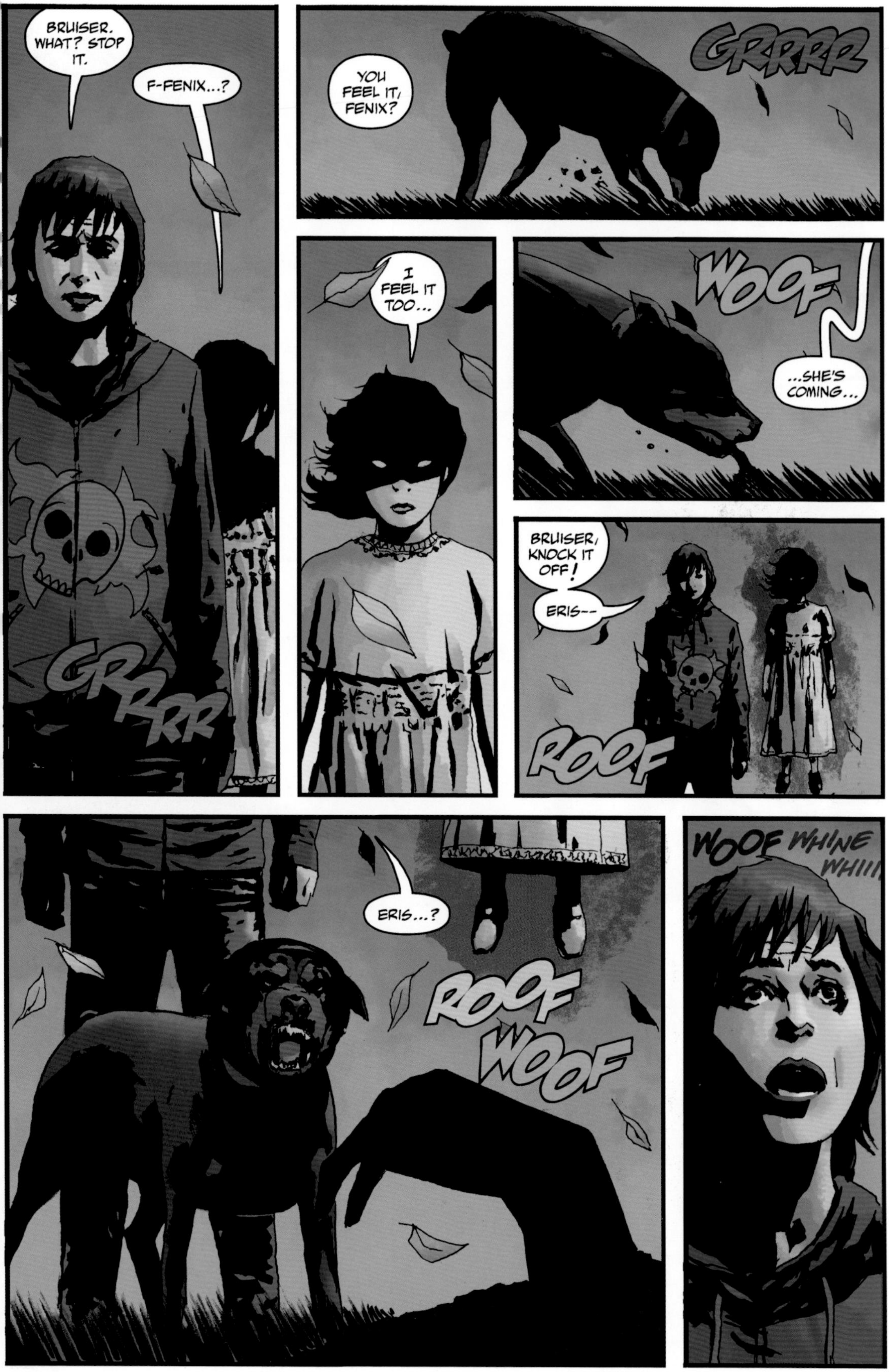
BRUISER. WHAT? STOP IT.
F-FENIX...?
GRRRR
GRRRR
YOU FEEL IT, FENIX?
I FEEL IT TOO...
WOOF
...SHE'S COMING...
BRUISER, KNOCK IT OFF!
ERIS--
ROOF
ERIS...?
ROOF
WOOF
WOOF WHINE
WHIII

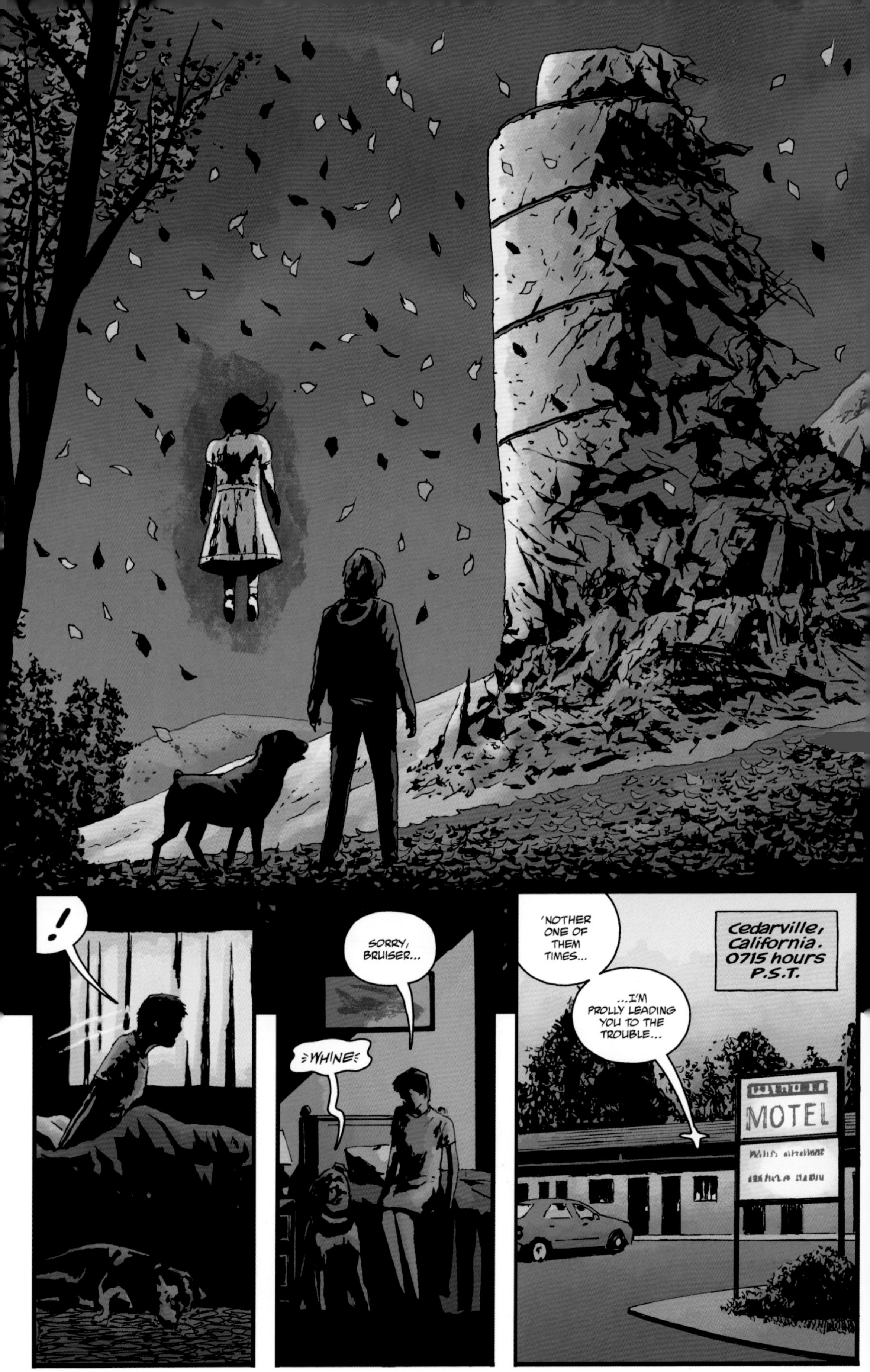
!
SORRY, BRUISER...
WHINE
Cedarville, California. 0715 hours P.S.T.
'NOTHER ONE OF THEM TIMES...
...I'M PROLLY LEADING YOU TO THE TROUBLE...
MOTEL

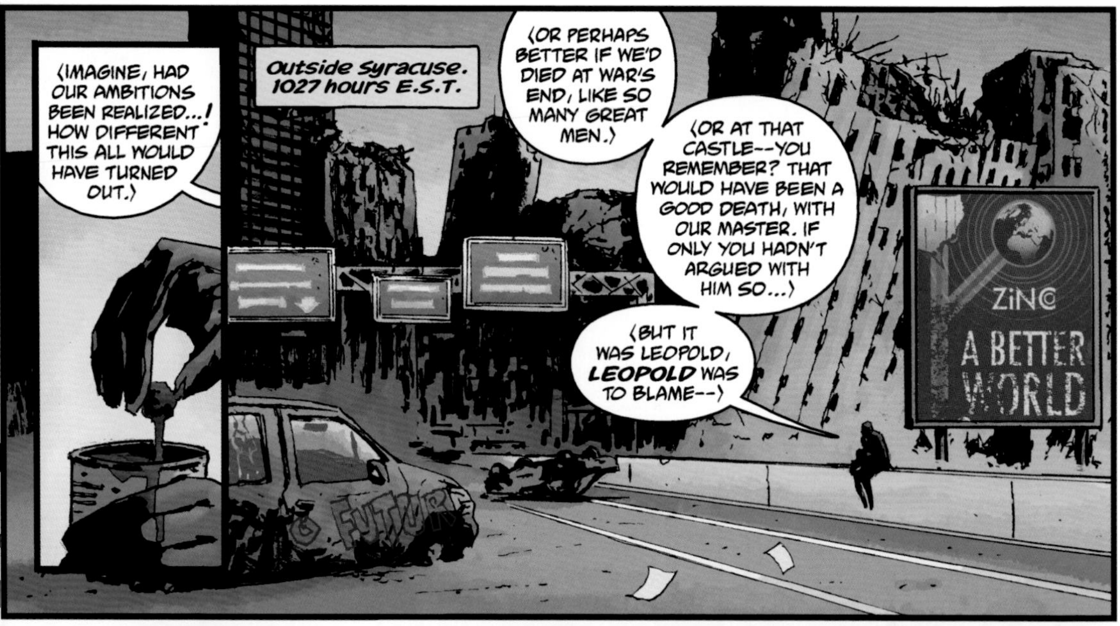

Outside Syracuse. 1027 hours E.S.T.
‹IMAGINE, HAD OUR AMBITIONS BEEN REALIZED...! HOW DIFFERENT THIS ALL WOULD HAVE TURNED OUT.›
‹OR PERHAPS BETTER IF WE'D DIED AT WAR'S END, LIKE SO MANY GREAT MEN.›
‹OR AT THAT CASTLE--YOU REMEMBER? THAT WOULD HAVE BEEN A GOOD DEATH, WITH OUR MASTER. IF ONLY YOU HADN'T ARGUED WITH HIM SO...›
‹BUT IT WAS LEOPOLD, LEOPOLD WAS TO BLAME--›
ZiNC
A BETTER WORLD

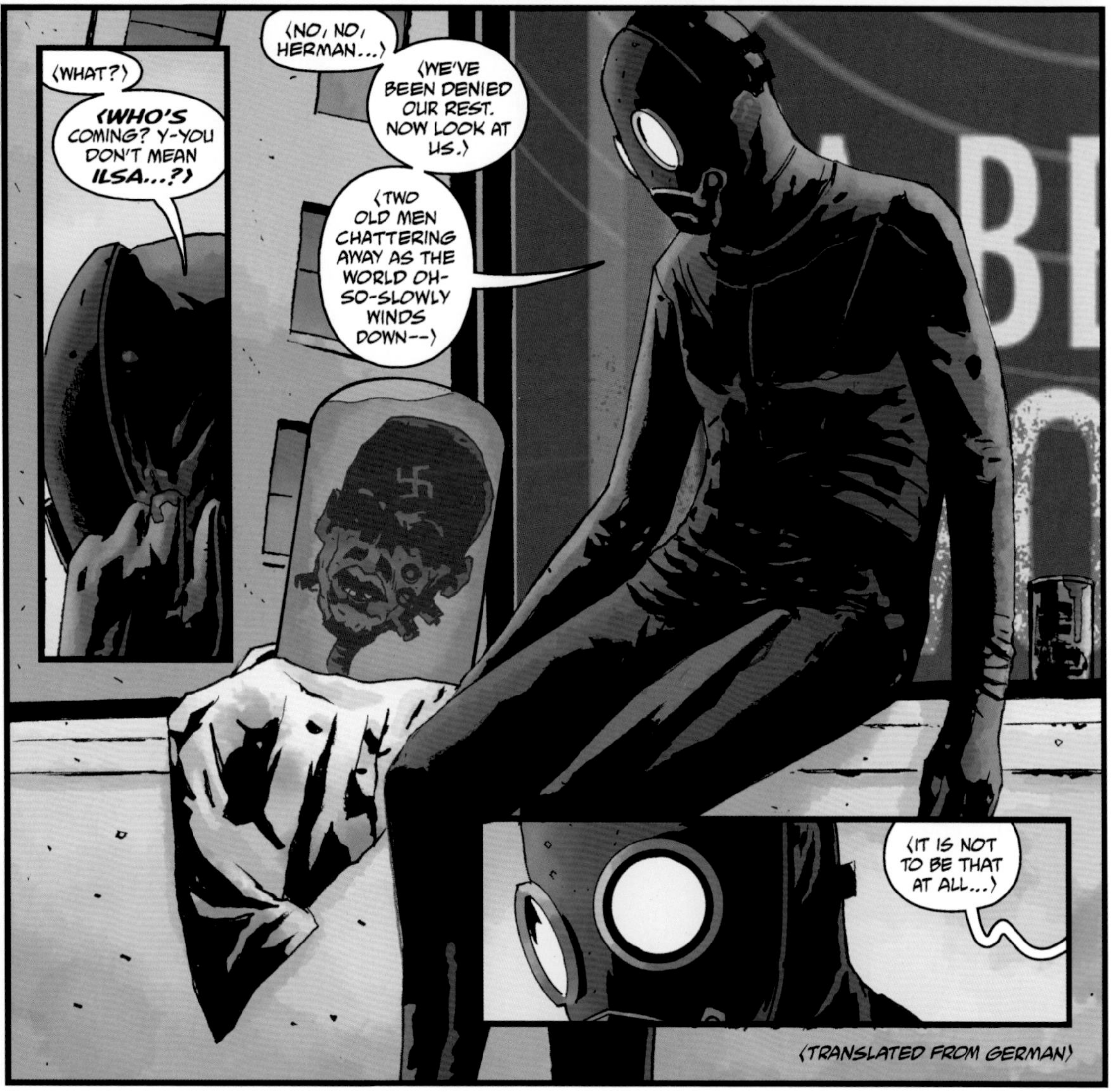

‹WHAT?›
‹WHO'S COMING? Y-YOU DON'T MEAN ILSA...?›
‹NO, NO, HERMAN...›
‹WE'VE BEEN DENIED OUR REST. NOW LOOK AT US.›
‹TWO OLD MEN CHATTERING AWAY AS THE WORLD OH-SO-SLOWLY WINDS DOWN--›
‹IT IS NOT TO BE THAT AT ALL...›
‹TRANSLATED FROM GERMAN›

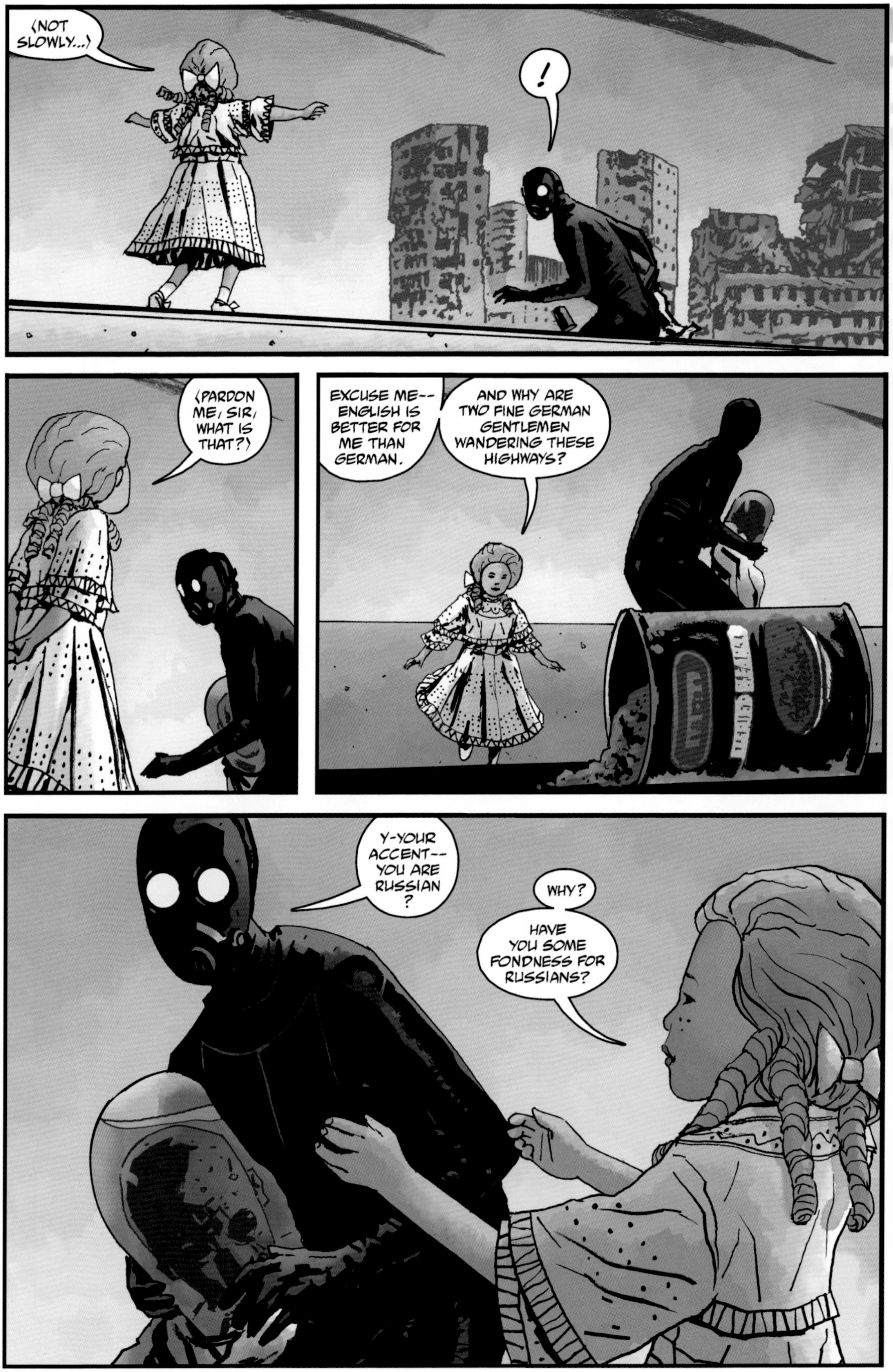

⟨NOT SLOWLY...⟩
!
⟨PARDON ME, SIR, WHAT IS THAT?⟩
EXCUSE ME-- ENGLISH IS BETTER FOR ME THAN GERMAN.
AND WHY ARE TWO FINE GERMAN GENTLEMEN WANDERING THESE HIGHWAYS?
Y-YOUR ACCENT-- YOU ARE RUSSIAN?
WHY?
HAVE YOU SOME FONDNESS FOR RUSSIANS?

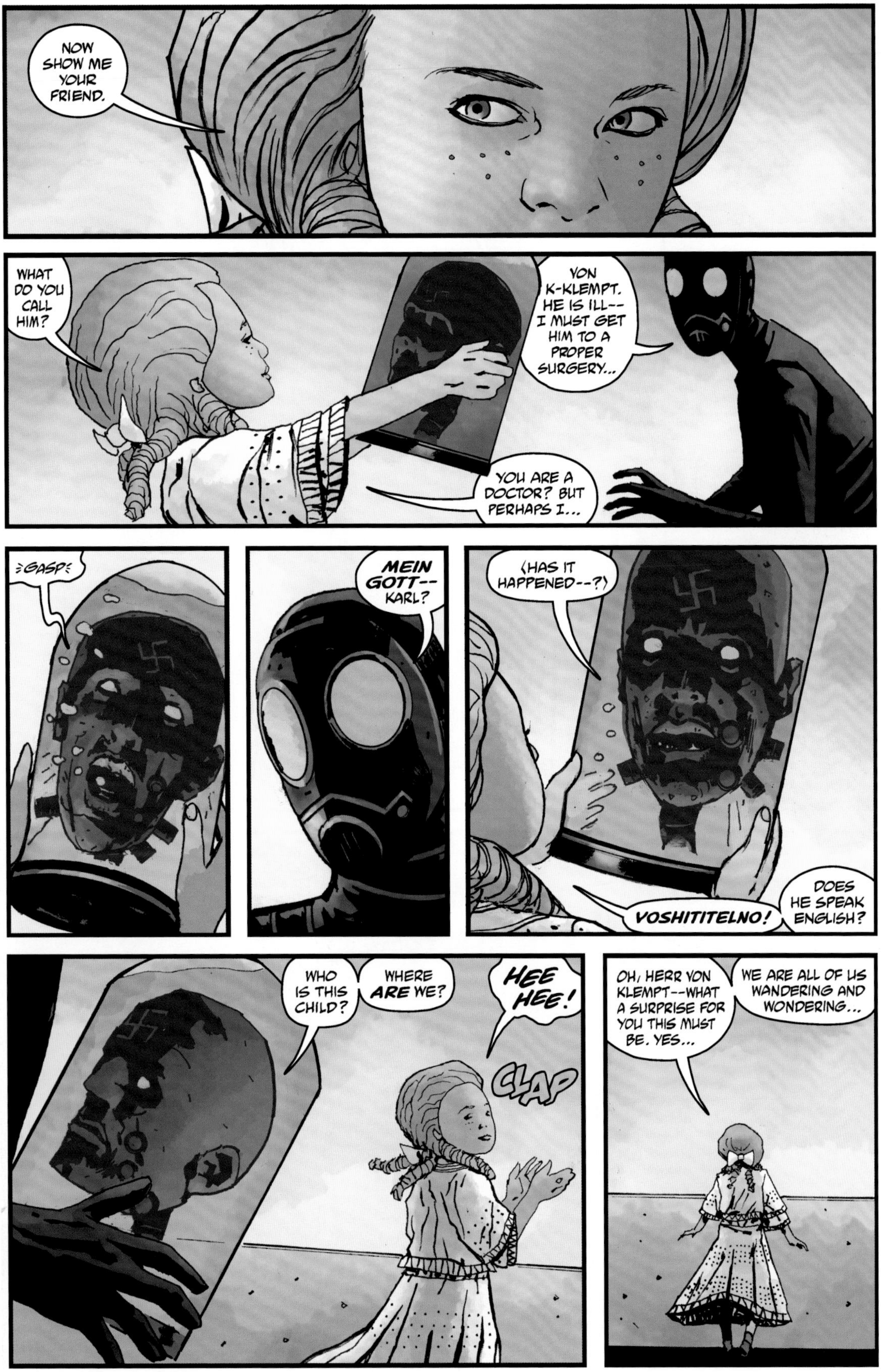
NOW SHOW ME YOUR FRIEND.
WHAT DO YOU CALL HIM?
VON K-KLEMPT. HE IS ILL-- I MUST GET HIM TO A PROPER SURGERY...
YOU ARE A DOCTOR? BUT PERHAPS I...
GASP
MEIN GOTT-- KARL?
‹HAS IT HAPPENED--?›
VOSHITITELNO!
DOES HE SPEAK ENGLISH?
WHO IS THIS CHILD?
WHERE ARE WE?
HEE HEE!
CLAP
OH, HERR VON KLEMPT--WHAT A SURPRISE FOR YOU THIS MUST BE. YES...
WE ARE ALL OF US WANDERING AND WONDERING...

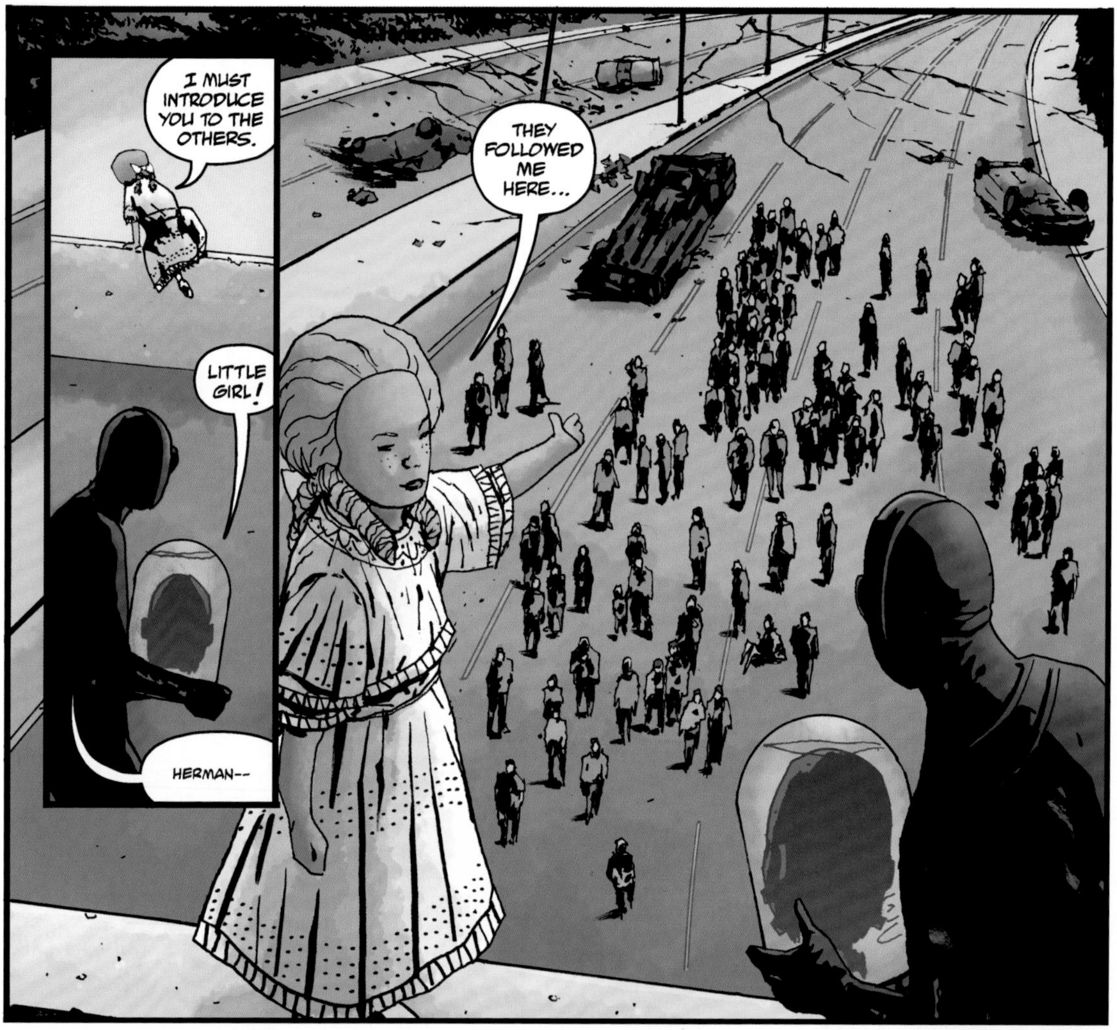
I MUST INTRODUCE YOU TO THE OTHERS.
LITTLE GIRL!
HERMAN--
THEY FOLLOWED ME HERE...

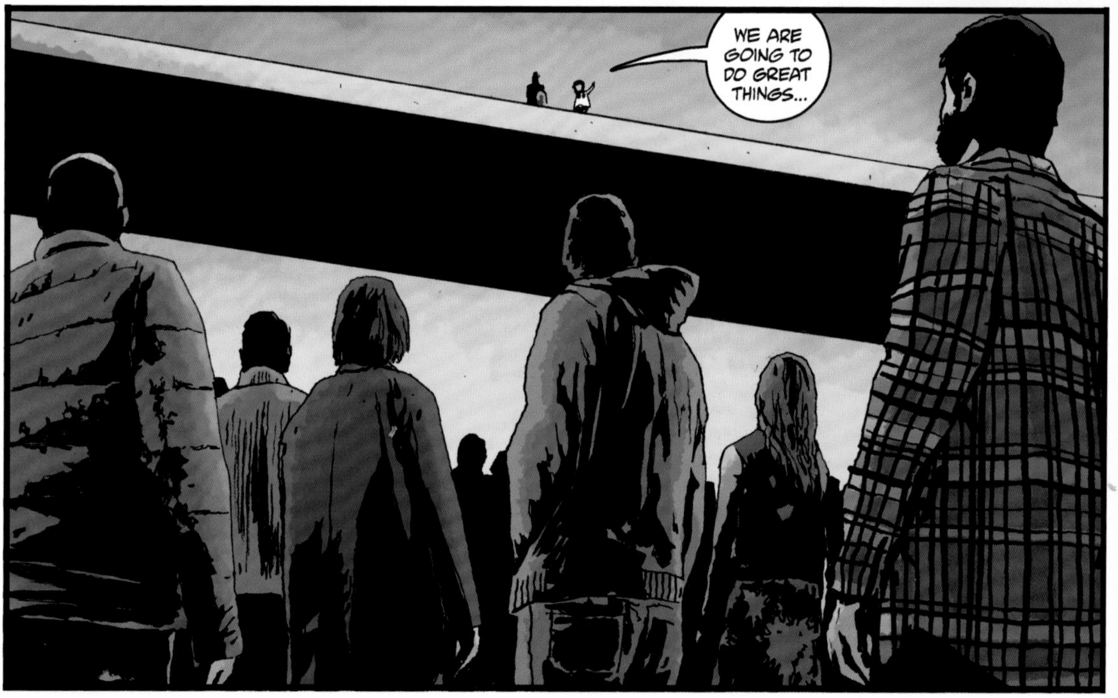
WE ARE GOING TO DO GREAT THINGS...

CHAPTER TWO

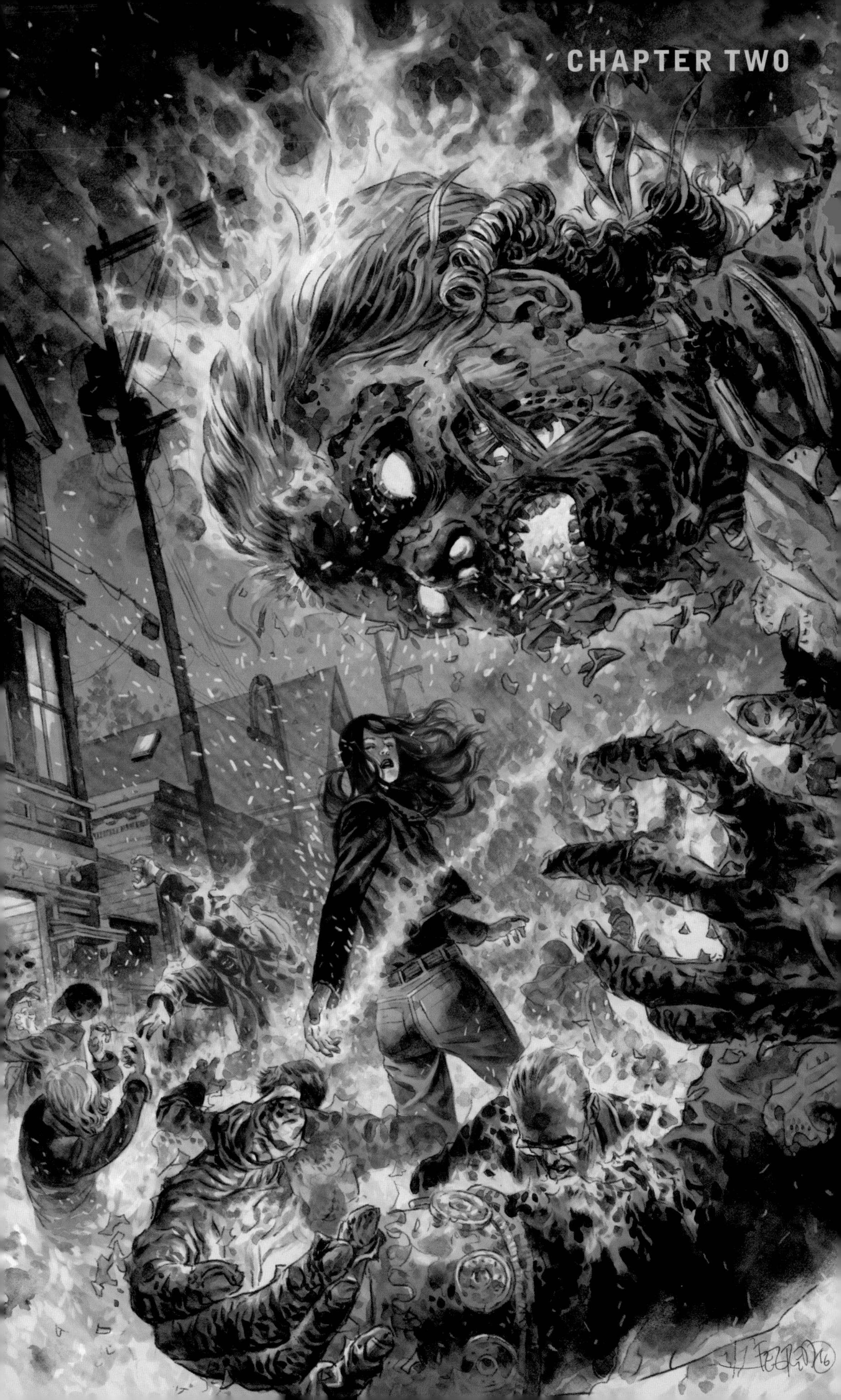

"FOR *YEARS, THEY*'VE TOLD YOU WE LIVE IN THE END TIMES."

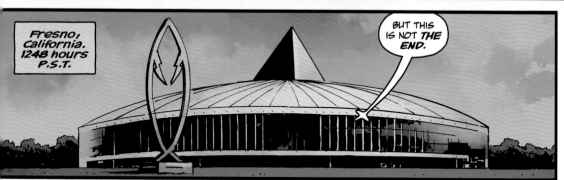

Fresno, California. 1248 hours P.S.T.

BUT THIS IS NOT *THE* END.

YOU KNOW THIS. *I* KNOW THIS.

NOW THERE ARE *OTHERS* ALL OVER THE *WORLD* WHO KNOW THIS.

"*THEY* HAVE SEEN THE SIGNS.

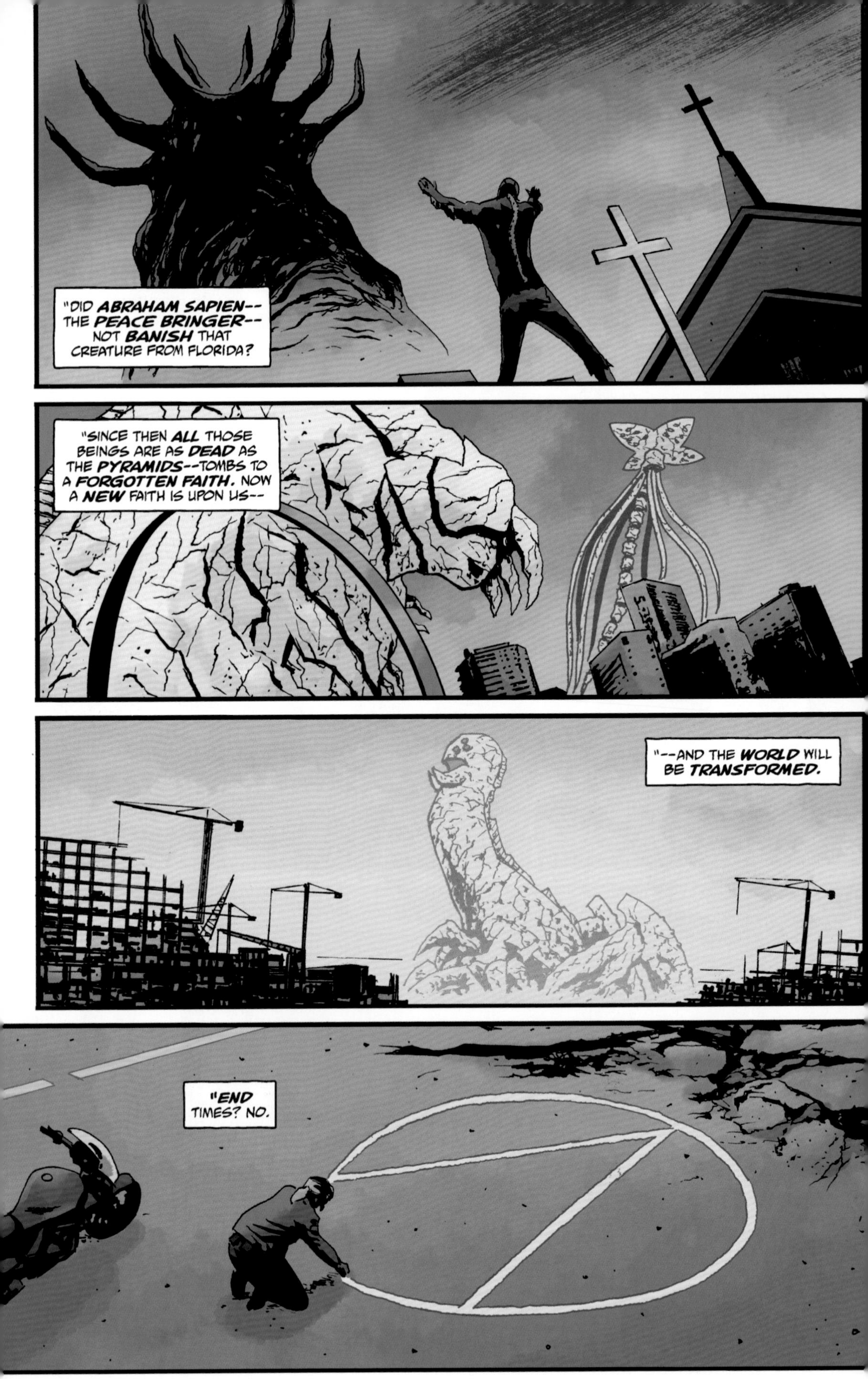
"DID ABRAHAM SAPIEN--
THE PEACE BRINGER--
NOT BANISH THAT
CREATURE FROM FLORIDA?
"SINCE THEN ALL THOSE
BEINGS ARE AS DEAD AS
THE PYRAMIDS--TOMBS TO
A FORGOTTEN FAITH. NOW
A NEW FAITH IS UPON US--
"--AND THE WORLD WILL
BE TRANSFORMED.
"END
TIMES? NO.

"THIS IS ONLY THE *END* OF A TIME OF *VIOLENCE*--

"--WHICH STARTED *LONG* BEFORE THOSE *CREATURES* CAME--AND HAS, WITH THEM, COME TO AN END.

"WE LIVE AT THE *BEGINNING,* BROTHERS AND SISTERS--OF A *NEW* AGE--AND WE WILL BE DELIVERED *PEACEFULLY* INTO THAT *NEW WORLD.*

"I WAS AS GUILTY AS *ANYONE*--MISREADING THE *SIGNS* WHEN THOSE TOWERING CREATURES *FIRST* APPEARED."

BUT I CAME TO RECOGNIZE THEM AS *AGENTS OF CHANGE*--A *SIGNAL*--

--A *WARNING* TO MAN THAT *THE OLD GODS* WERE PAST--

"--AND *WE* NEEDED TO LOOK *FORWARD.*"

WHO'S THE GIRL?

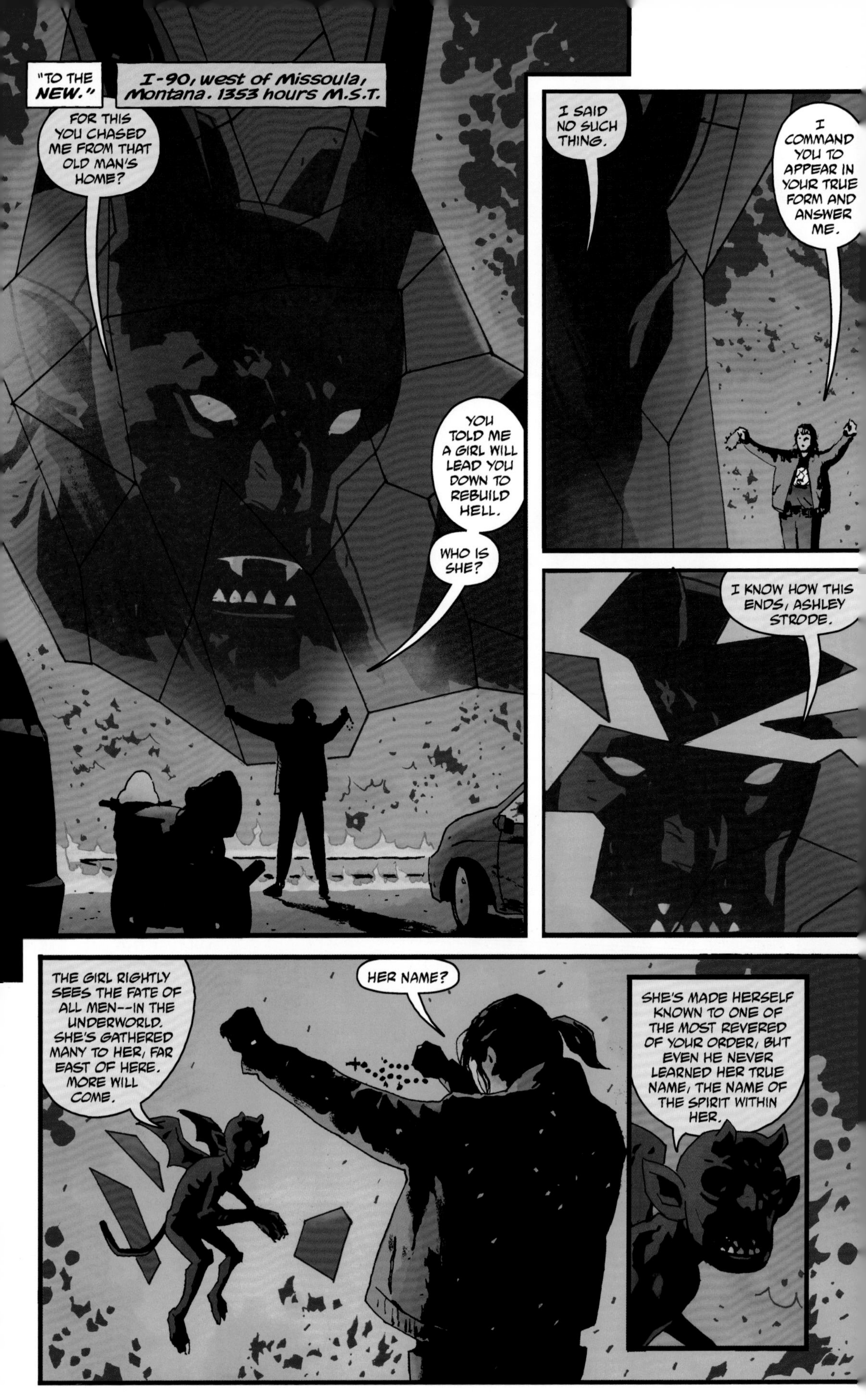
"TO THE NEW."
I-90, west of Missoula, Montana. 1353 hours M.S.T.
FOR THIS YOU CHASED ME FROM THAT OLD MAN'S HOME?
YOU TOLD ME A GIRL WILL LEAD YOU DOWN TO REBUILD HELL.
WHO IS SHE?
I SAID NO SUCH THING.
I COMMAND YOU TO APPEAR IN YOUR TRUE FORM AND ANSWER ME.
I KNOW HOW THIS ENDS, ASHLEY STRODE.
THE GIRL RIGHTLY SEES THE FATE OF ALL MEN--IN THE UNDERWORLD. SHE'S GATHERED MANY TO HER, FAR EAST OF HERE. MORE WILL COME.
HER NAME?
SHE'S MADE HERSELF KNOWN TO ONE OF THE MOST REVERED OF YOUR ORDER, BUT EVEN HE NEVER LEARNED HER TRUE NAME, THE NAME OF THE SPIRIT WITHIN HER.

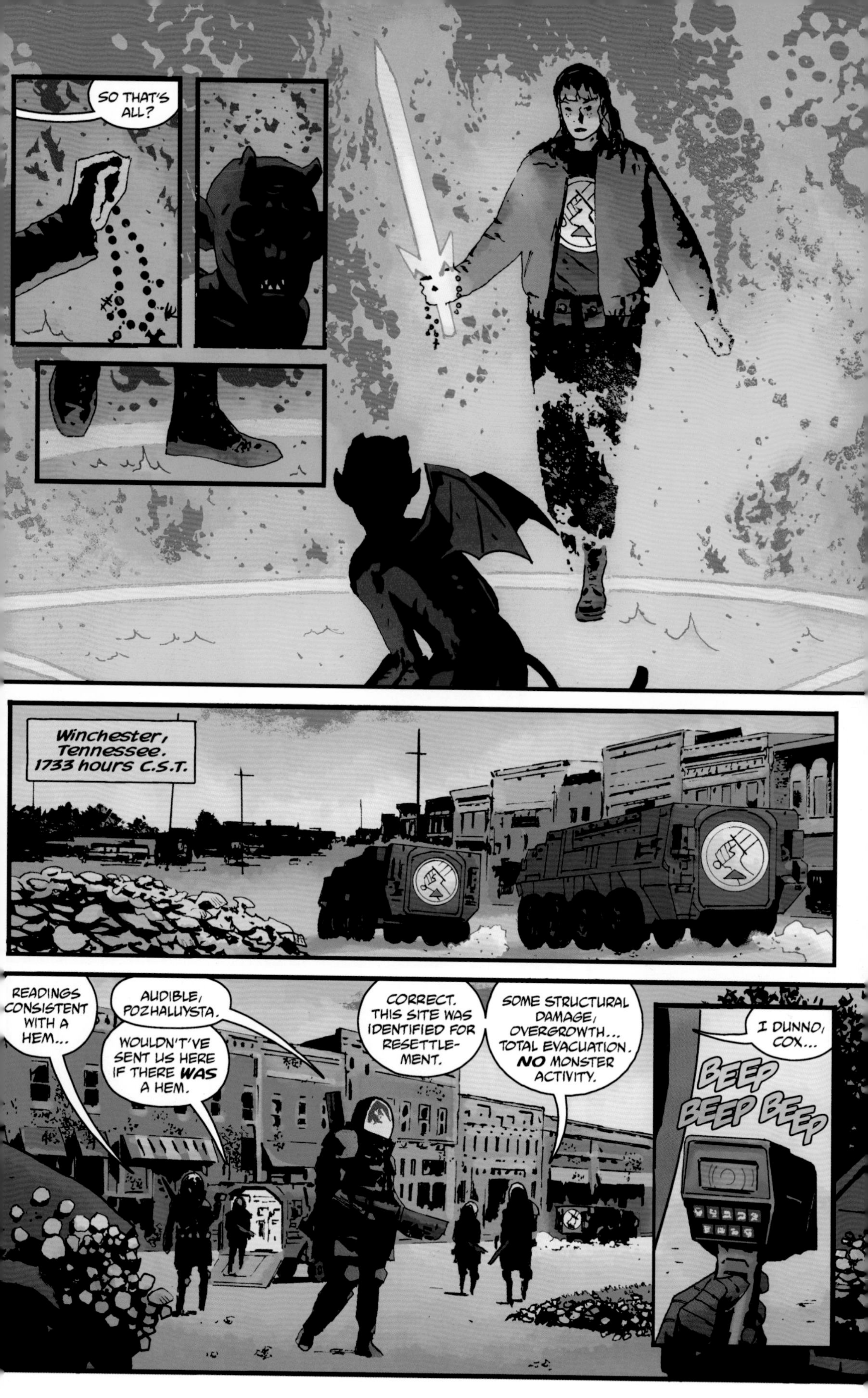
SO THAT'S ALL?
Winchester, Tennessee. 1733 hours C.S.T.
READINGS CONSISTENT WITH A HEM...
AUDIBLE, POZHALUYSTA.
WOULDN'T'VE SENT US HERE IF THERE WAS A HEM.
CORRECT. THIS SITE WAS IDENTIFIED FOR RESETTLE-MENT.
SOME STRUCTURAL DAMAGE, OVERGROWTH... TOTAL EVACUATION. NO MONSTER ACTIVITY.
I DUNNO, COX...
BEEP BEEP BEEP BEEP

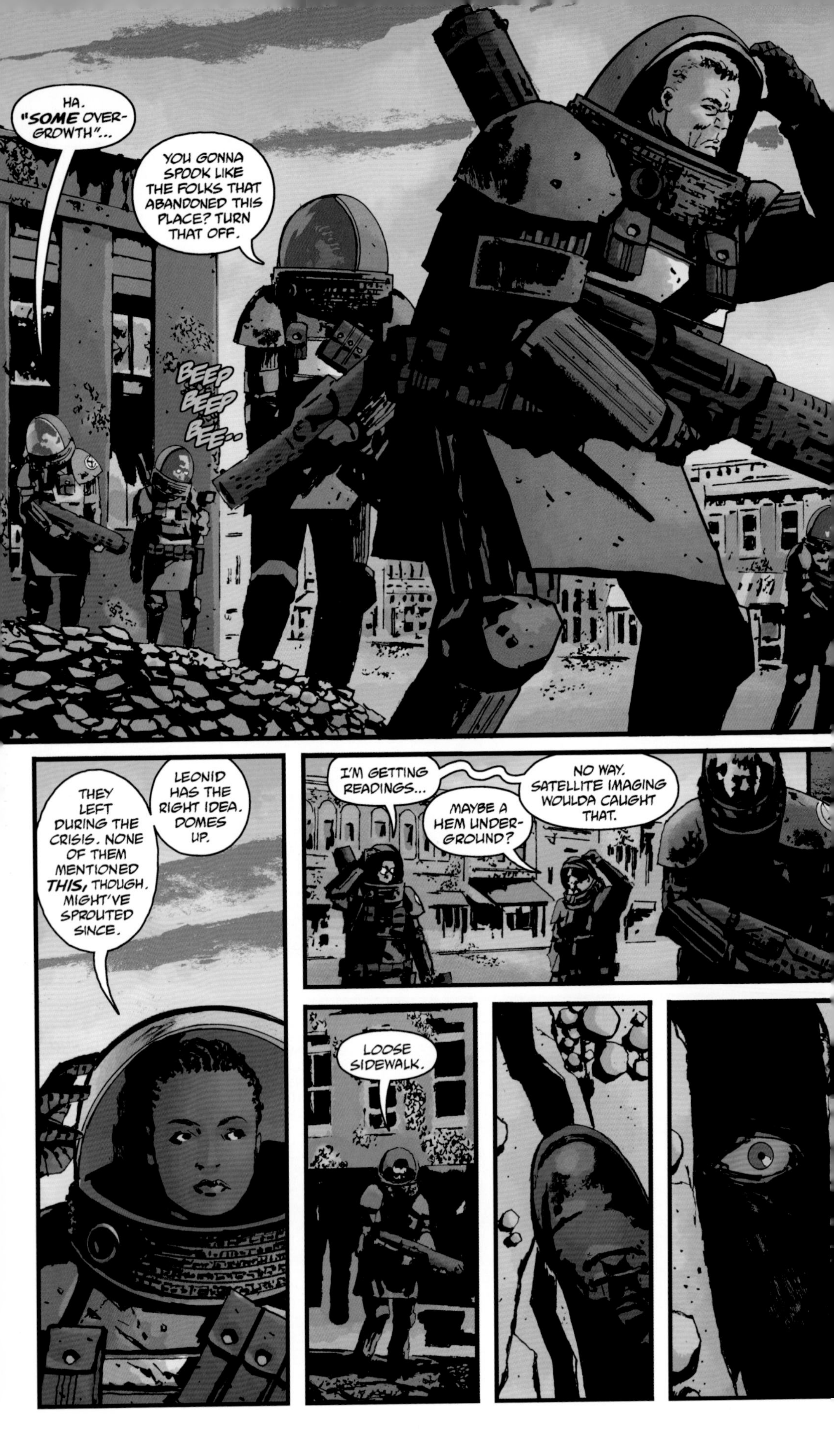
HA. "SOME OVER-GROWTH"...
YOU GONNA SPOOK LIKE THE FOLKS THAT ABANDONED THIS PLACE? TURN THAT OFF.
BEEP BEEP BEE...
LEONID HAS THE RIGHT IDEA. DOMES UP.
THEY LEFT DURING THE CRISIS. NONE OF THEM MENTIONED THIS, THOUGH. MIGHT'VE SPROUTED SINCE.
I'M GETTING READINGS...
MAYBE A HEM UNDER-GROUND?
NO WAY. SATELLITE IMAGING WOULDA CAUGHT THAT.
LOOSE SIDEWALK.

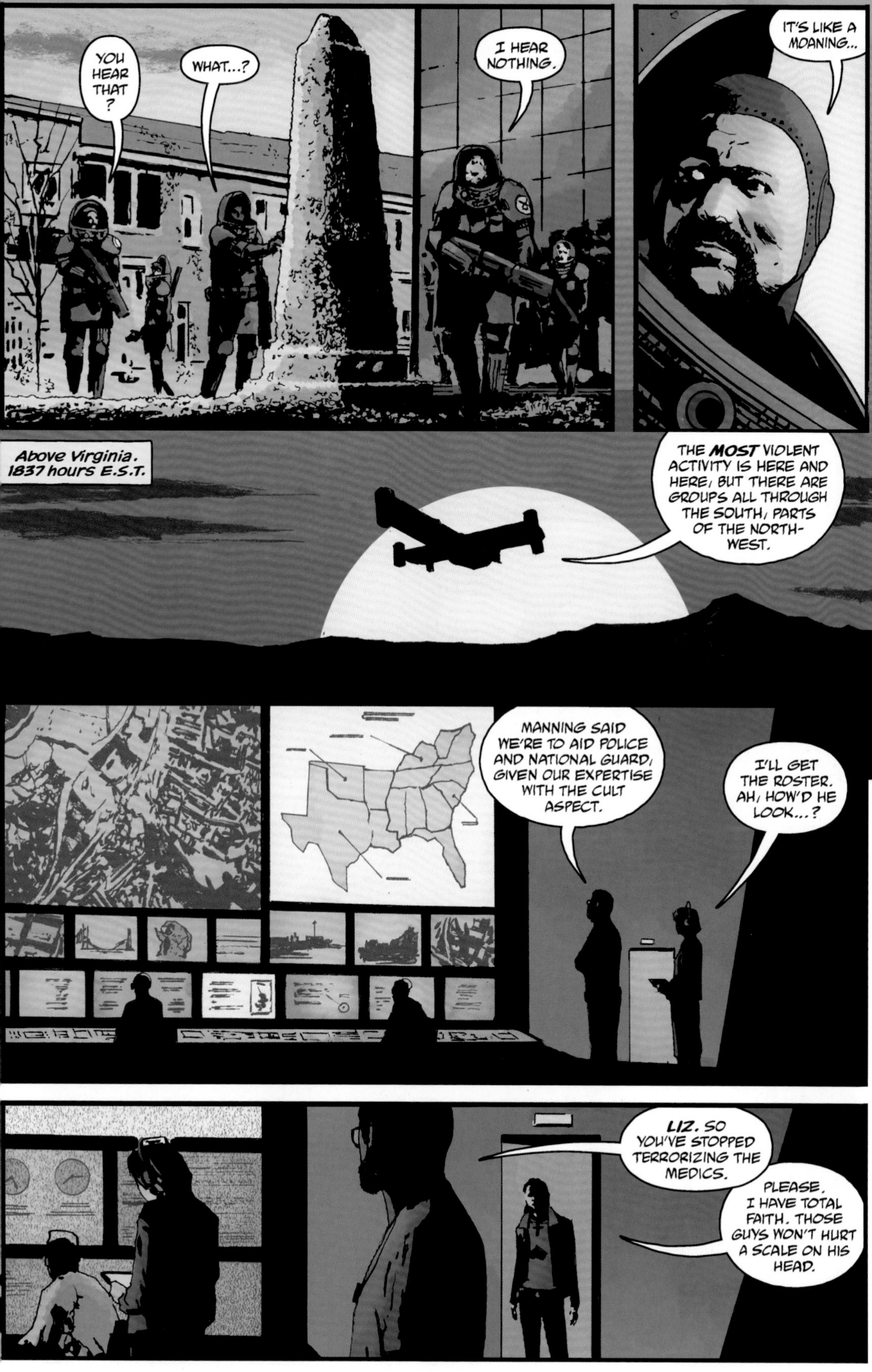
YOU HEAR THAT ?
WHAT...?
I HEAR NOTHING.
IT'S LIKE A MOANING...
Above Virginia. 1837 hours E.S.T.
THE MOST VIOLENT ACTIVITY IS HERE AND HERE, BUT THERE ARE GROUPS ALL THROUGH THE SOUTH, PARTS OF THE NORTH-WEST.
MANNING SAID WE'RE TO AID POLICE AND NATIONAL GUARD, GIVEN OUR EXPERTISE WITH THE CULT ASPECT.
I'LL GET THE ROSTER. AH, HOW'D HE LOOK...?
LIZ. SO YOU'VE STOPPED TERRORIZING THE MEDICS.
PLEASE. I HAVE TOTAL FAITH. THOSE GUYS WON'T HURT A SCALE ON HIS HEAD.

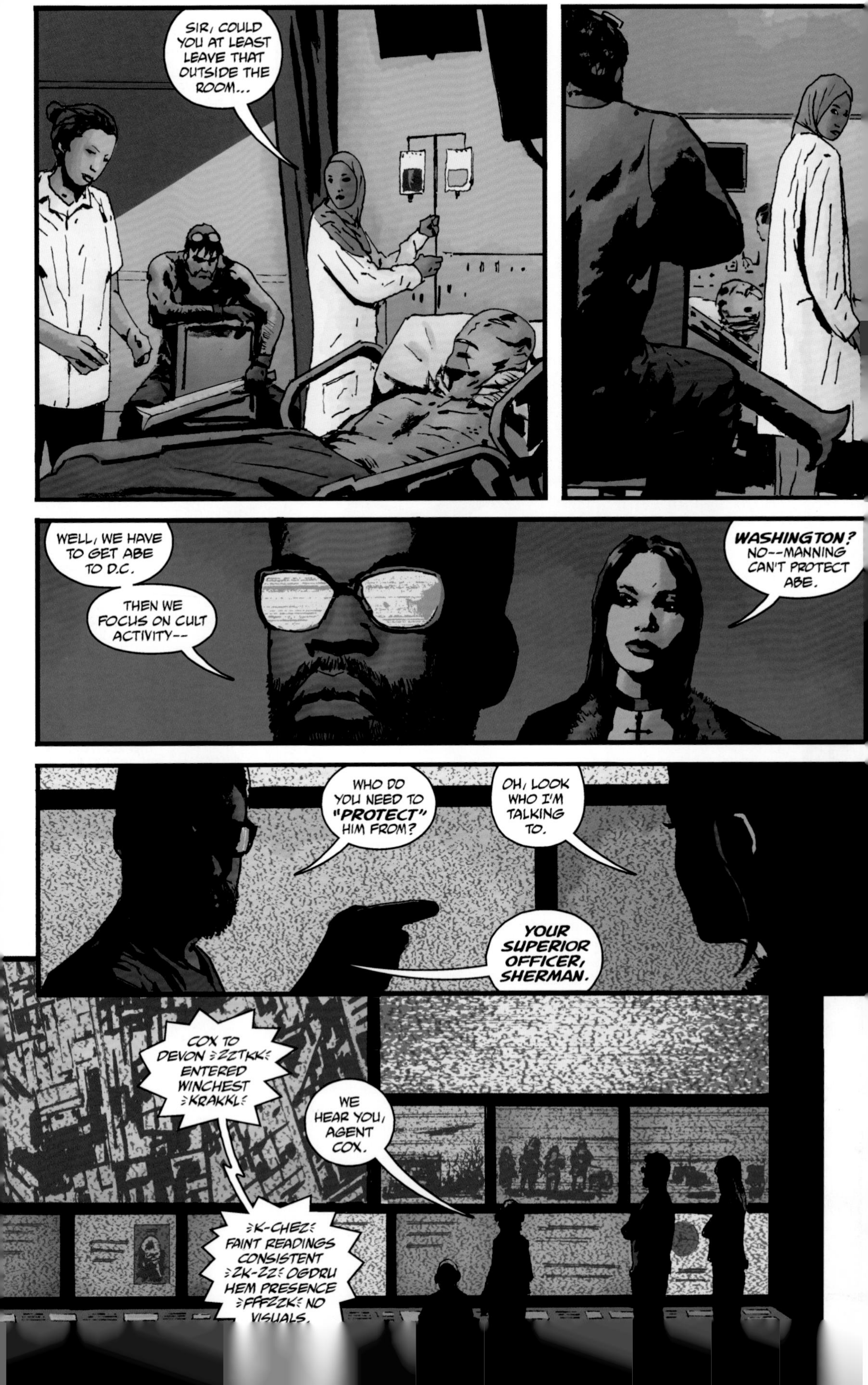
SIR, COULD YOU AT LEAST LEAVE THAT OUTSIDE THE ROOM...
WELL, WE HAVE TO GET ABE TO D.C.
THEN WE FOCUS ON CULT ACTIVITY--
WASHINGTON? NO--MANNING CAN'T PROTECT ABE.
WHO DO YOU NEED TO "PROTECT" HIM FROM?
OH, LOOK WHO I'M TALKING TO.
YOUR SUPERIOR OFFICER, SHERMAN.
COX TO DEVON ƷZZTKKƸ ENTERED WINCHEST ƷKRAKKLƸ
WE HEAR YOU, AGENT COX.
ƷK-CHEZƸ FAINT READINGS CONSISTENT ƷZK-ZZƸ OGDRU HEM PRESENCE ƷFFFZZKƸ NO VISUALS.

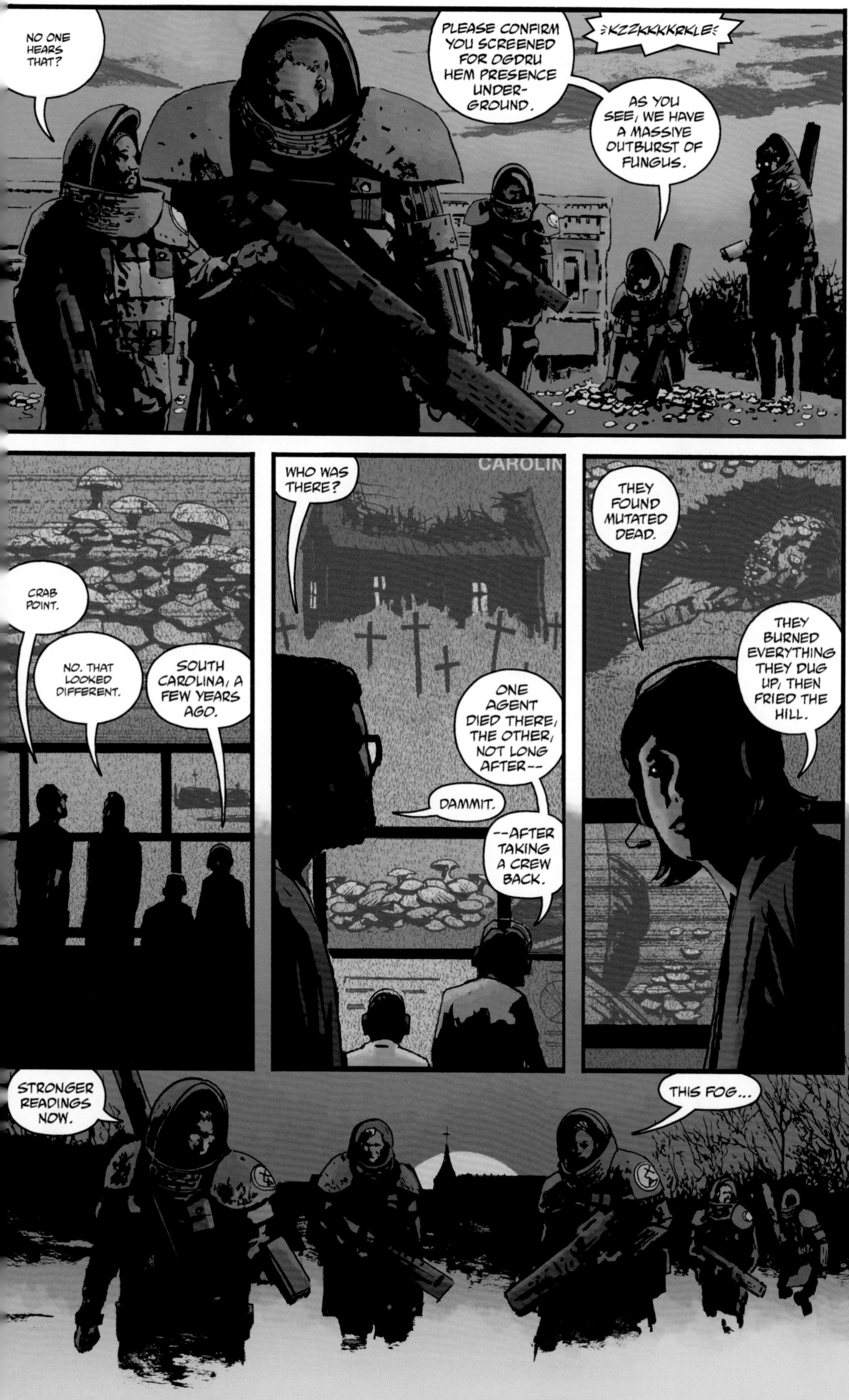
NO ONE HEARS THAT?
PLEASE CONFIRM YOU SCREENED FOR OGDRU HEM PRESENCE UNDER-GROUND.
KZZKKKKRKLE
AS YOU SEE, WE HAVE A MASSIVE OUTBURST OF FUNGUS.
CRAB POINT.
NO. THAT LOOKED DIFFERENT.
SOUTH CAROLINA, A FEW YEARS AGO.
CAROLIN
WHO WAS THERE?
ONE AGENT DIED THERE, THE OTHER, NOT LONG AFTER--
DAMMIT.
--AFTER TAKING A CREW BACK.
THEY FOUND MUTATED DEAD.
THEY BURNED EVERYTHING THEY DUG UP, THEN FRIED THE HILL.
STRONGER READINGS NOW.
THIS FOG...

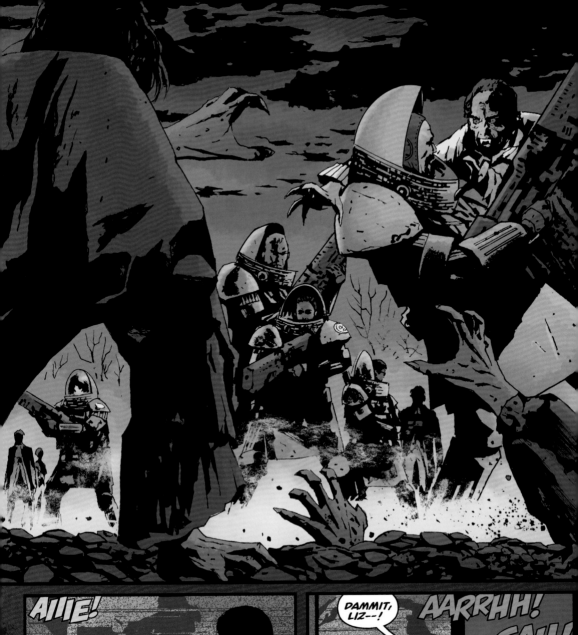

AllIE!

GAHH!
LEONID!!
ARRGH!

DAMMIT, LIZ--!

AARRHH!
GAH!

--YOU CAN'T *GET* THERE FAST ENOUGH!

"I WAS IN NEW CASTLE-- PENNSYLVANIA. MOSTLY UNTOUCHED. LIFE WENT ON, YOU KNOW...?"

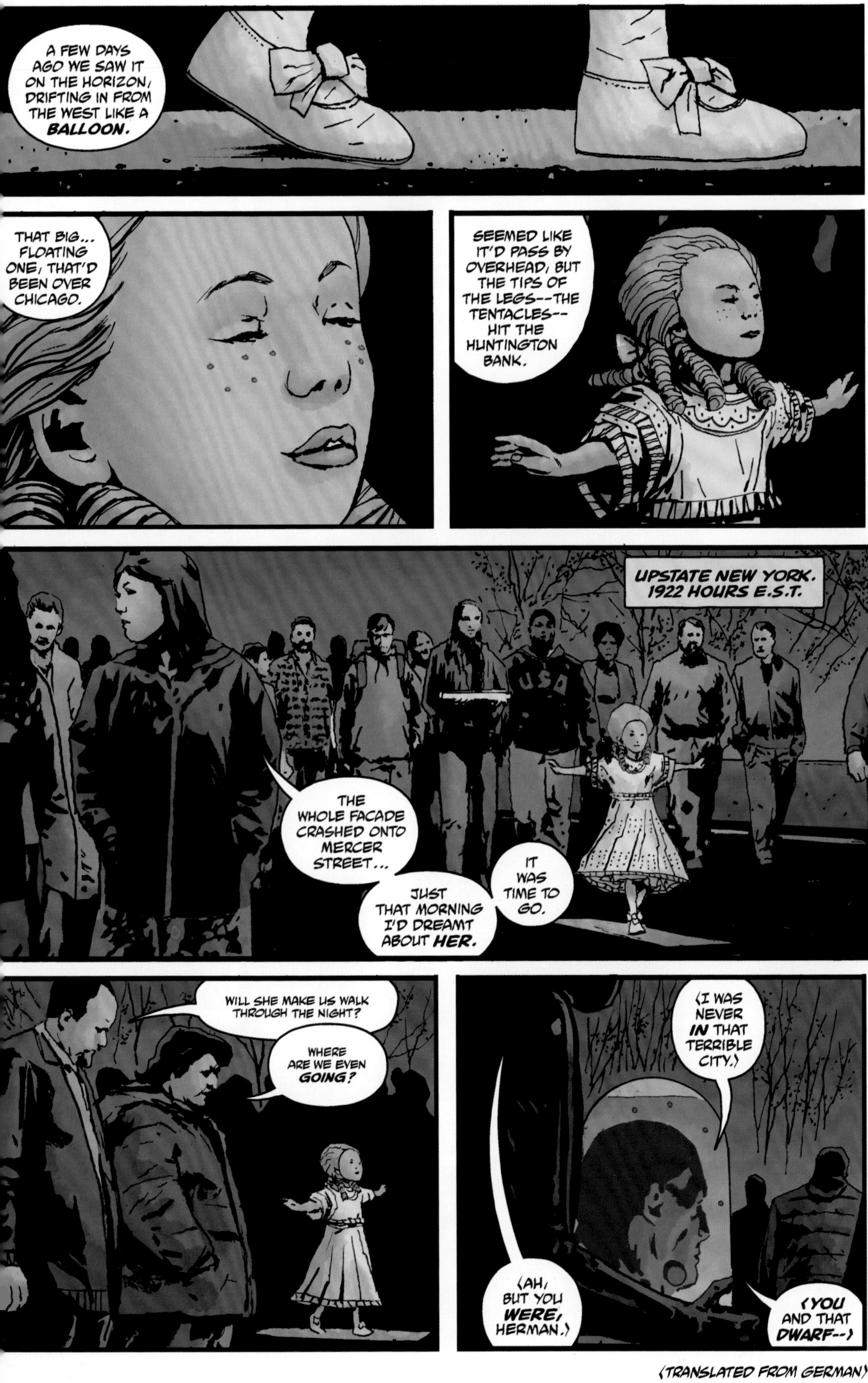

A FEW DAYS AGO WE SAW IT ON THE HORIZON, DRIFTING IN FROM THE WEST LIKE A BALLOON.
THAT BIG... FLOATING ONE, THAT'D BEEN OVER CHICAGO.
SEEMED LIKE IT'D PASS BY OVERHEAD, BUT THE TIPS OF THE LEGS--THE TENTACLES--HIT THE HUNTINGTON BANK.
UPSTATE NEW YORK. 1922 HOURS E.S.T.
USA
THE WHOLE FACADE CRASHED ONTO MERCER STREET...
JUST THAT MORNING I'D DREAMT ABOUT HER.
IT WAS TIME TO GO.
WILL SHE MAKE US WALK THROUGH THE NIGHT?
WHERE ARE WE EVEN GOING?
‹I WAS NEVER IN THAT TERRIBLE CITY.›
‹AH, BUT YOU WERE, HERMAN.›
‹YOU AND THAT DWARF--›

‹TRANSLATED FROM GERMAN›

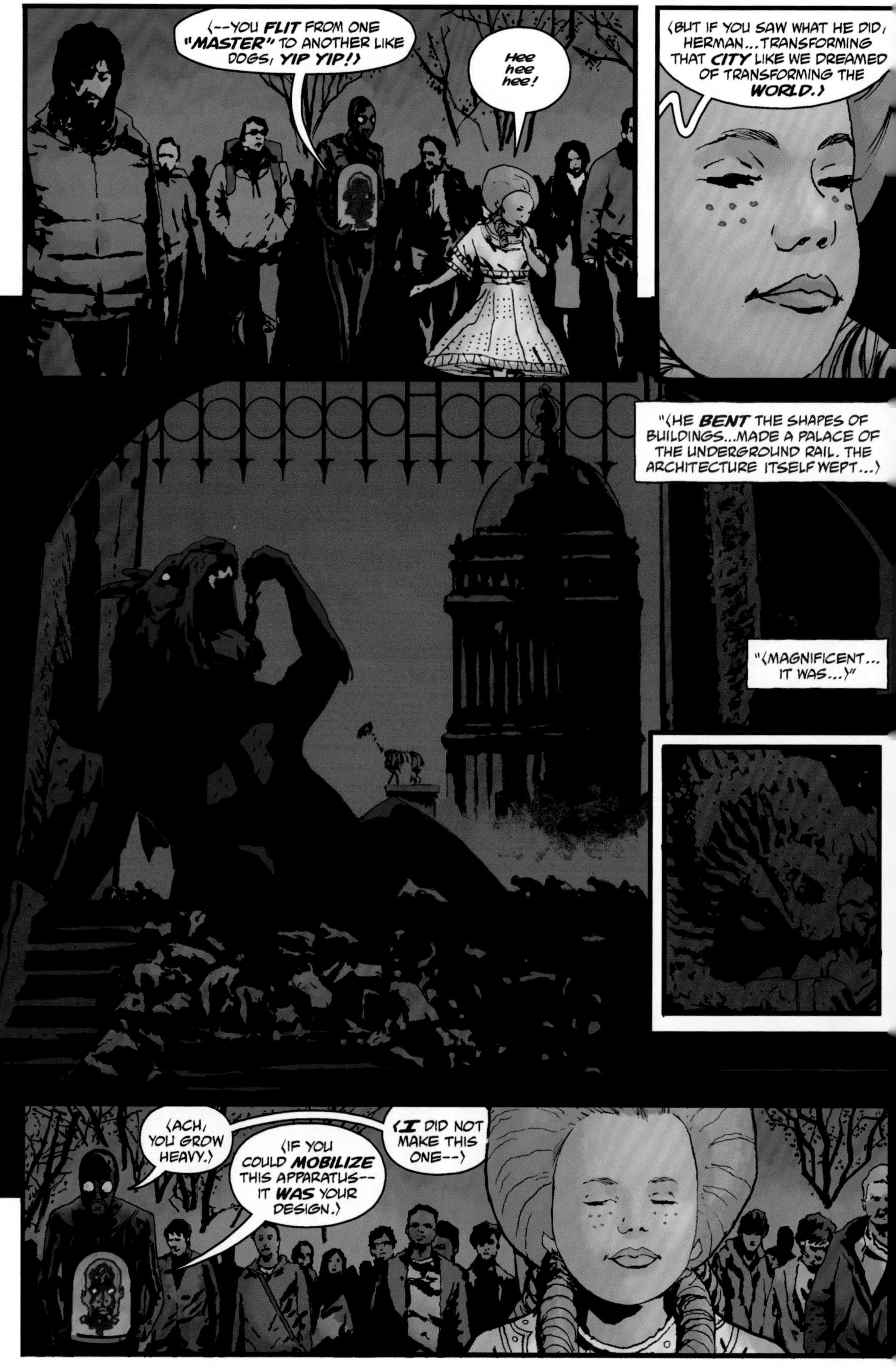

⟨--YOU FLIT FROM ONE "MASTER" TO ANOTHER LIKE DOGS, YIP YIP!⟩
Hee hee hee!
⟨BUT IF YOU SAW WHAT HE DID, HERMAN... TRANSFORMING THAT CITY LIKE WE DREAMED OF TRANSFORMING THE WORLD.⟩
"⟨HE BENT THE SHAPES OF BUILDINGS...MADE A PALACE OF THE UNDERGROUND RAIL. THE ARCHITECTURE ITSELF WEPT...⟩
"⟨MAGNIFICENT... IT WAS...⟩"
⟨ACH, YOU GROW HEAVY.⟩
⟨IF YOU COULD MOBILIZE THIS APPARATUS-- IT WAS YOUR DESIGN.⟩
⟨I DID NOT MAKE THIS ONE--⟩

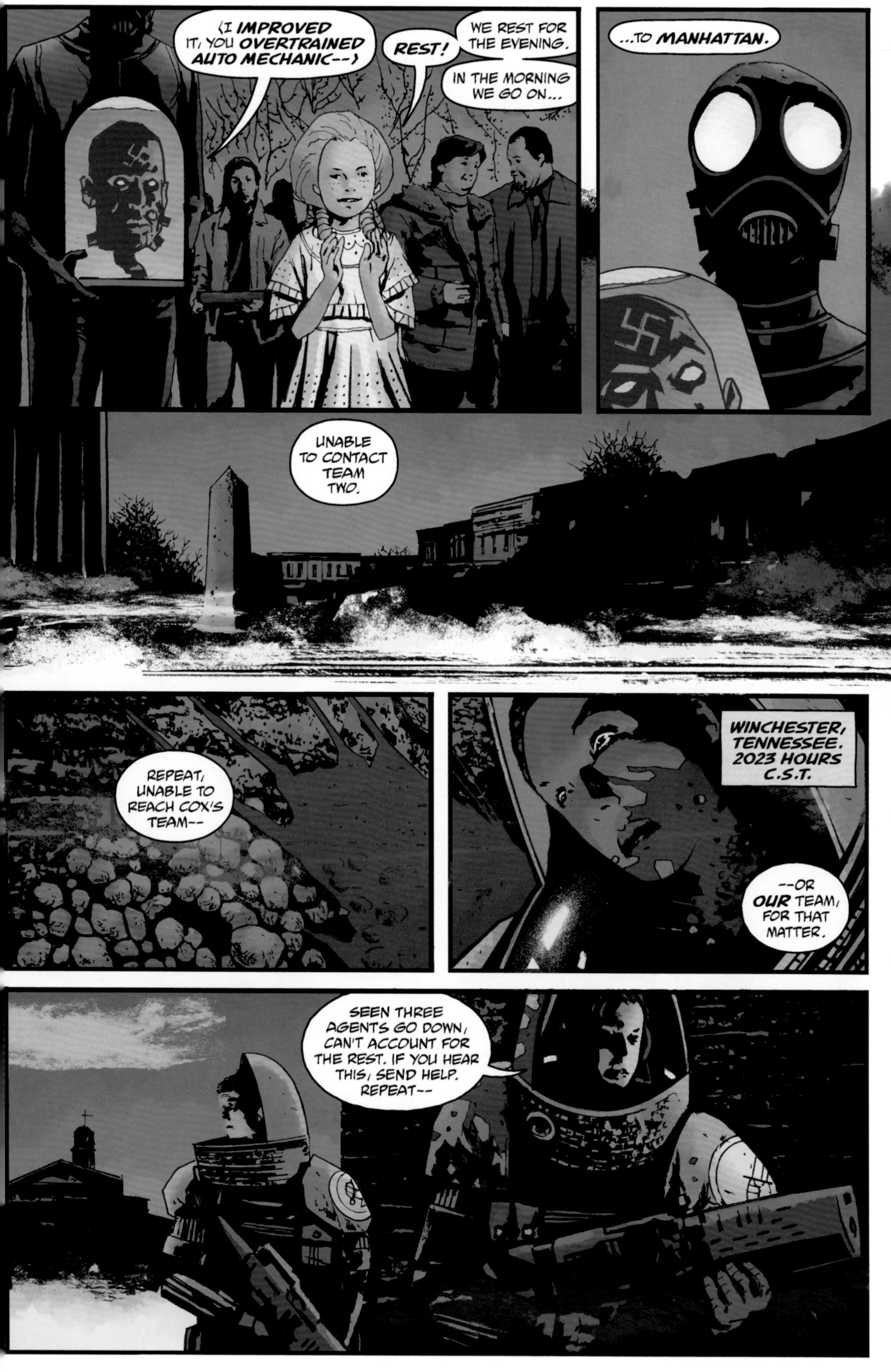
⟨I IMPROVED IT, YOU OVERTRAINED AUTO MECHANIC--⟩
REST!
WE REST FOR THE EVENING.
IN THE MORNING WE GO ON...
...TO MANHATTAN.
UNABLE TO CONTACT TEAM TWO.
REPEAT, UNABLE TO REACH COX'S TEAM--
WINCHESTER, TENNESSEE. 2023 HOURS C.S.T.
--OR OUR TEAM, FOR THAT MATTER.
SEEN THREE AGENTS GO DOWN, CAN'T ACCOUNT FOR THE REST. IF YOU HEAR THIS, SEND HELP. REPEAT--

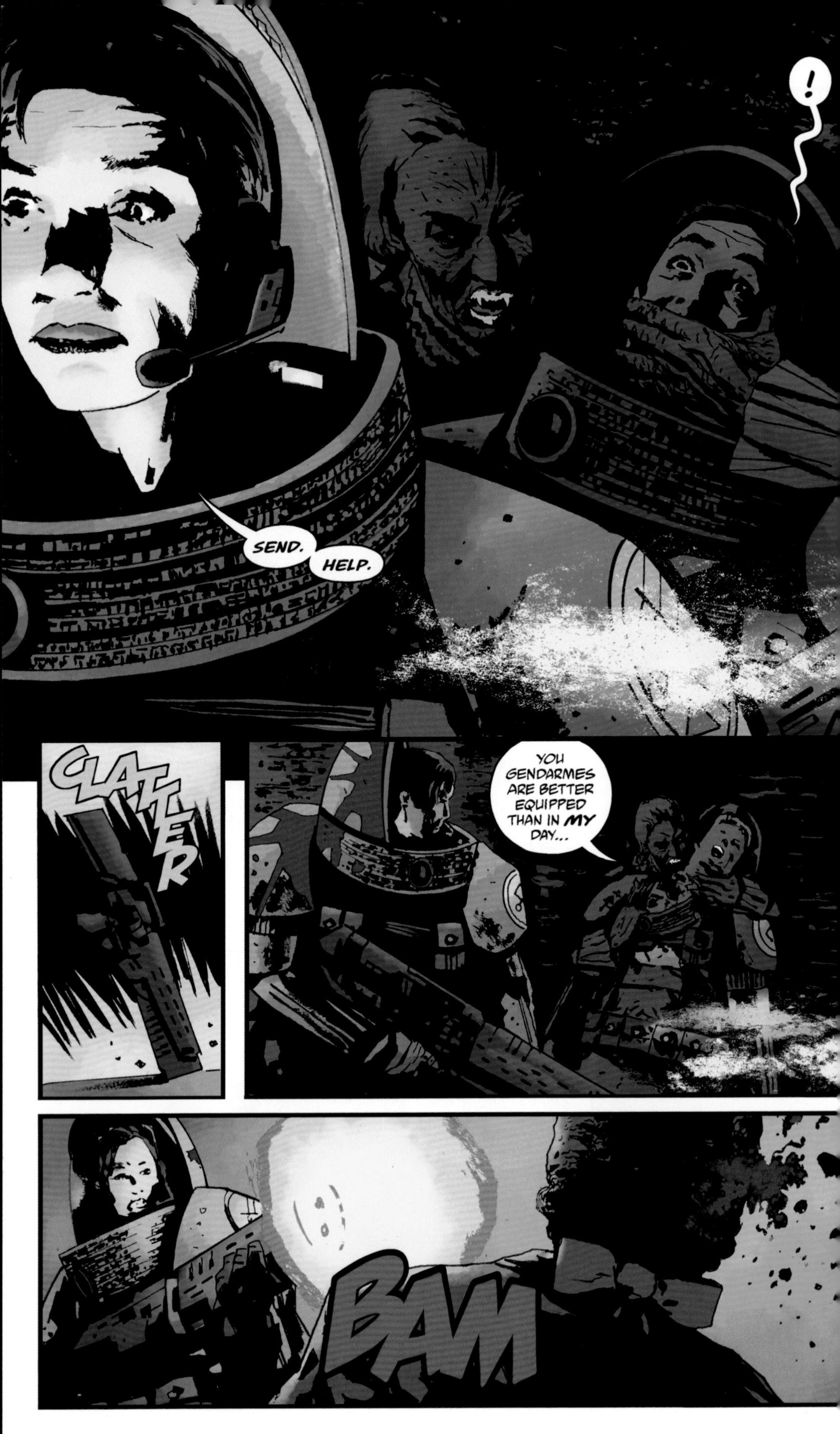
!
SEND.
HELP.
CLATTER
YOU GENDARMES ARE BETTER EQUIPPED THAN IN MY DAY...
BAM

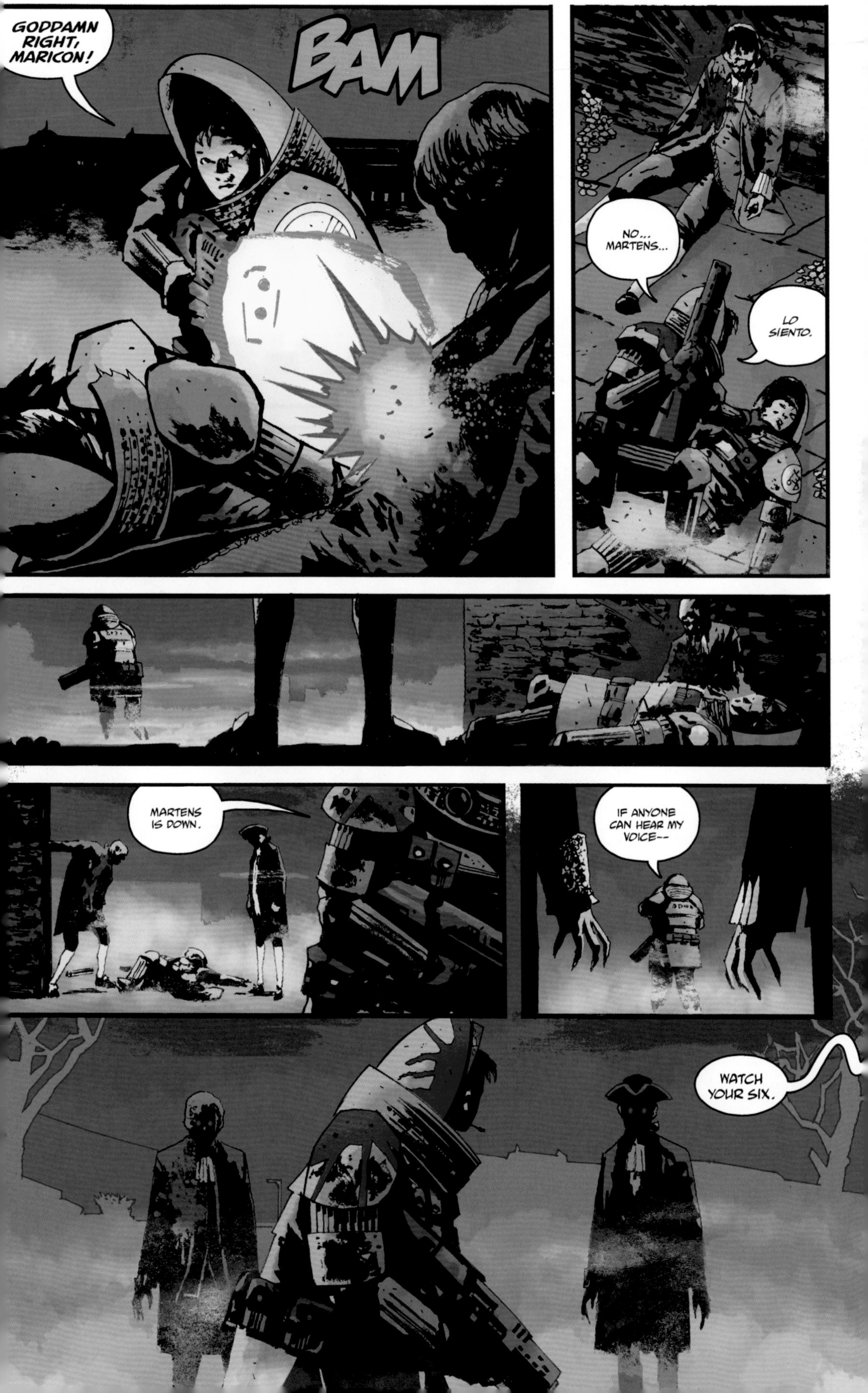
GODDAMN RIGHT, MARICON!
BAM
NO... MARTENS...
LO SIENTO.
MARTENS IS DOWN.
IF ANYONE CAN HEAR MY VOICE--
WATCH YOUR SIX.

FOOOOSH

RAT-TAT-TAT

YOU MADE IT...

JESUS, YOU MADE IT...

SORRY, KEPT HAVING TO SLOW DOWN TO CHECK THE G.P.S....

VAMPIRES. NEVER SEEN ANYTHING LIKE IT...

I HAVE.

NOT LIKE THIS.

RATATA-TATA

⟨MY GOD.⟩

⟨LOOK WHAT'S BECOME OF US...⟩

WHY, MIGHT I ASK--

SPLOOSH

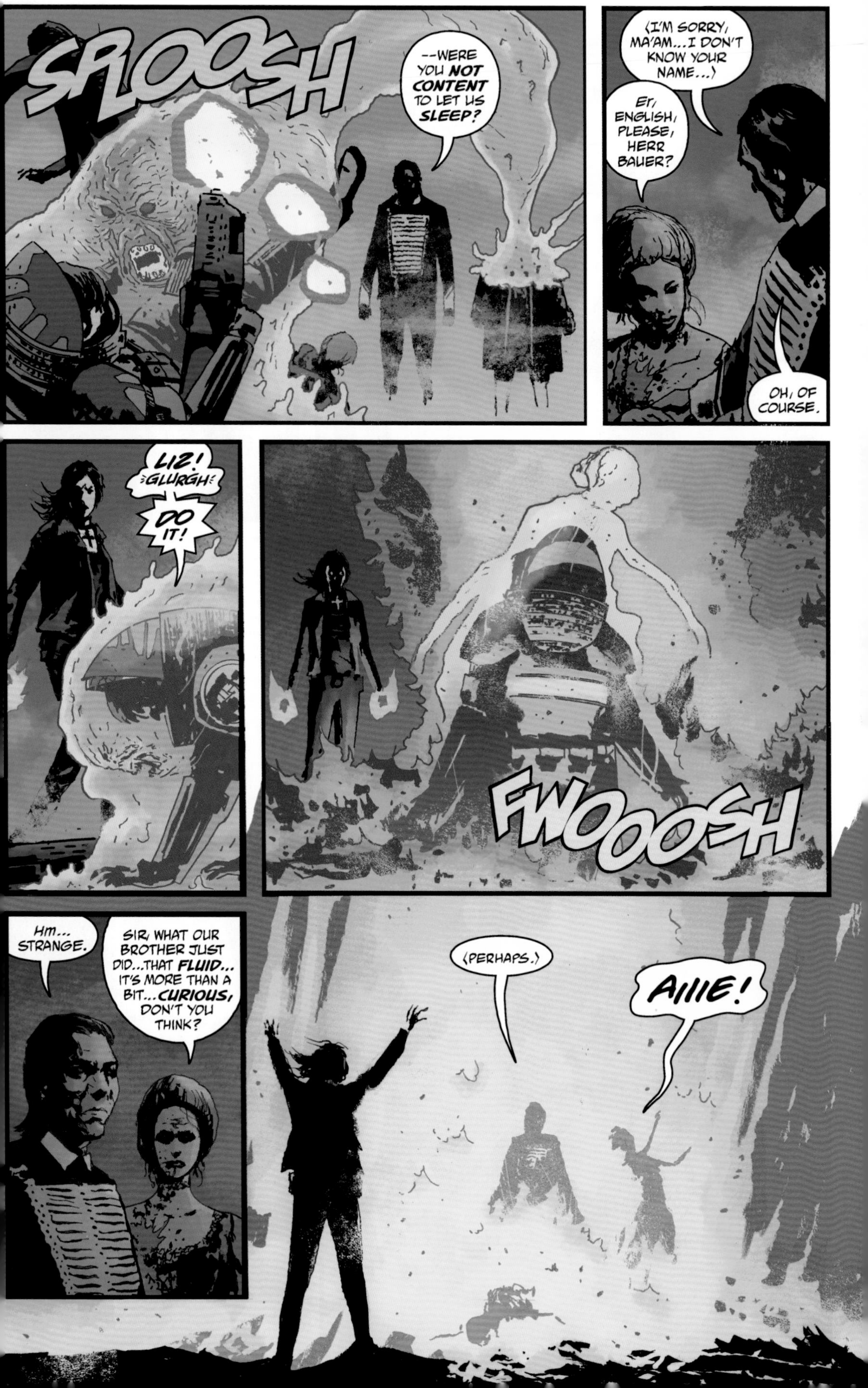
SPLOOSH
--WERE YOU NOT CONTENT TO LET US SLEEP?
(I'M SORRY, MA'AM... I DON'T KNOW YOUR NAME...)
Er, ENGLISH, PLEASE, HERR BAUER?
OH, OF COURSE.
LIZ! GLURGH DO IT!
FWOOOSH
Hm... STRANGE.
SIR, WHAT OUR BROTHER JUST DID...THAT FLUID... IT'S MORE THAN A BIT...CURIOUS, DON'T YOU THINK?
(PERHAPS.)
AIIIE!

FIRE?

WE HID SO *PATIENTLY*-- FOR *CENTURIES.* BUT THERE WERE *OTHERS,* DEEPER STILL.

EVEN *OUR* ELDERS DIDN'T KNOW OF THEM.

IT WAS *FIRE* THAT DID IT...

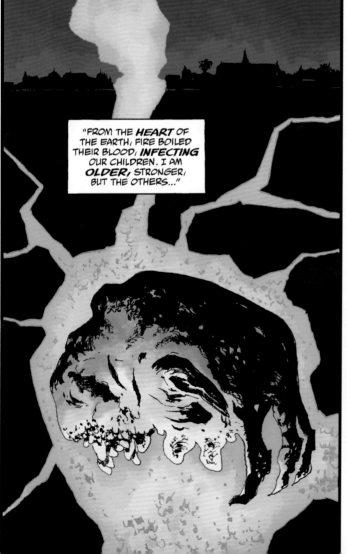

"FROM THE *HEART* OF THE EARTH, FIRE BOILED THEIR BLOOD, *INFECTING* OUR CHILDREN. I AM *OLDER,* STRONGER, BUT THE OTHERS..."

HEINRICH, LUDLOW, THE COLONISTS... THEY DEFENDED THIS GROUND WHEN THE VAMPIRE KILLER CAME.

THEN AFTER ALL THOSE YEARS SPENT *WAITING* FOR JUDGMENT DAY--THEY ARE TURNED INTO--INTO *WHAT?*

NOW JUDGMENT DAY HAS BEEN--

THOK

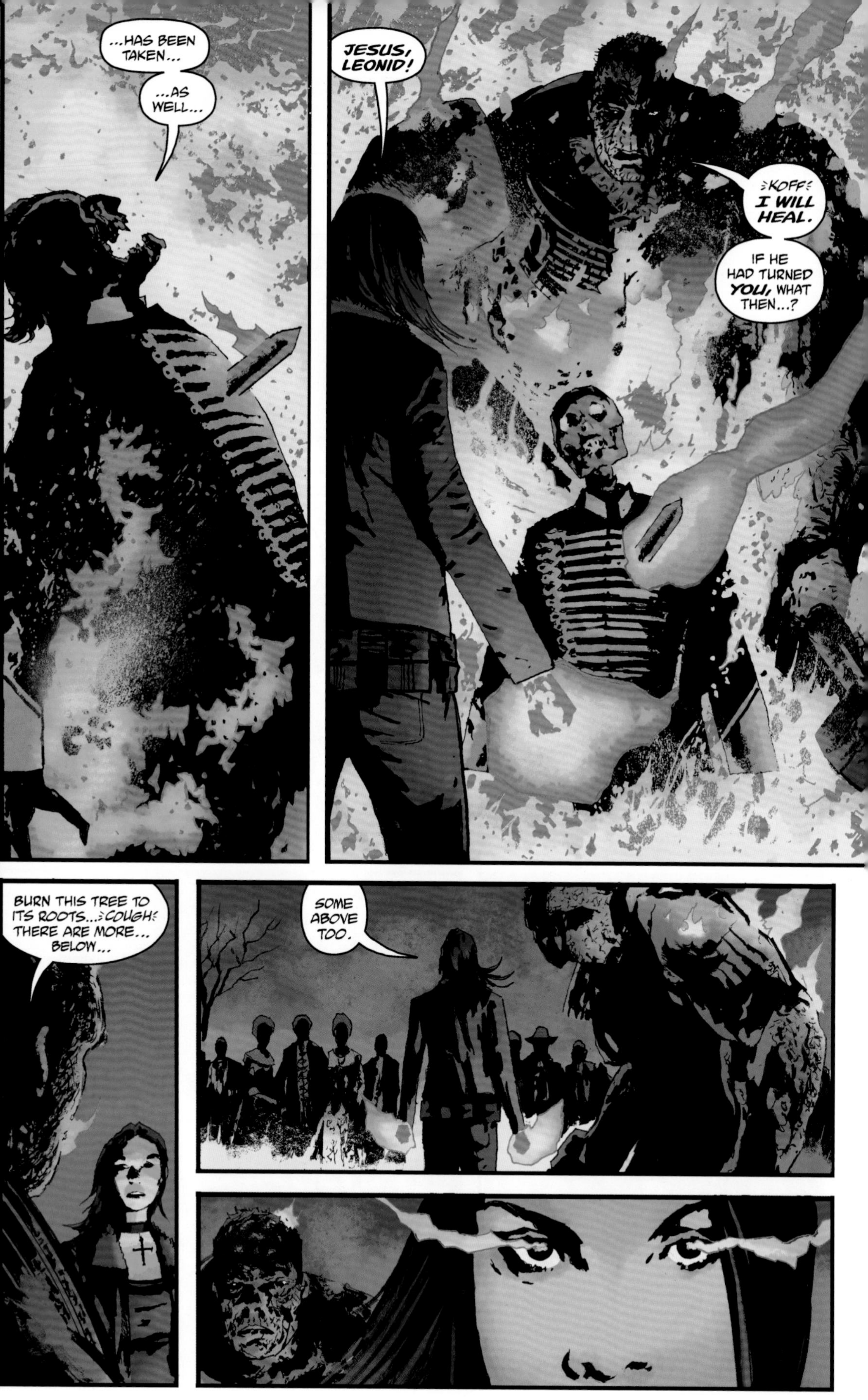
...HAS BEEN TAKEN...
...AS WELL...
JESUS, LEONID!
KOFF I WILL HEAL.
IF HE HAD TURNED YOU, WHAT THEN...?
BURN THIS TREE TO ITS ROOTS... COUGH THERE ARE MORE... BELOW...
SOME ABOVE TOO.

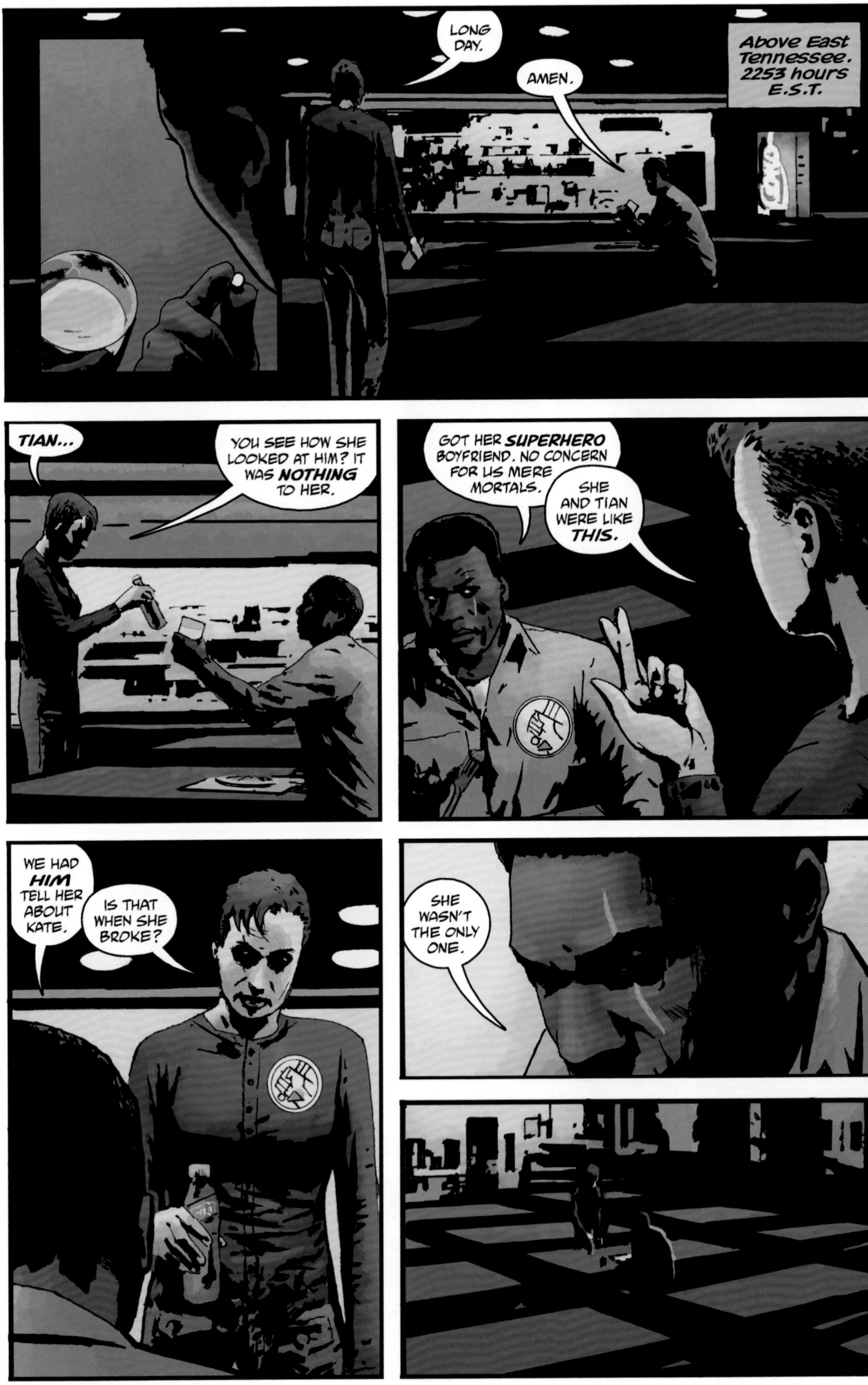
Above East Tennessee. 2253 hours E.S.T.
LONG DAY.
AMEN.
TIAN...
YOU SEE HOW SHE LOOKED AT HIM? IT WAS NOTHING TO HER.
GOT HER SUPERHERO BOYFRIEND. NO CONCERN FOR US MERE MORTALS.
SHE AND TIAN WERE LIKE THIS.
WE HAD HIM TELL HER ABOUT KATE.
IS THAT WHEN SHE BROKE?
SHE WASN'T THE ONLY ONE.

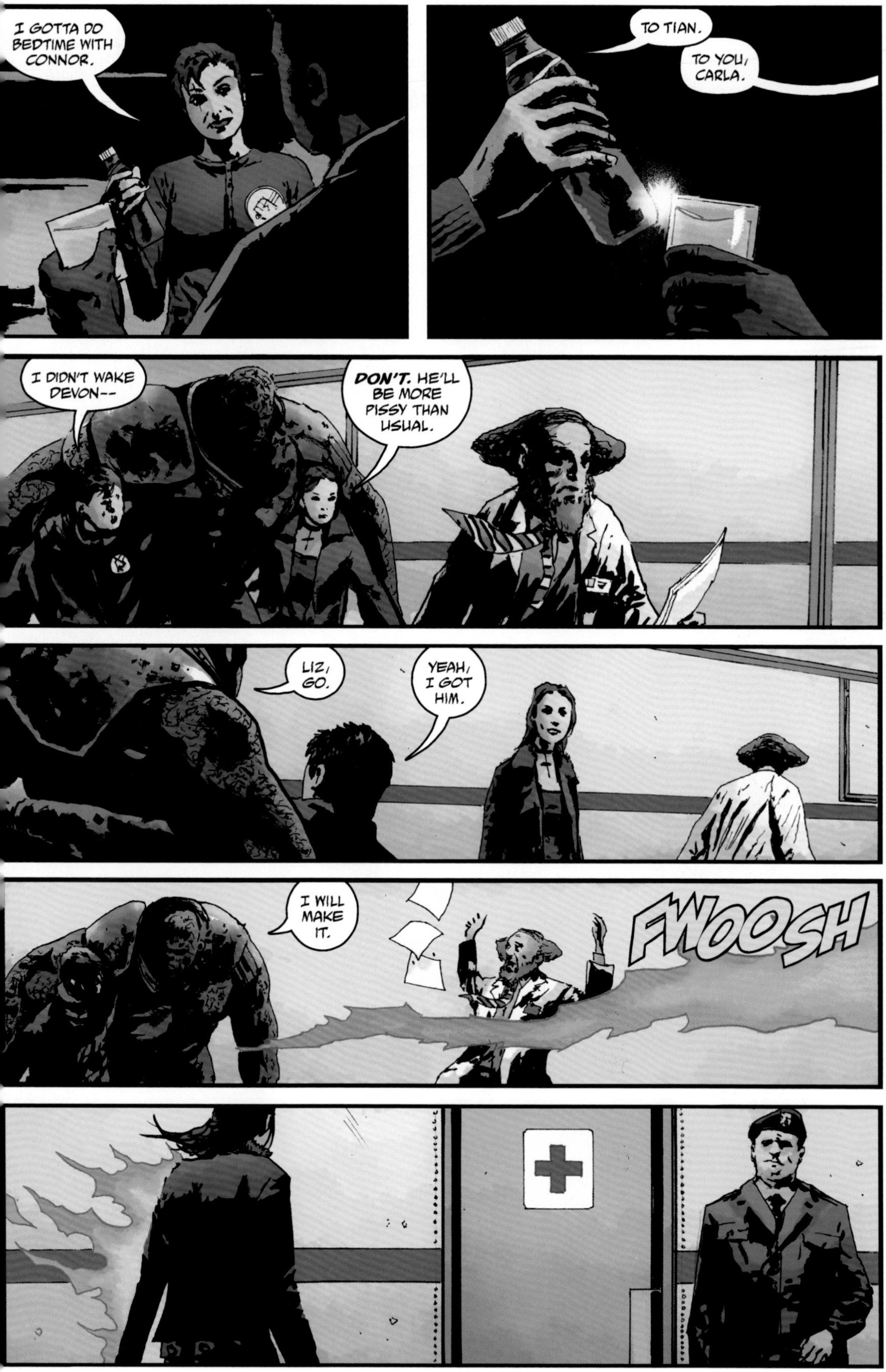
I GOTTA DO BEDTIME WITH CONNOR.
TO TIAN.
TO YOU, CARLA.
I DIDN'T WAKE DEVON--
DON'T. HE'LL BE MORE PISSY THAN USUAL.
LIZ, GO.
YEAH, I GOT HIM.
I WILL MAKE IT.
FWOOSH

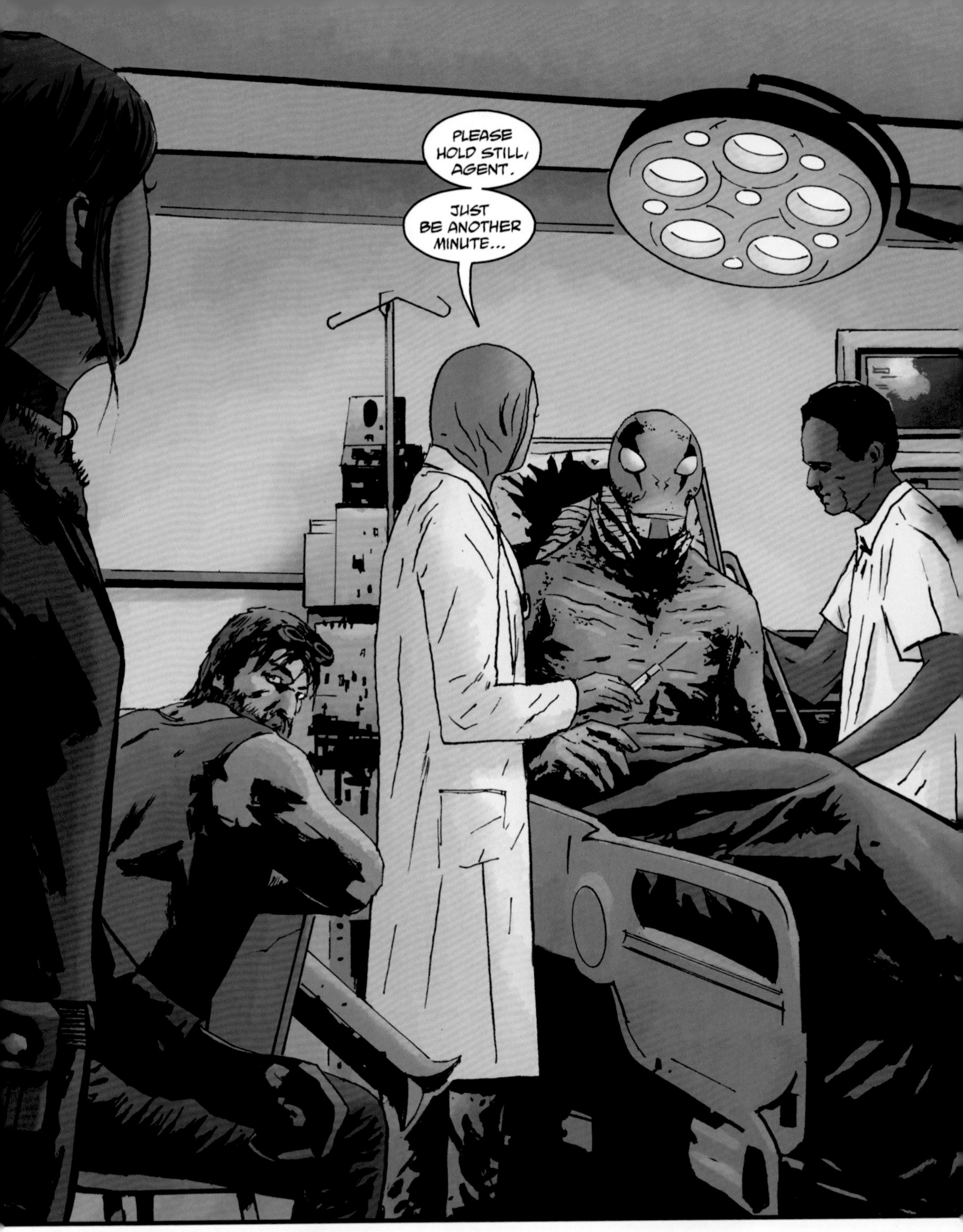
PLEASE HOLD STILL, AGENT.
JUST BE ANOTHER MINUTE...

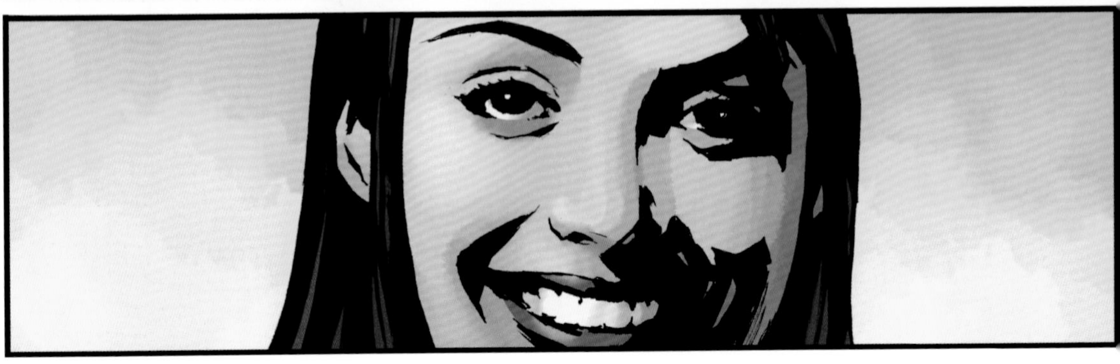

CHAPTER THREE

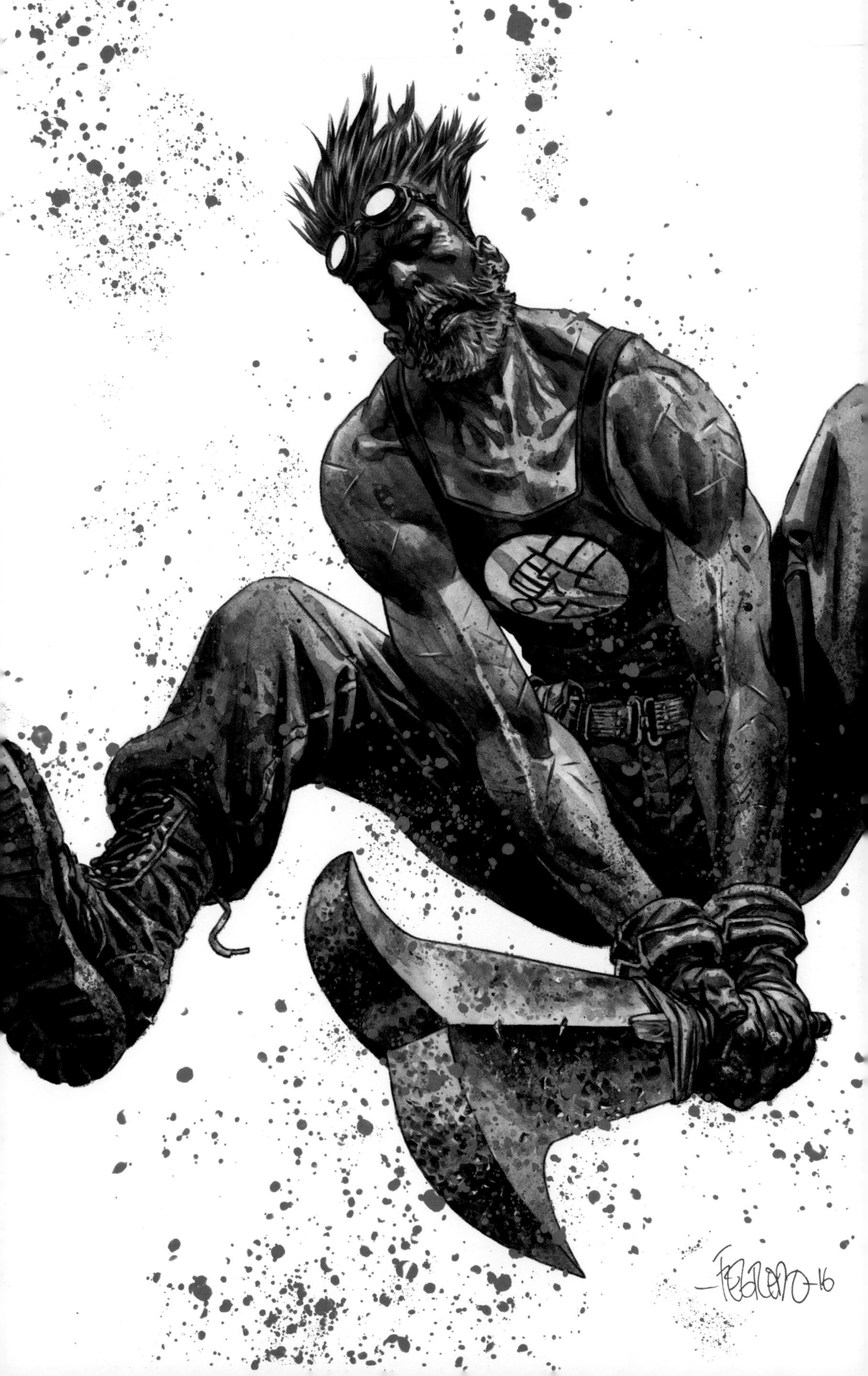

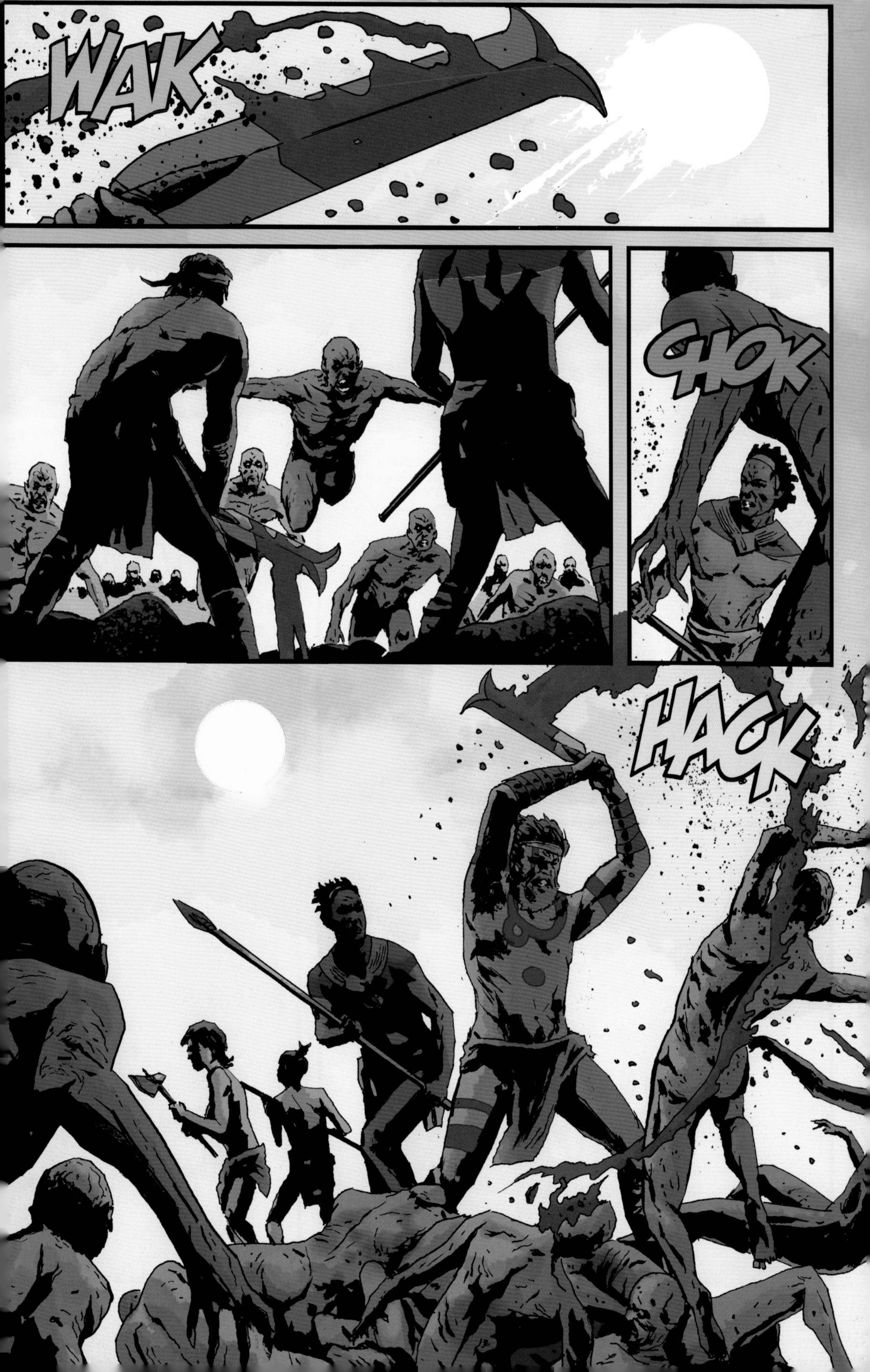
WAK
CHOK
HACK

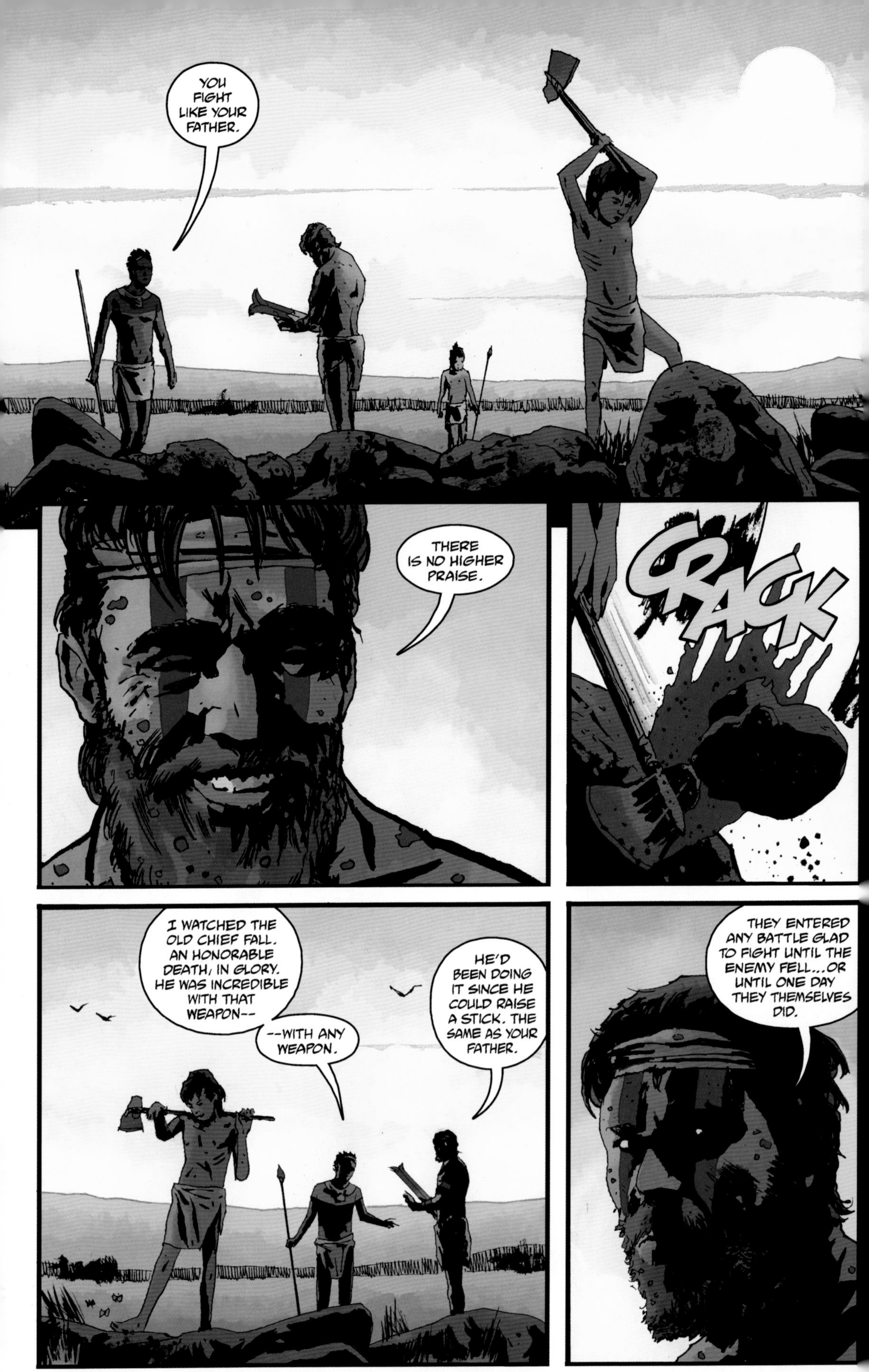
YOU FIGHT LIKE YOUR FATHER.
THERE IS NO HIGHER PRAISE.
CRACK
I WATCHED THE OLD CHIEF FALL. AN HONORABLE DEATH, IN GLORY. HE WAS INCREDIBLE WITH THAT WEAPON--
--WITH ANY WEAPON.
HE'D BEEN DOING IT SINCE HE COULD RAISE A STICK. THE SAME AS YOUR FATHER.
THEY ENTERED ANY BATTLE GLAD TO FIGHT UNTIL THE ENEMY FELL...OR UNTIL ONE DAY THEY THEMSELVES DID.

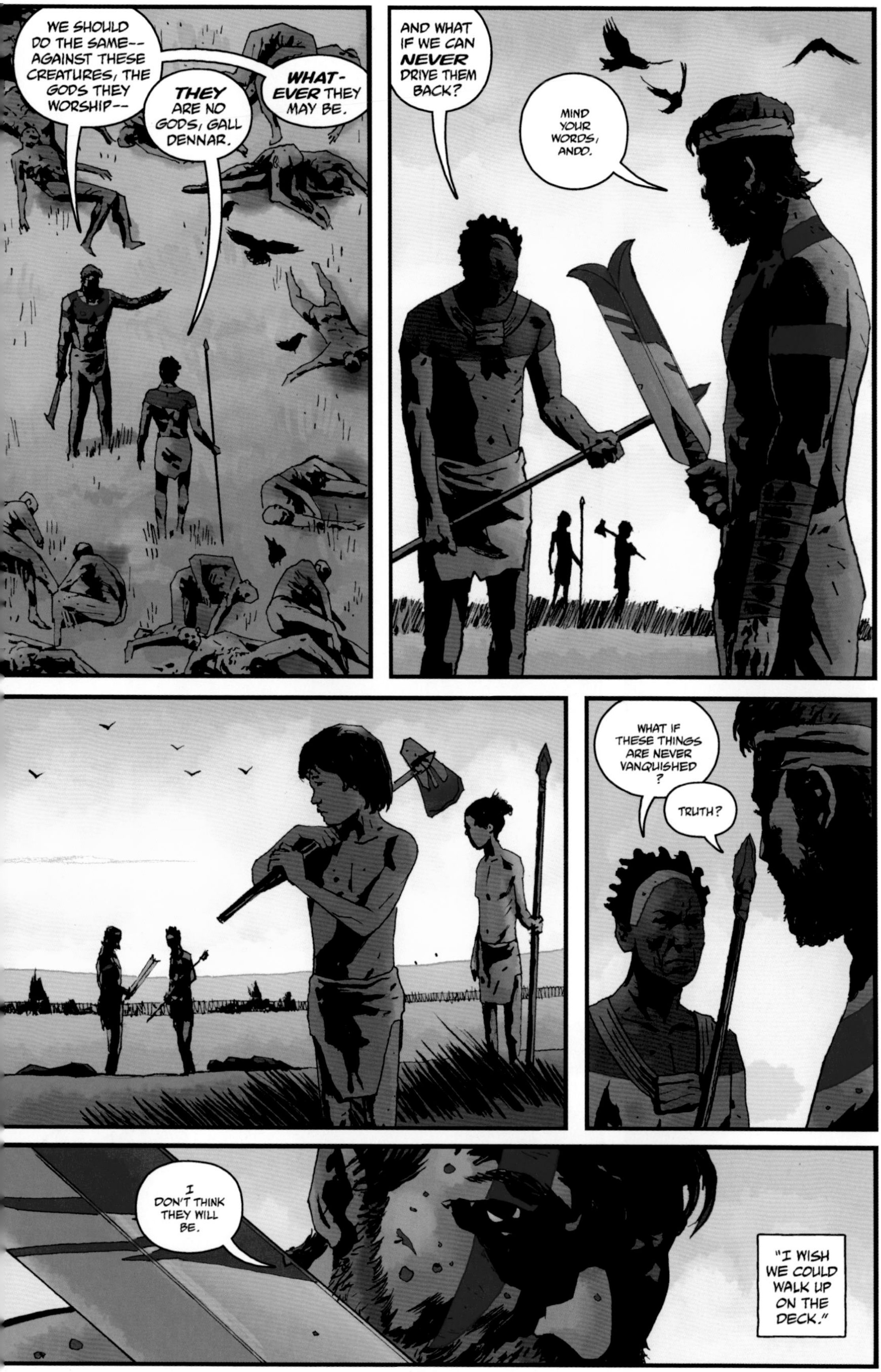
WE SHOULD DO THE SAME-- AGAINST THESE CREATURES, THE GODS THEY WORSHIP--
THEY ARE NO GODS, GALL DENNAR.
WHAT-EVER THEY MAY BE.
AND WHAT IF WE CAN NEVER DRIVE THEM BACK?
MIND YOUR WORDS, ANDO.
WHAT IF THESE THINGS ARE NEVER VANQUISHED?
TRUTH?
I DON'T THINK THEY WILL BE.
"I WISH WE COULD WALK UP ON THE DECK."

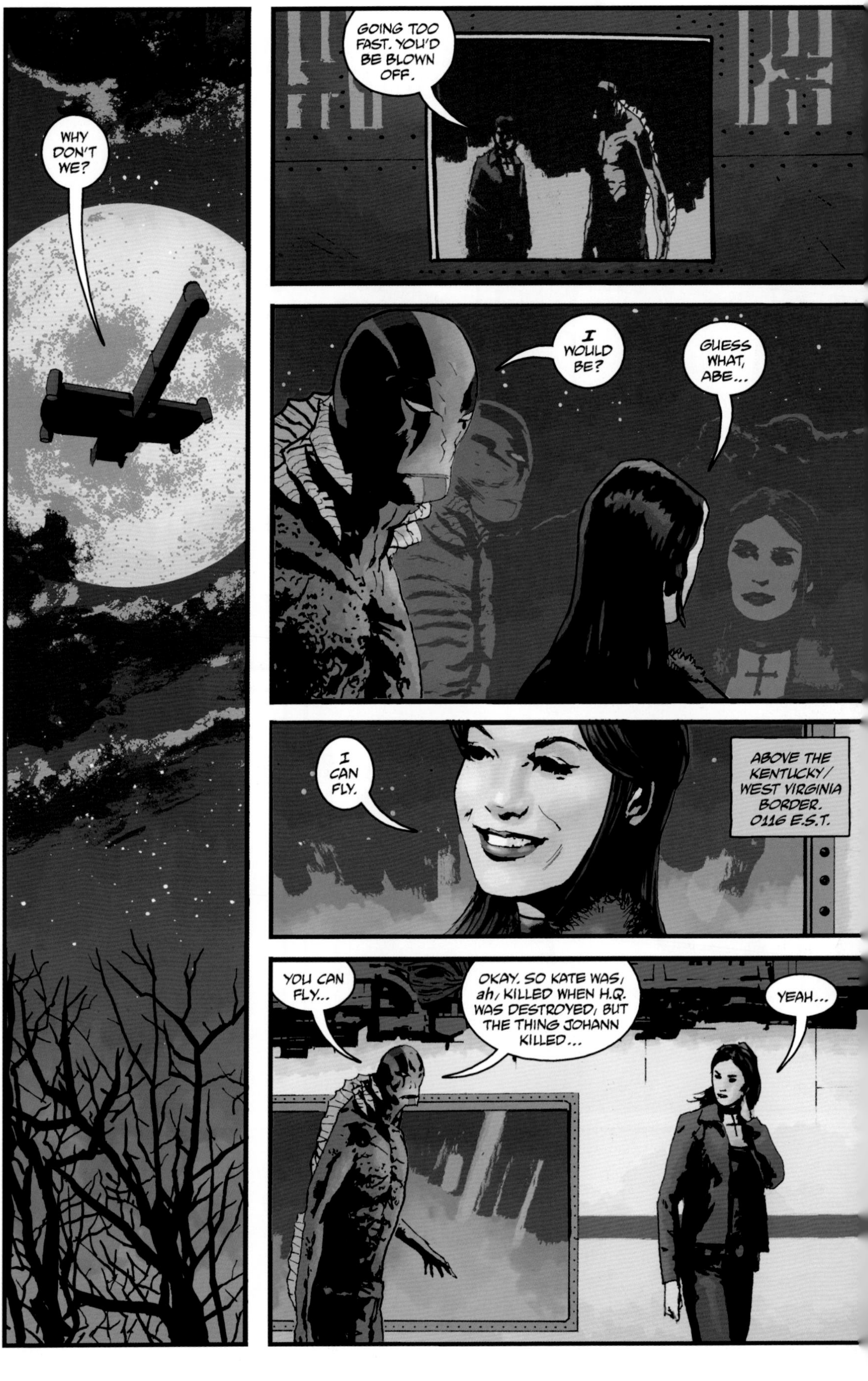
WHY DON'T WE?
GOING TOO FAST. YOU'D BE BLOWN OFF.
I WOULD BE?
GUESS WHAT, ABE...
ABOVE THE KENTUCKY/ WEST VIRGINIA BORDER. 0116 E.S.T.
I CAN FLY.
YOU CAN FLY...
OKAY. SO KATE WAS, ah, KILLED WHEN H.Q. WAS DESTROYED, BUT THE THING JOHANN KILLED...
YEAH...

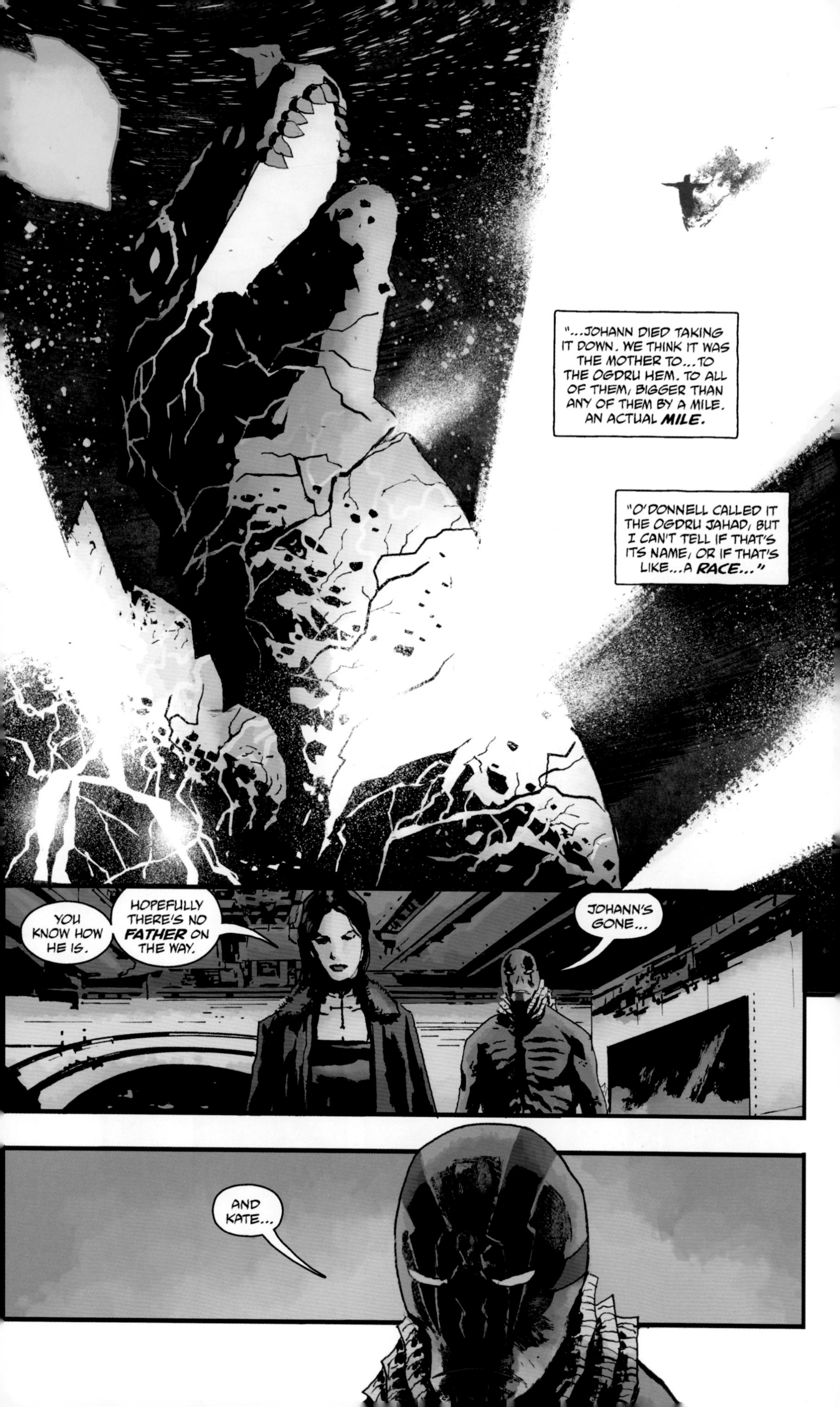
"...JOHANN DIED TAKING IT DOWN. WE THINK IT WAS THE MOTHER TO...TO THE OGDRU HEM. TO ALL OF THEM, BIGGER THAN ANY OF THEM BY A MILE. AN ACTUAL **MILE.**
"O'DONNELL CALLED IT THE OGDRU JAHAD, BUT I CAN'T TELL IF THAT'S ITS NAME, OR IF THAT'S LIKE...A **RACE...**"
YOU KNOW HOW HE IS.
HOPEFULLY THERE'S NO **FATHER** ON THE WAY.
JOHANN'S GONE...
AND KATE...

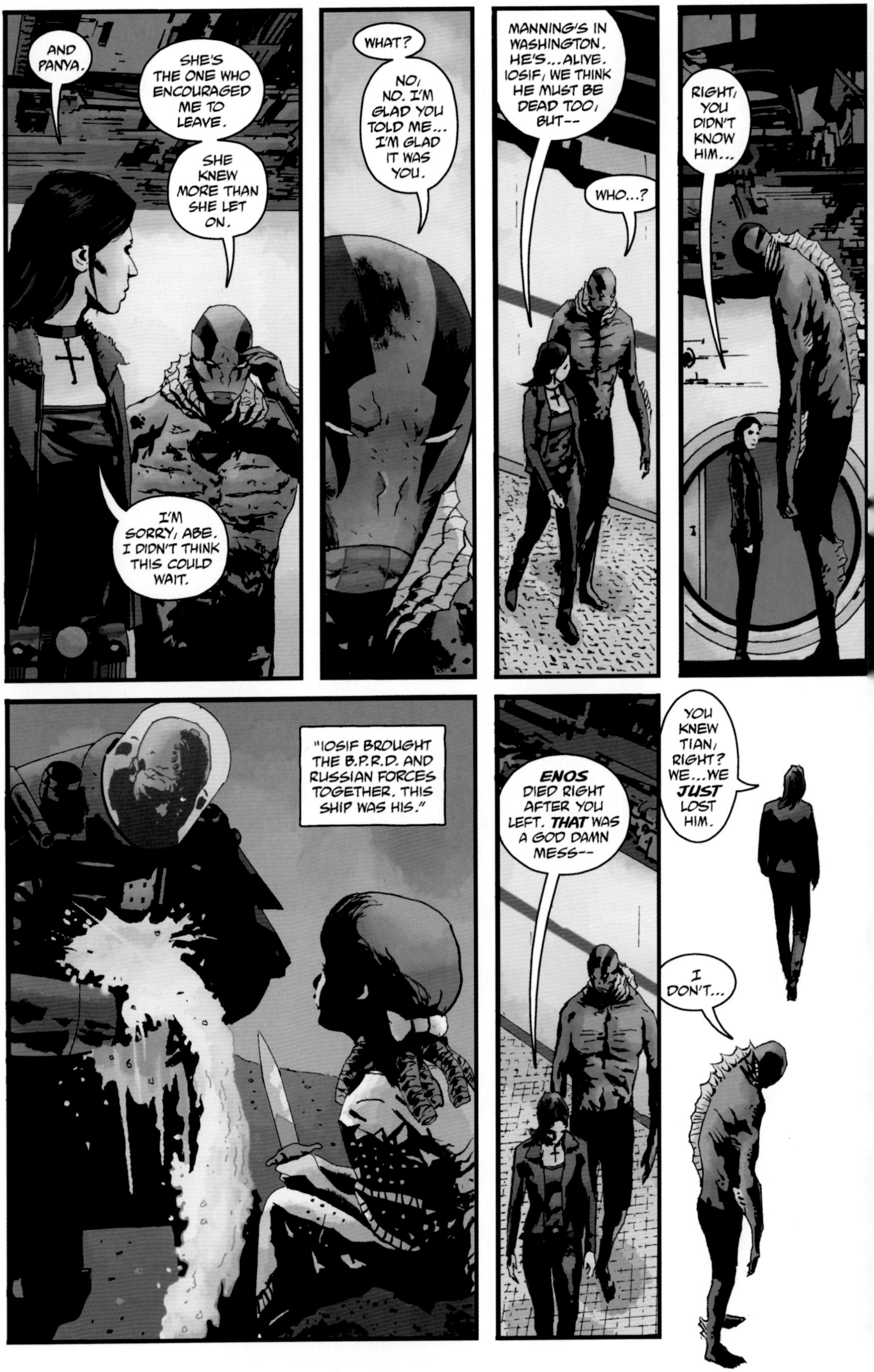

AND PANYA.
SHE'S THE ONE WHO ENCOURAGED ME TO LEAVE.
SHE KNEW MORE THAN SHE LET ON.
I'M SORRY, ABE. I DIDN'T THINK THIS COULD WAIT.
WHAT?
NO, NO. I'M GLAD YOU TOLD ME... I'M GLAD IT WAS YOU.
MANNING'S IN WASHINGTON. HE'S...ALIVE. IOSIF, WE THINK HE MUST BE DEAD TOO, BUT--
WHO...?
RIGHT, YOU DIDN'T KNOW HIM...
"IOSIF BROUGHT THE B.P.R.D. AND RUSSIAN FORCES TOGETHER. THIS SHIP WAS HIS."
ENOS DIED RIGHT AFTER YOU LEFT. THAT WAS A GOD DAMN MESS--
YOU KNEW TIAN, RIGHT? WE...WE JUST LOST HIM.
I DON'T...

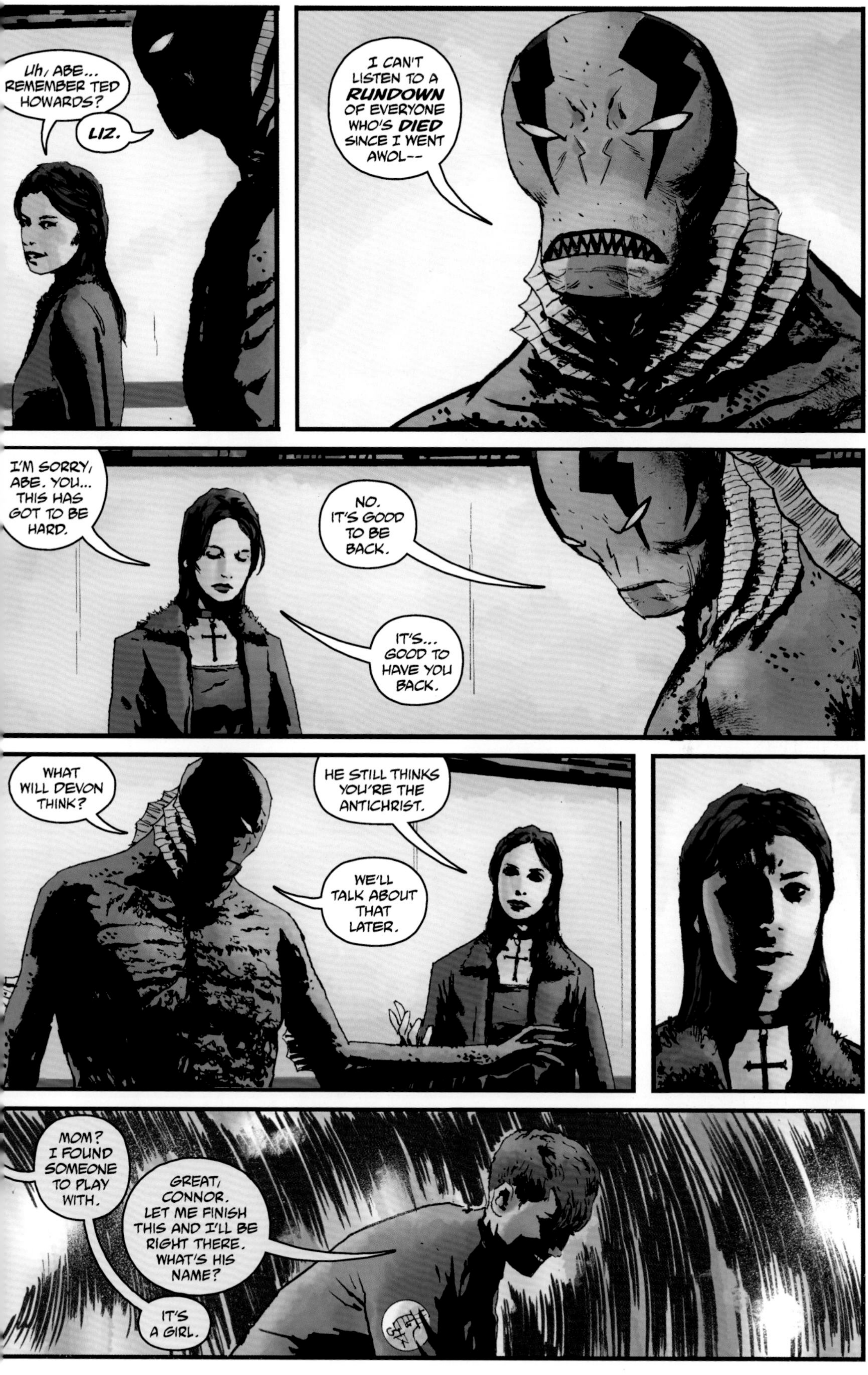
UH, ABE... REMEMBER TED HOWARDS?
LIZ.
I CAN'T LISTEN TO A RUNDOWN OF EVERYONE WHO'S DIED SINCE I WENT AWOL--
I'M SORRY, ABE. YOU... THIS HAS GOT TO BE HARD.
NO. IT'S GOOD TO BE BACK.
IT'S... GOOD TO HAVE YOU BACK.
WHAT WILL DEVON THINK?
HE STILL THINKS YOU'RE THE ANTICHRIST.
WE'LL TALK ABOUT THAT LATER.
MOM? I FOUND SOMEONE TO PLAY WITH.
GREAT, CONNOR. LET ME FINISH THIS AND I'LL BE RIGHT THERE. WHAT'S HIS NAME?
IT'S A GIRL.

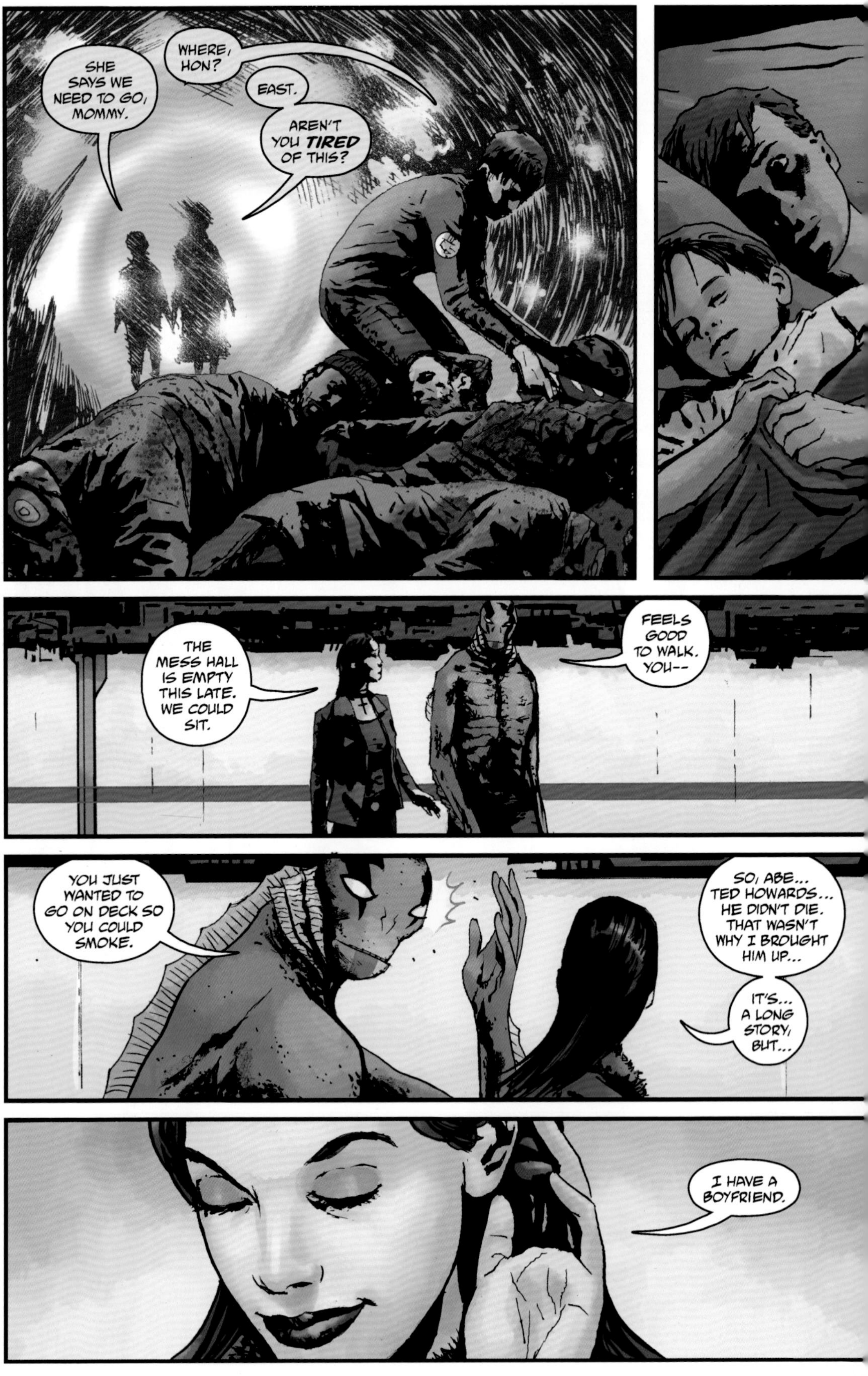
SHE SAYS WE NEED TO GO, MOMMY.
WHERE, HON?
EAST.
AREN'T YOU TIRED OF THIS?
THE MESS HALL IS EMPTY THIS LATE. WE COULD SIT.
FEELS GOOD TO WALK. YOU--
YOU JUST WANTED TO GO ON DECK SO YOU COULD SMOKE.
SO, ABE... TED HOWARDS... HE DIDN'T DIE. THAT WASN'T WHY I BROUGHT HIM UP...
IT'S... A LONG STORY, BUT...
I HAVE A BOYFRIEND.

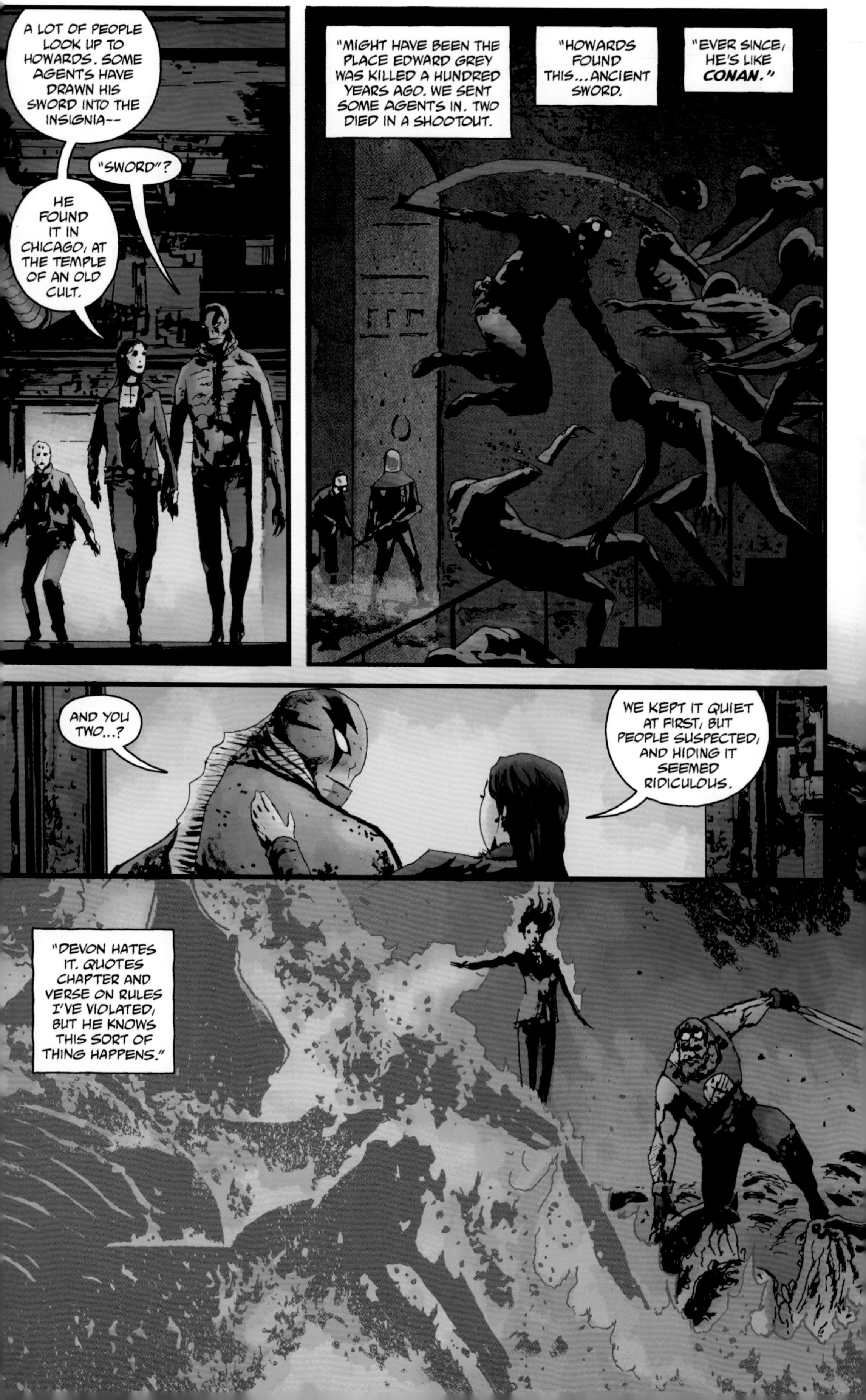
A LOT OF PEOPLE LOOK UP TO HOWARDS. SOME AGENTS HAVE DRAWN HIS SWORD INTO THE INSIGNIA--
"SWORD"?
HE FOUND IT IN CHICAGO, AT THE TEMPLE OF AN OLD CULT.
"MIGHT HAVE BEEN THE PLACE EDWARD GREY WAS KILLED A HUNDRED YEARS AGO. WE SENT SOME AGENTS IN. TWO DIED IN A SHOOTOUT.
"HOWARDS FOUND THIS... ANCIENT SWORD.
"EVER SINCE, HE'S LIKE **CONAN**."
AND YOU TWO...?
WE KEPT IT QUIET AT FIRST, BUT PEOPLE SUSPECTED, AND HIDING IT SEEMED RIDICULOUS.
"DEVON HATES IT. QUOTES CHAPTER AND VERSE ON RULES I'VE VIOLATED, BUT HE KNOWS THIS SORT OF THING HAPPENS."

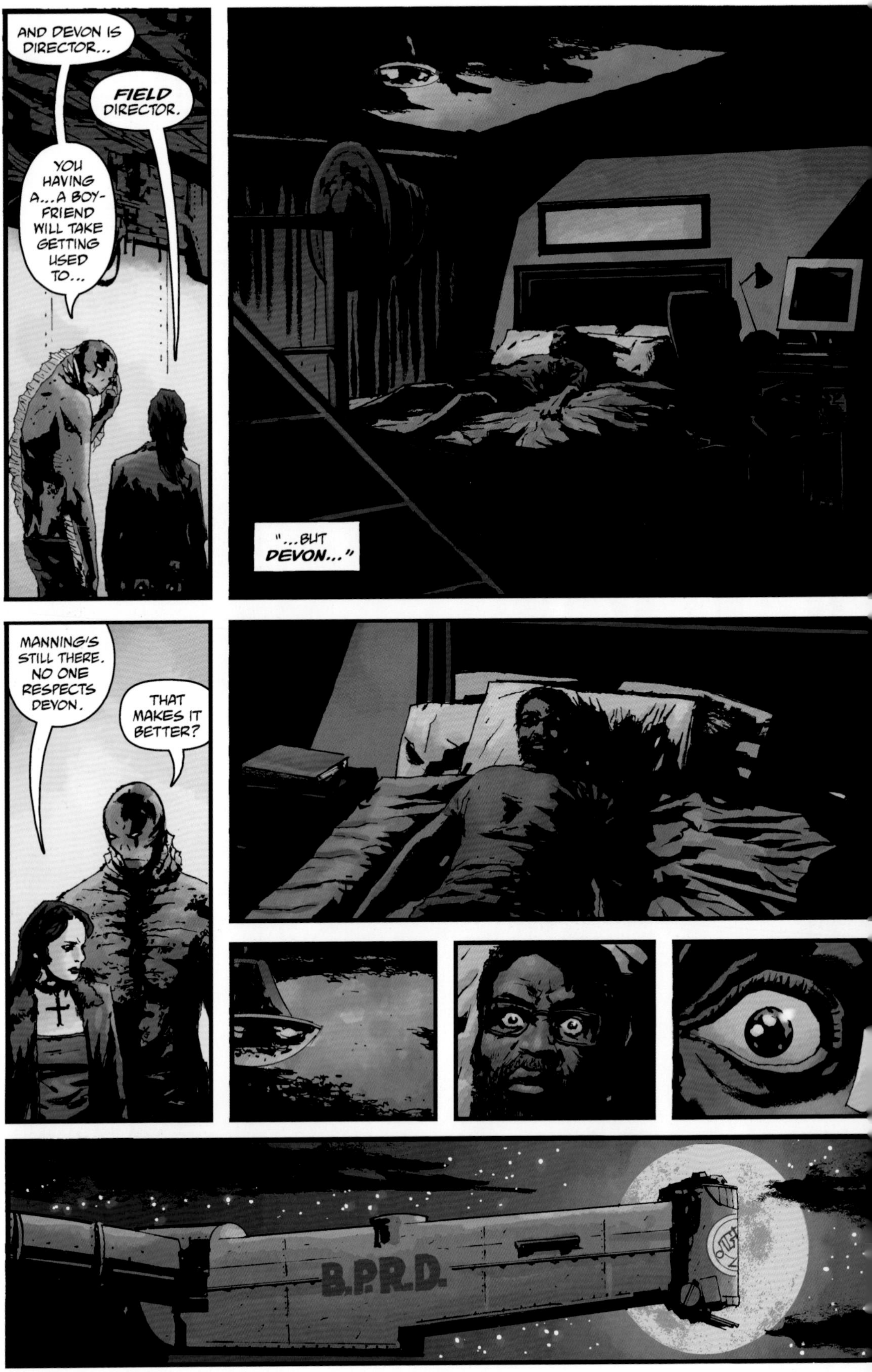
AND DEVON IS DIRECTOR...
FIELD DIRECTOR.
YOU HAVING A...A BOY-FRIEND WILL TAKE GETTING USED TO...
"...BUT DEVON..."
MANNING'S STILL THERE. NO ONE RESPECTS DEVON.
THAT MAKES IT BETTER?
B.P.R.D.

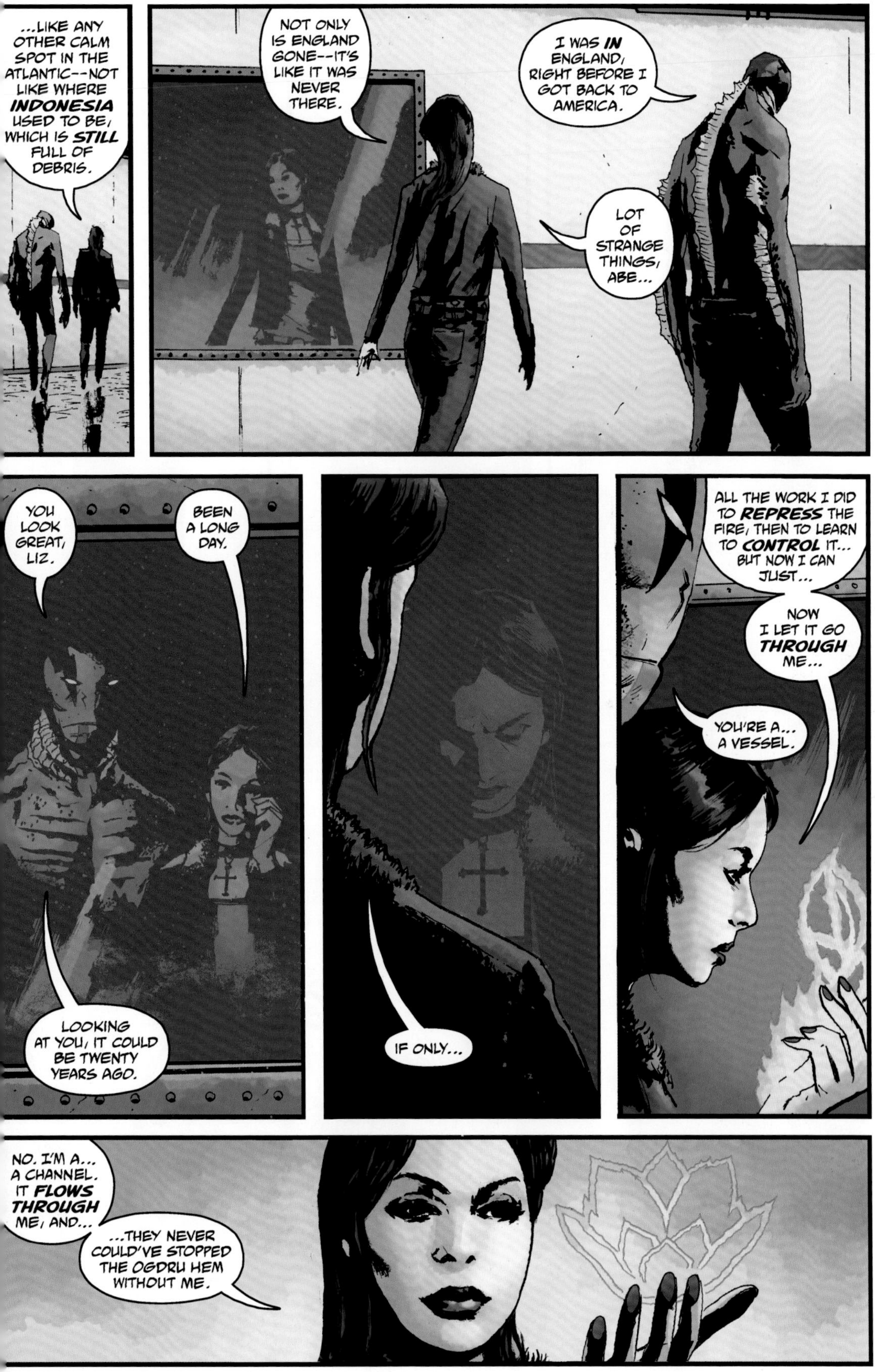
...LIKE ANY OTHER CALM SPOT IN THE ATLANTIC--NOT LIKE WHERE INDONESIA USED TO BE, WHICH IS STILL FULL OF DEBRIS.
NOT ONLY IS ENGLAND GONE--IT'S LIKE IT WAS NEVER THERE.
I WAS IN ENGLAND, RIGHT BEFORE I GOT BACK TO AMERICA.
LOT OF STRANGE THINGS, ABE...
YOU LOOK GREAT, LIZ.
BEEN A LONG DAY.
LOOKING AT YOU, IT COULD BE TWENTY YEARS AGO.
IF ONLY...
ALL THE WORK I DID TO REPRESS THE FIRE, THEN TO LEARN TO CONTROL IT... BUT NOW I CAN JUST...
NOW I LET IT GO THROUGH ME...
YOU'RE A... A VESSEL.
NO. I'M A... A CHANNEL. IT FLOWS THROUGH ME, AND...
...THEY NEVER COULD'VE STOPPED THE OGDRU HEM WITHOUT ME.

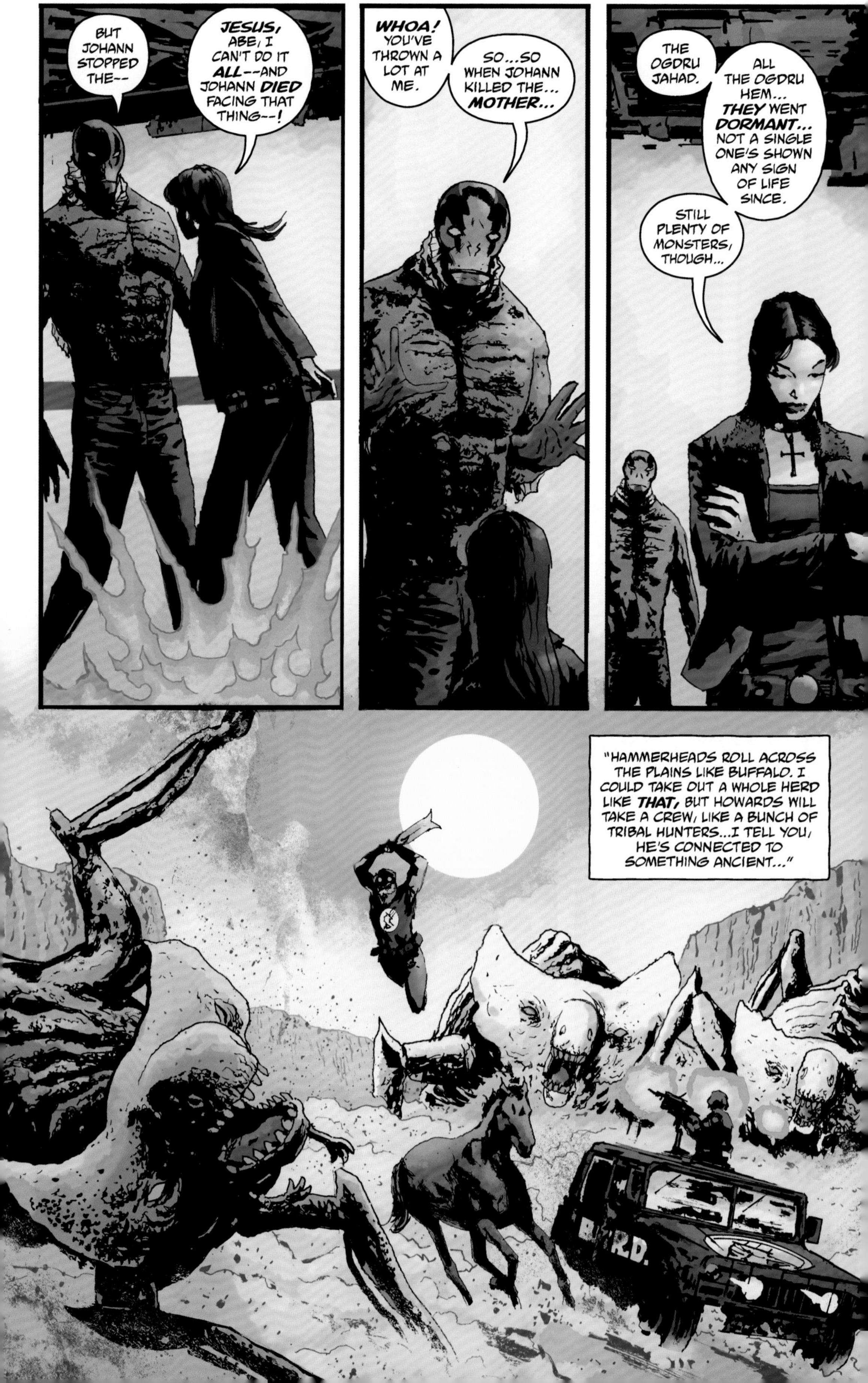
BUT JOHANN STOPPED THE--
JESUS, ABE, I CAN'T DO IT ALL--AND JOHANN DIED FACING THAT THING--!
WHOA! YOU'VE THROWN A LOT AT ME.
SO...SO WHEN JOHANN KILLED THE... MOTHER...
THE OGDRU JAHAD.
ALL THE OGDRU HEM... THEY WENT DORMANT... NOT A SINGLE ONE'S SHOWN ANY SIGN OF LIFE SINCE.
STILL PLENTY OF MONSTERS, THOUGH...
"HAMMERHEADS ROLL ACROSS THE PLAINS LIKE BUFFALO. I COULD TAKE OUT A WHOLE HERD LIKE THAT, BUT HOWARDS WILL TAKE A CREW, LIKE A BUNCH OF TRIBAL HUNTERS...I TELL YOU, HE'S CONNECTED TO SOMETHING ANCIENT..."
B.P.R.D.

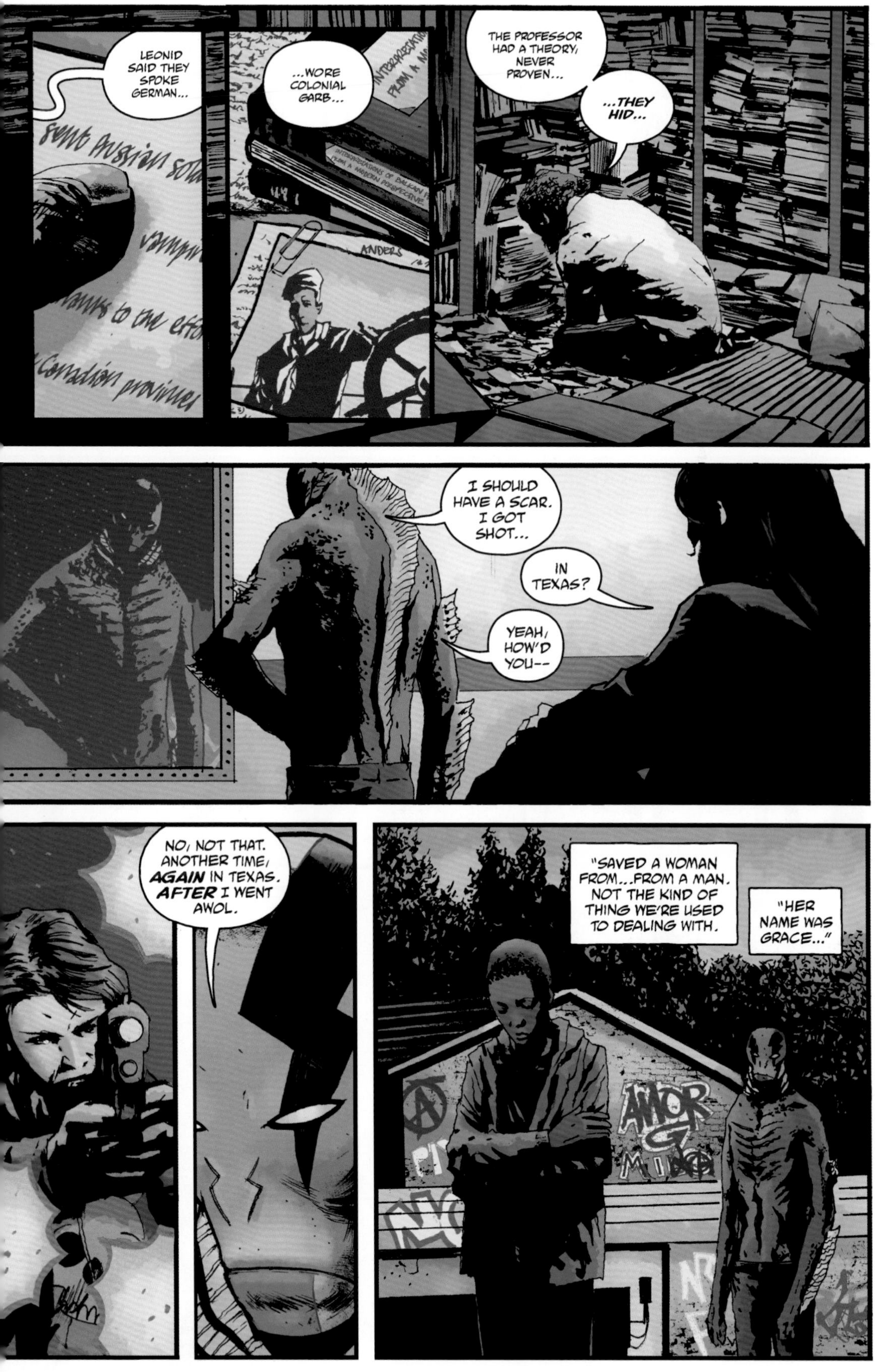
LEONID SAID THEY SPOKE GERMAN...
...WORE COLONIAL GARB...
THE PROFESSOR HAD A THEORY, NEVER PROVEN...
...THEY HID...
I SHOULD HAVE A SCAR. I GOT SHOT...
IN TEXAS?
YEAH, HOW'D YOU--
NO, NOT THAT. ANOTHER TIME, AGAIN IN TEXAS. AFTER I WENT AWOL.
"SAVED A WOMAN FROM...FROM A MAN. NOT THE KIND OF THING WE'RE USED TO DEALING WITH.
"HER NAME WAS GRACE..."

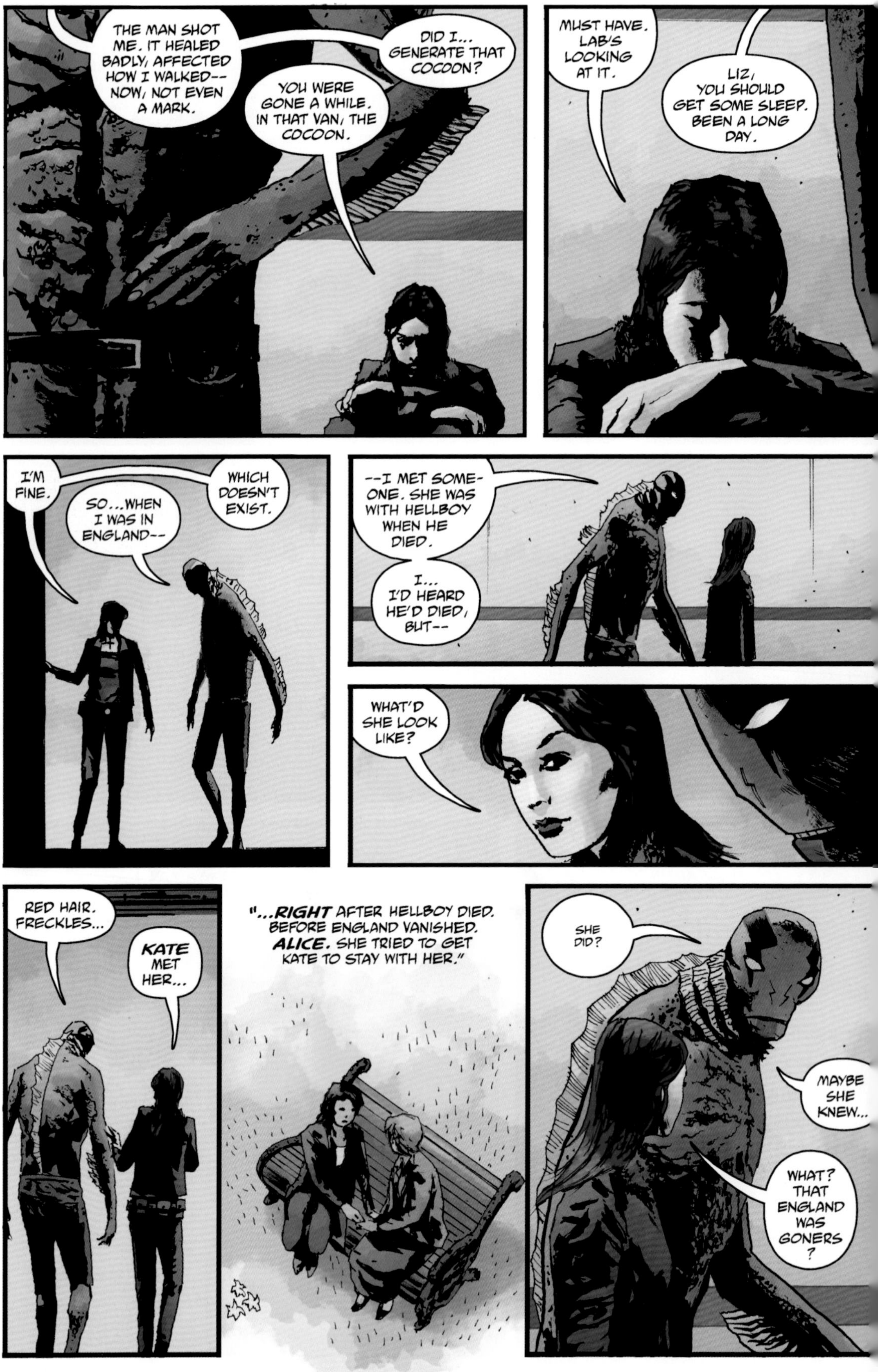
THE MAN SHOT ME. IT HEALED BADLY, AFFECTED HOW I WALKED-- NOW, NOT EVEN A MARK.
DID I... GENERATE THAT COCOON?
YOU WERE GONE A WHILE. IN THAT VAN, THE COCOON.
MUST HAVE. LAB'S LOOKING AT IT.
LIZ, YOU SHOULD GET SOME SLEEP. BEEN A LONG DAY.
I'M FINE.
WHICH DOESN'T EXIST.
SO...WHEN I WAS IN ENGLAND--
--I MET SOME-ONE. SHE WAS WITH HELLBOY WHEN HE DIED.
I... I'D HEARD HE'D DIED, BUT--
WHAT'D SHE LOOK LIKE?
RED HAIR. FRECKLES...
KATE MET HER...
"...RIGHT AFTER HELLBOY DIED. BEFORE ENGLAND VANISHED. ALICE. SHE TRIED TO GET KATE TO STAY WITH HER."
SHE DID?
MAYBE SHE KNEW...
WHAT? THAT ENGLAND WAS GONERS ?

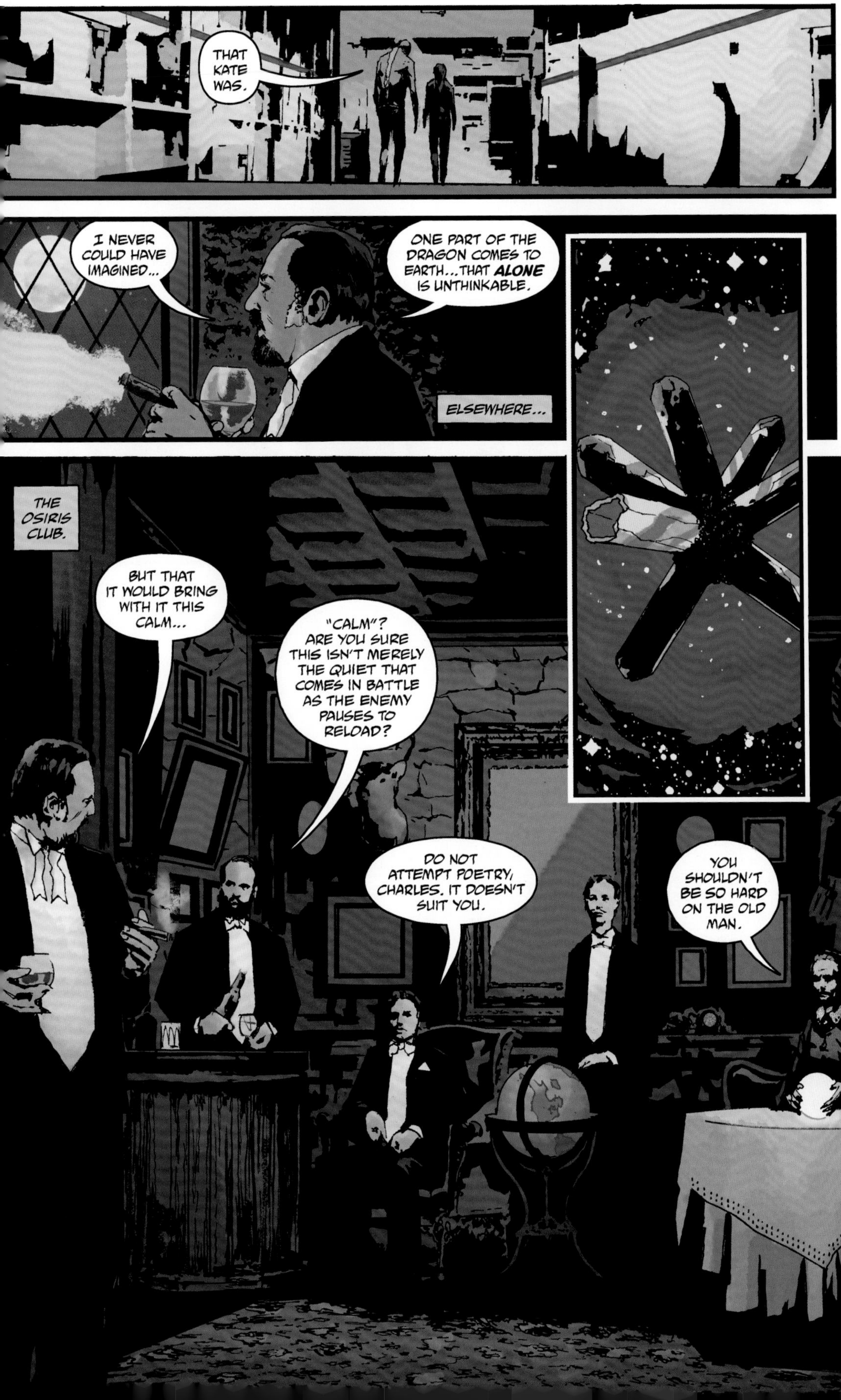

THAT KATE WAS.
I NEVER COULD HAVE IMAGINED...
ONE PART OF THE DRAGON COMES TO EARTH...THAT ALONE IS UNTHINKABLE.
ELSEWHERE...
THE OSIRIS CLUB.
BUT THAT IT WOULD BRING WITH IT THIS CALM...
"CALM"? ARE YOU SURE THIS ISN'T MERELY THE QUIET THAT COMES IN BATTLE AS THE ENEMY PAUSES TO RELOAD?
DO NOT ATTEMPT POETRY, CHARLES. IT DOESN'T SUIT YOU.
YOU SHOULDN'T BE SO HARD ON THE OLD MAN.

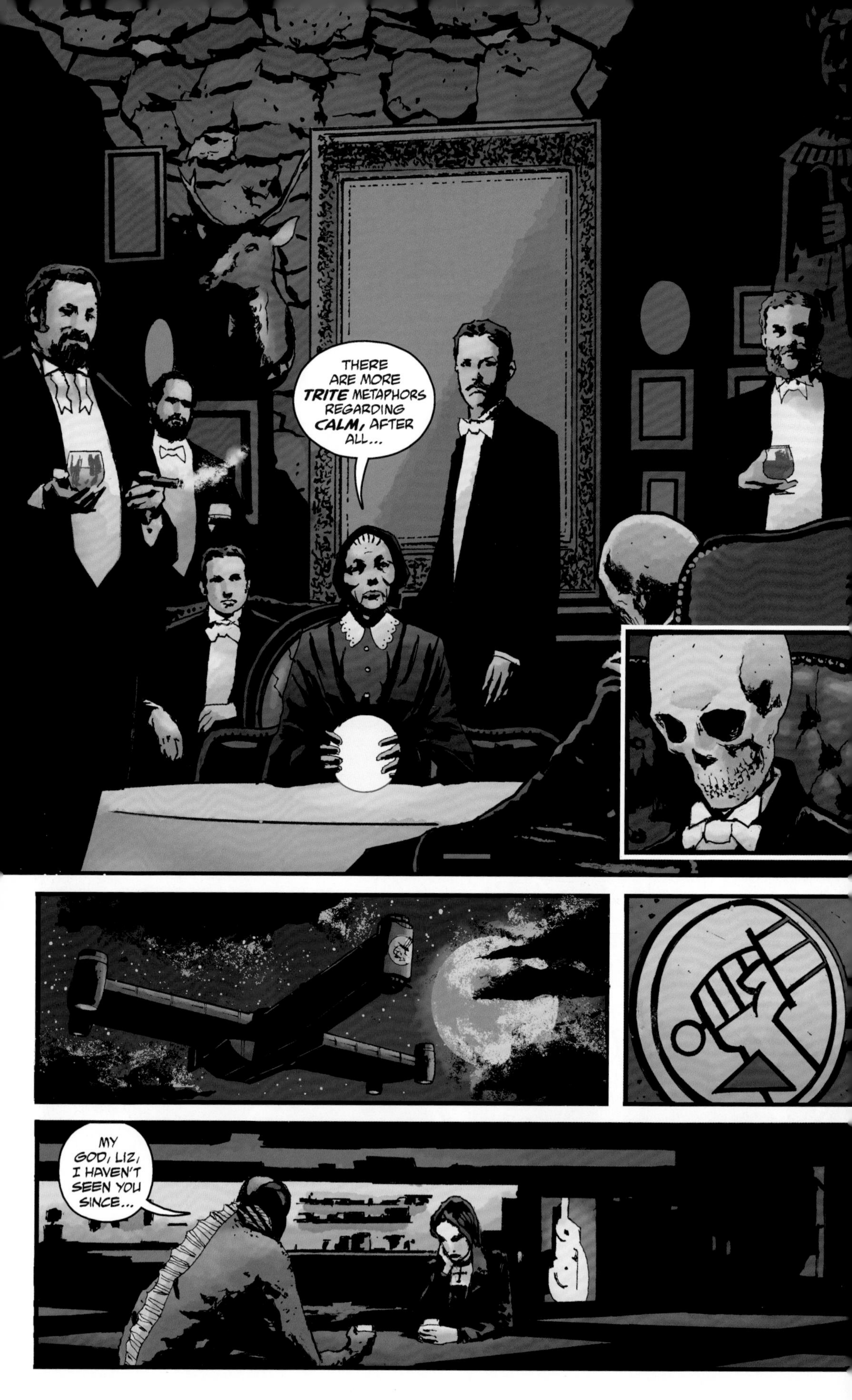
THERE ARE MORE TRITE METAPHORS REGARDING CALM, AFTER ALL...
MY GOD, LIZ, I HAVEN'T SEEN YOU SINCE...

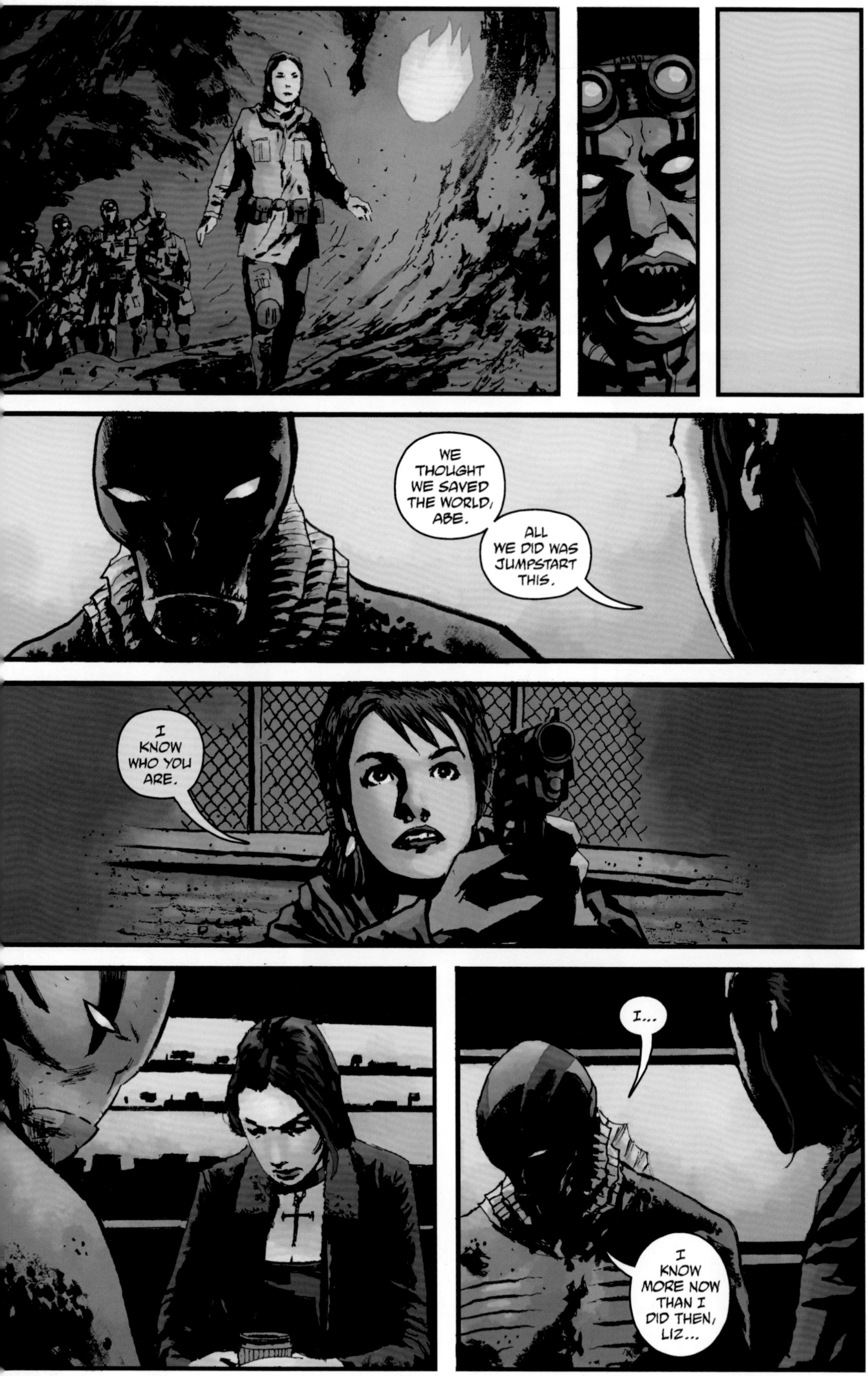
WE THOUGHT WE SAVED THE WORLD, ABE.
ALL WE DID WAS JUMPSTART THIS.
I KNOW WHO YOU ARE.
I...
I KNOW MORE NOW THAN I DID THEN, LIZ...

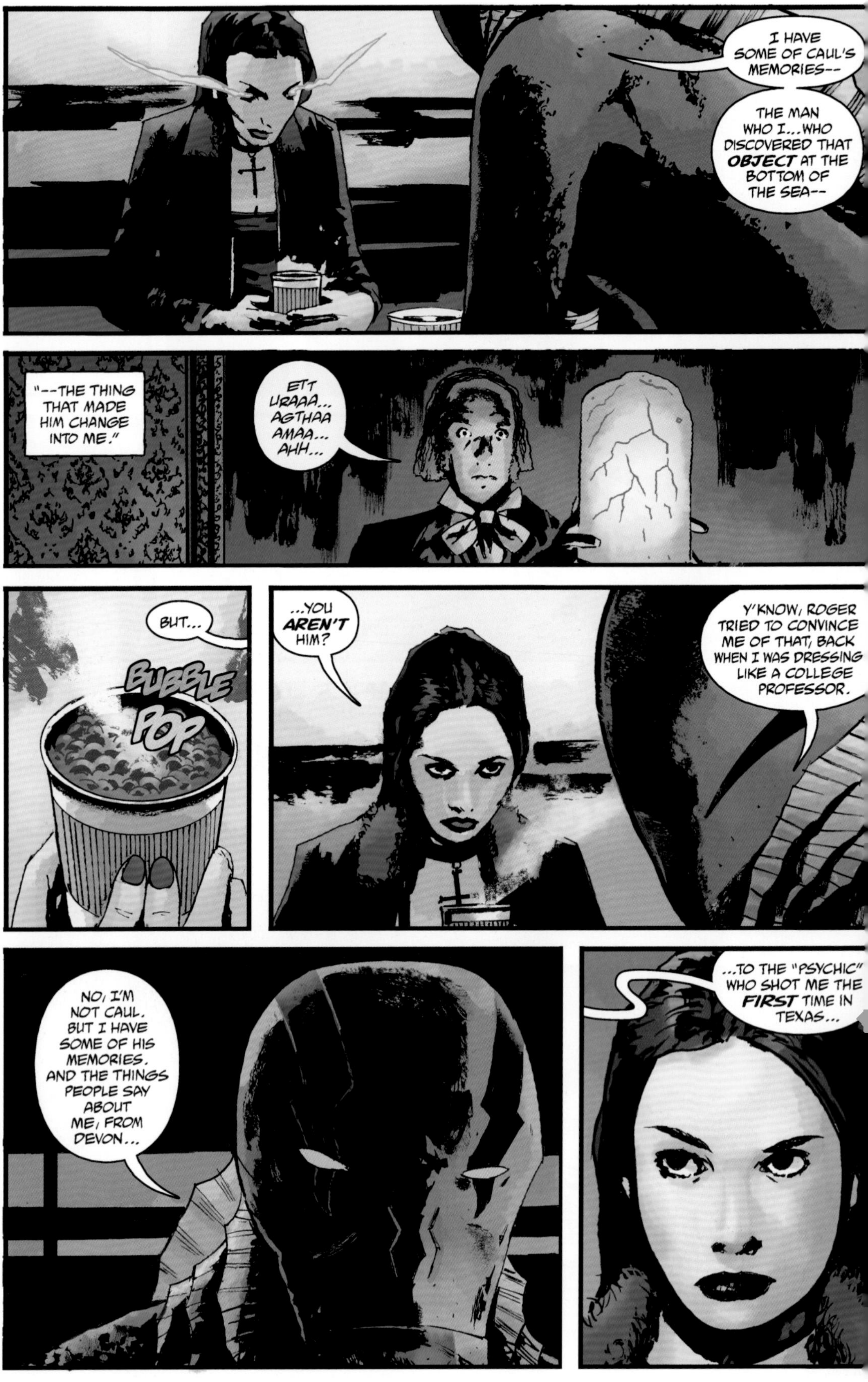
I HAVE SOME OF CAUL'S MEMORIES--
THE MAN WHO I...WHO DISCOVERED THAT OBJECT AT THE BOTTOM OF THE SEA--
"--THE THING THAT MADE HIM CHANGE INTO ME."
ETT URAAA... AGTHAA AMAA... AHH...
BUT...
BUBBLE
POP
...YOU AREN'T HIM?
Y'KNOW, ROGER TRIED TO CONVINCE ME OF THAT, BACK WHEN I WAS DRESSING LIKE A COLLEGE PROFESSOR.
NO, I'M NOT CAUL. BUT I HAVE SOME OF HIS MEMORIES. AND THE THINGS PEOPLE SAY ABOUT ME, FROM DEVON...
...TO THE "PSYCHIC" WHO SHOT ME THE FIRST TIME IN TEXAS...

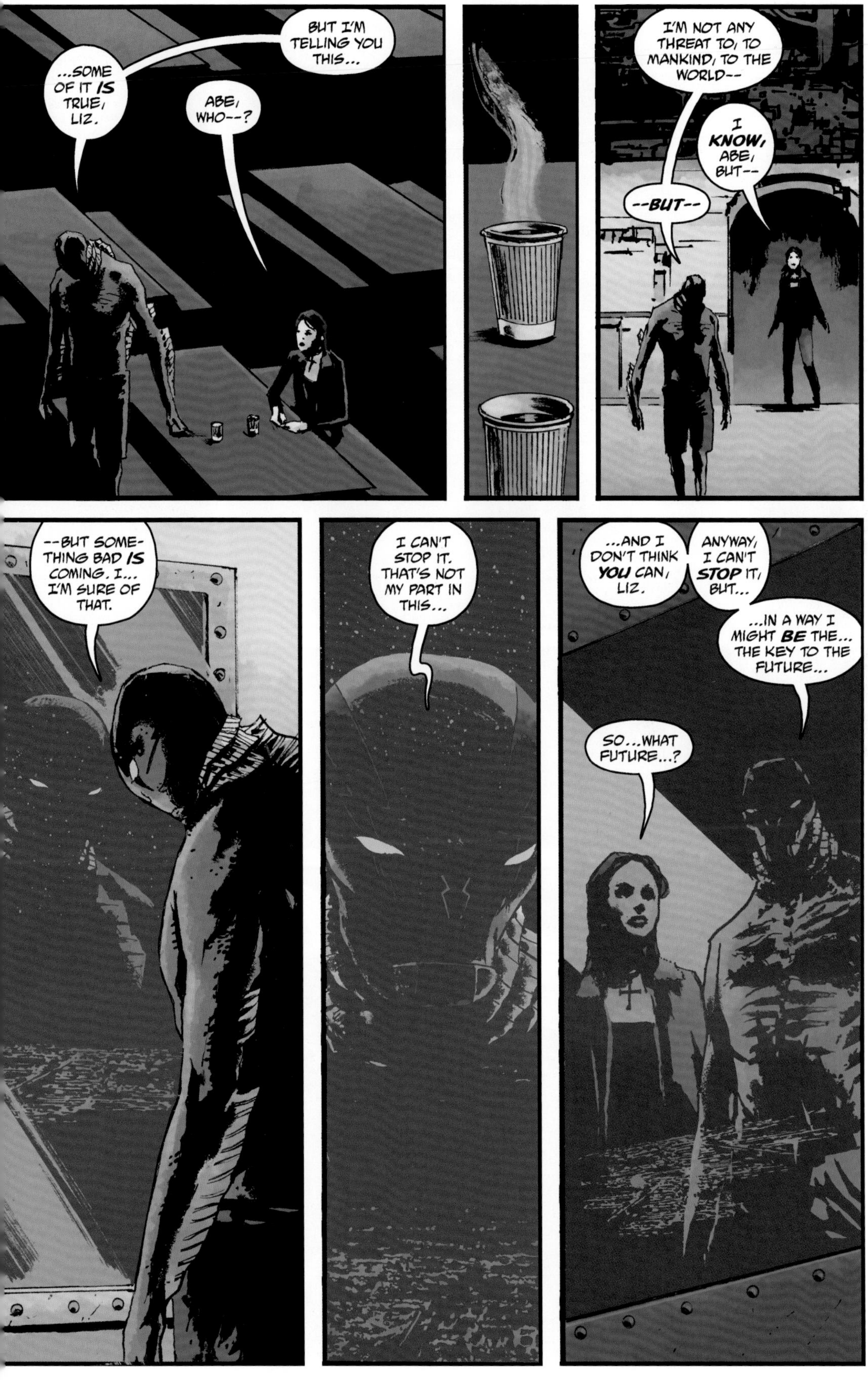
...SOME OF IT IS TRUE, LIZ.
BUT I'M TELLING YOU THIS...
ABE, WHO--?
I'M NOT ANY THREAT TO, TO MANKIND, TO THE WORLD--
I KNOW, ABE, BUT--
--BUT--
--BUT SOME-THING BAD IS COMING. I... I'M SURE OF THAT.
I CAN'T STOP IT. THAT'S NOT MY PART IN THIS...
ANYWAY, I CAN'T STOP IT, BUT...
...AND I DON'T THINK YOU CAN, LIZ.
...IN A WAY I MIGHT BE THE... THE KEY TO THE FUTURE...
SO...WHAT FUTURE...?

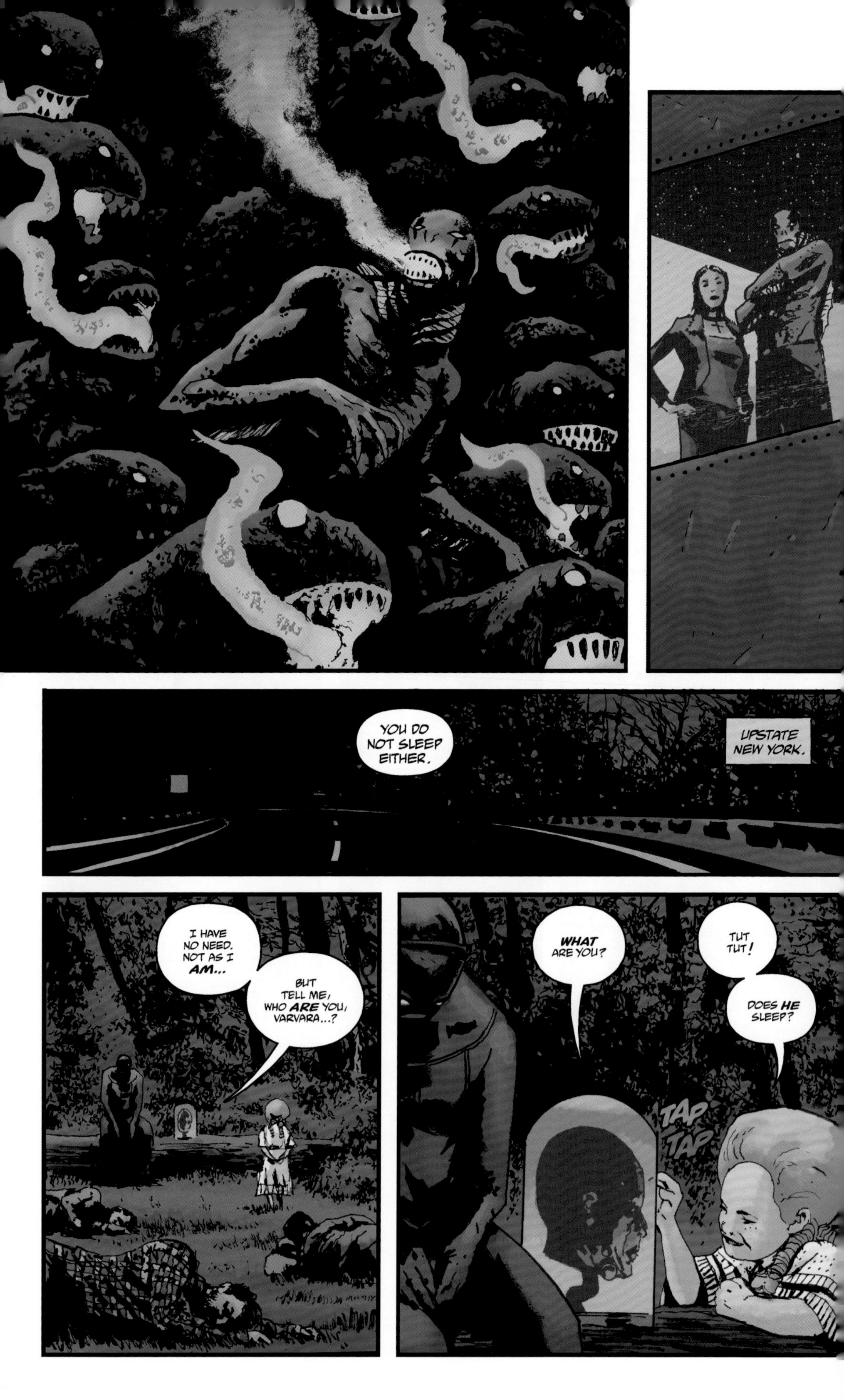
UPSTATE NEW YORK.
YOU DO NOT SLEEP EITHER.
I HAVE NO NEED. NOT AS I AM...
BUT TELL ME, WHO ARE YOU, VARVARA...?
WHAT ARE YOU?
TUT TUT!
DOES HE SLEEP?
TAP TAP

WHO CAN TELL.

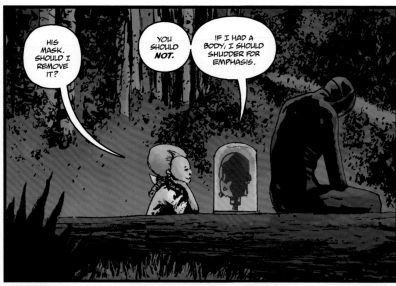

HIS MASK. SHOULD I REMOVE IT?

YOU SHOULD *NOT*.

IF I HAD A BODY, I SHOULD SHUDDER FOR EMPHASIS.

HEE HEE HEE!

HEH!

WE'LL GET YOU INTO A MORE COMFORTABLE ROOM, ah, LATER TODAY.

WE'LL KEEP AN EYE ON YOU FOR ANOTHER FEW HOURS...

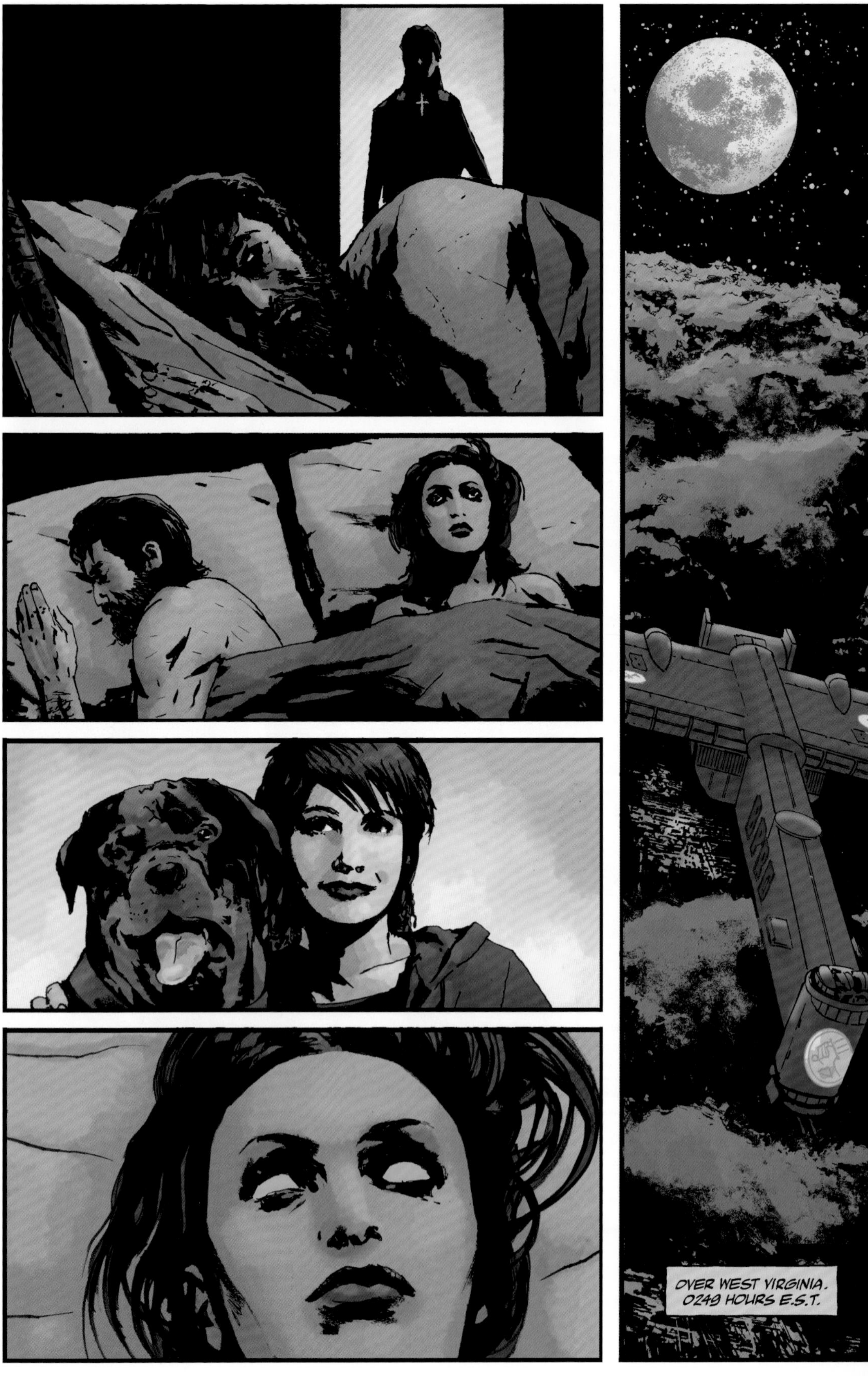
OVER WEST VIRGINIA.
0249 HOURS E.S.T.

CHAPTER FOUR

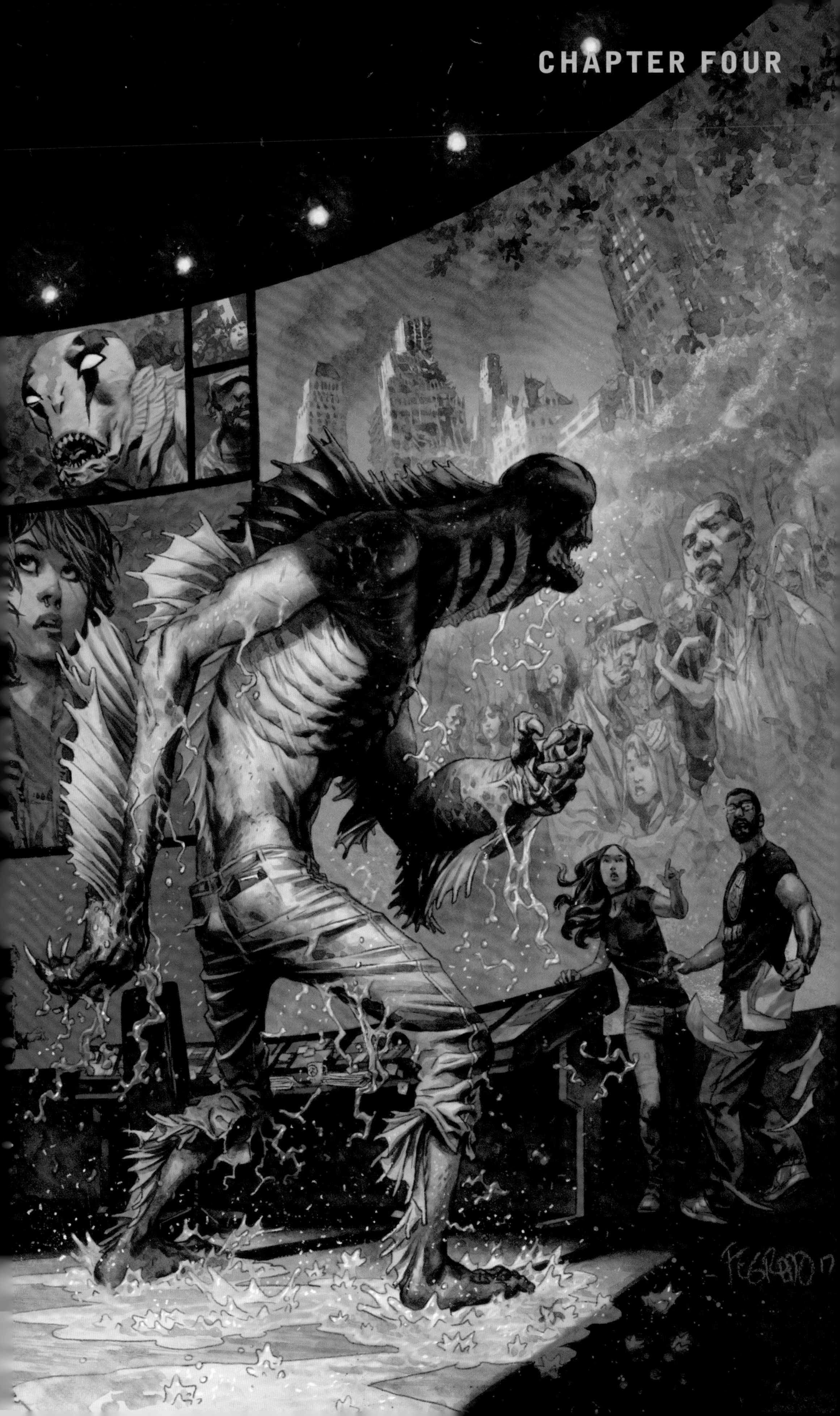

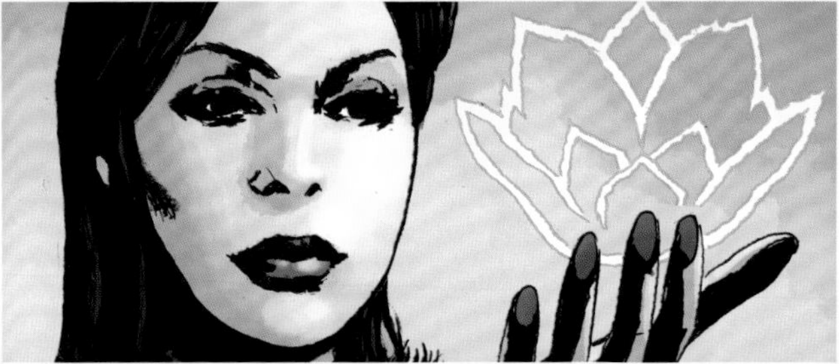

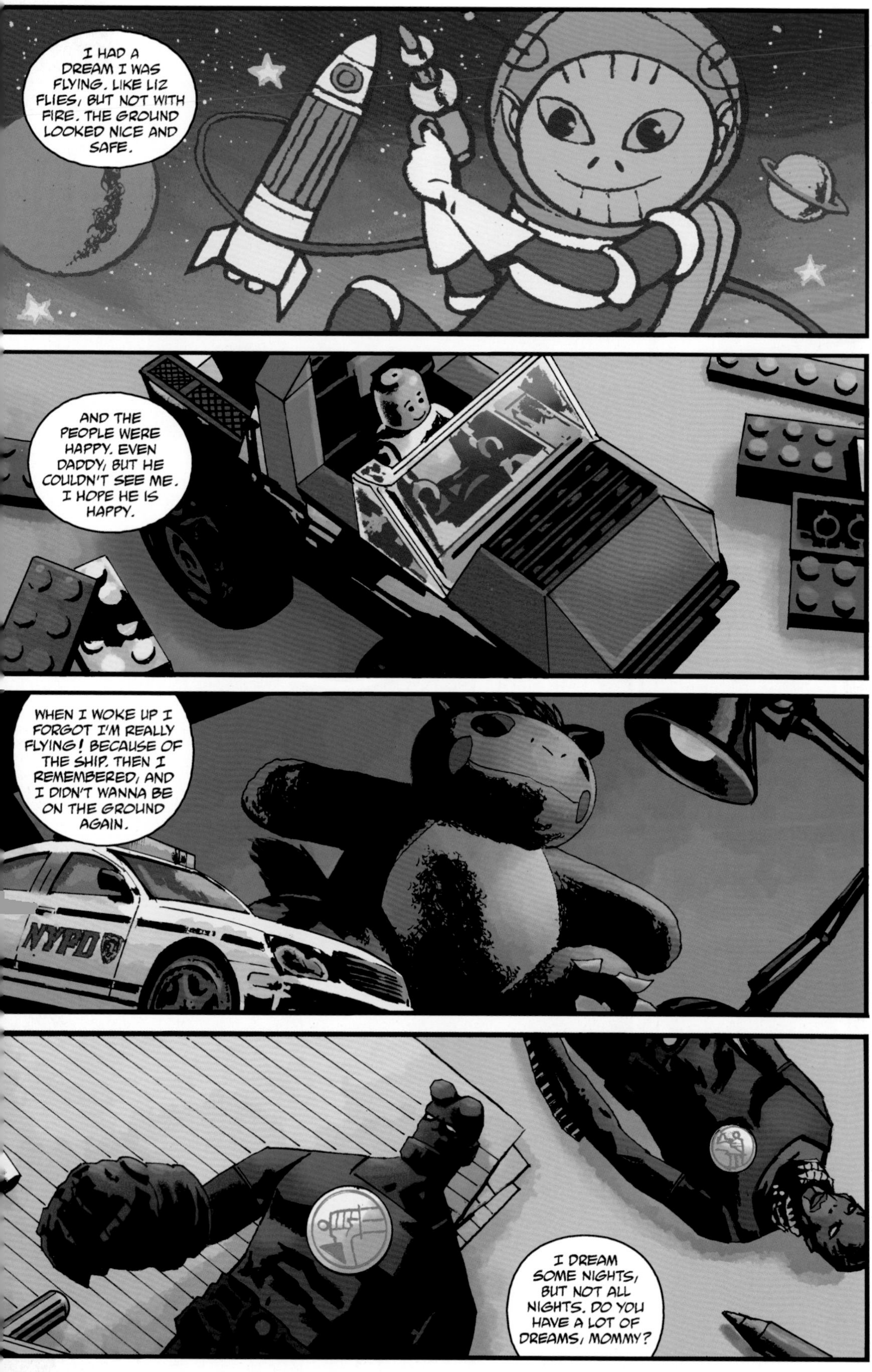
I HAD A DREAM I WAS FLYING. LIKE LIZ FLIES, BUT NOT WITH FIRE. THE GROUND LOOKED NICE AND SAFE.
AND THE PEOPLE WERE HAPPY. EVEN DADDY, BUT HE COULDN'T SEE ME. I HOPE HE IS HAPPY.
WHEN I WOKE UP I FORGOT I'M REALLY FLYING! BECAUSE OF THE SHIP. THEN I REMEMBERED, AND I DIDN'T WANNA BE ON THE GROUND AGAIN.
NYPD
I DREAM SOME NIGHTS, BUT NOT ALL NIGHTS. DO YOU HAVE A LOT OF DREAMS, MOMMY?

OVER SOUTHERN OHIO. 0719 HOURS E.S.T.

IT'S DIFFERENT WHEN YOU'RE OLDER, HON.

"WE GOT JACK'S TEST RESULTS..."

TCH-CHNK

...REGULAR OLD STAPH INFECTION. MAY REQUIRE SURGERY, BUT HE'LL BE FINE.

PHEW. CHRIST, MAN, IMAGINE IF YOU'D PASSED SOMETHING ON TO HIM WHILE YOU WERE ON LEAVE...?

TELL ME ABOUT IT. ONE TO THE HEAD, PLEASE.

I FEAR YOU...MISUNDERSTOOD WHAT I SAID ABOUT THIS PLACE. WE MAY ALL PERISH WITHIN ITS BOUNDARIES...

THOSE SOLDIERS WON'T LET US THROUGH...

WEEHAWKEN, NEW JERSEY. 0732 E.S.T.

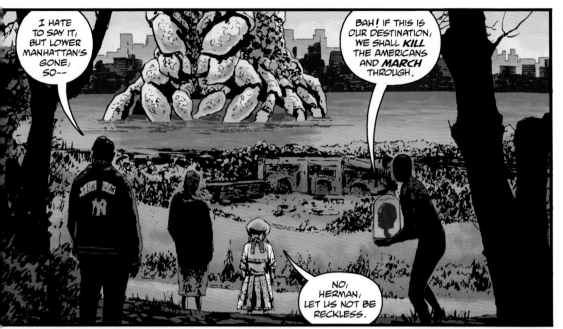

I HATE TO SAY IT, BUT LOWER MANHATTAN'S GONE, SO--

BAH! IF THIS IS OUR DESTINATION, WE SHALL *KILL* THE AMERICANS AND *MARCH* THROUGH.

NO, HERMAN, LET US NOT BE RECKLESS.

I...COULD NOT BEAR TO LOSE ANY OF YOU.

OVER INDIANAPOLIS. 0742 HOURS E.S.T.

WE'RE GOING TO COLORADO REGARDING ANOTHER MATTER. MEET US THERE IF YOU LIKE.

WAIT--GETTING ME IS *OPTIONAL*?

DEVON, WE NEED TO TALK-- *CLEAR THE ROOM.*

"*CLEAR THE ROOM*"? WHAT--?

STAZZ, *REMOVE* HER!

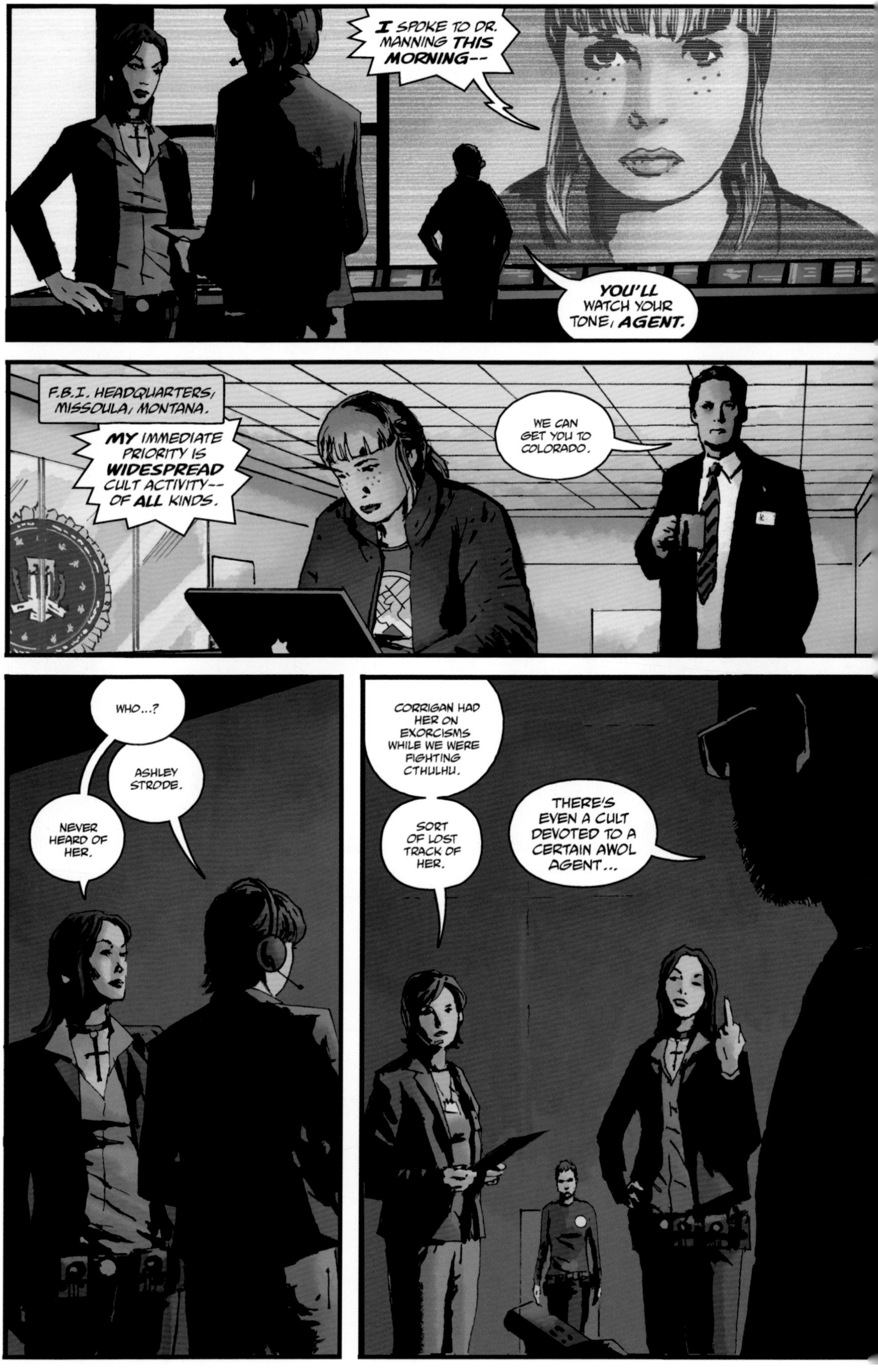
I SPOKE TO DR. MANNING THIS MORNING--
YOU'LL WATCH YOUR TONE, AGENT.
F.B.I. HEADQUARTERS, MISSOULA, MONTANA.
MY IMMEDIATE PRIORITY IS WIDESPREAD CULT ACTIVITY-- OF ALL KINDS.
WE CAN GET YOU TO COLORADO.
WHO...?
ASHLEY STRODE.
NEVER HEARD OF HER.
CORRIGAN HAD HER ON EXORCISMS WHILE WE WERE FIGHTING CTHULHU.
SORT OF LOST TRACK OF HER.
THERE'S EVEN A CULT DEVOTED TO A CERTAIN AWOL AGENT...

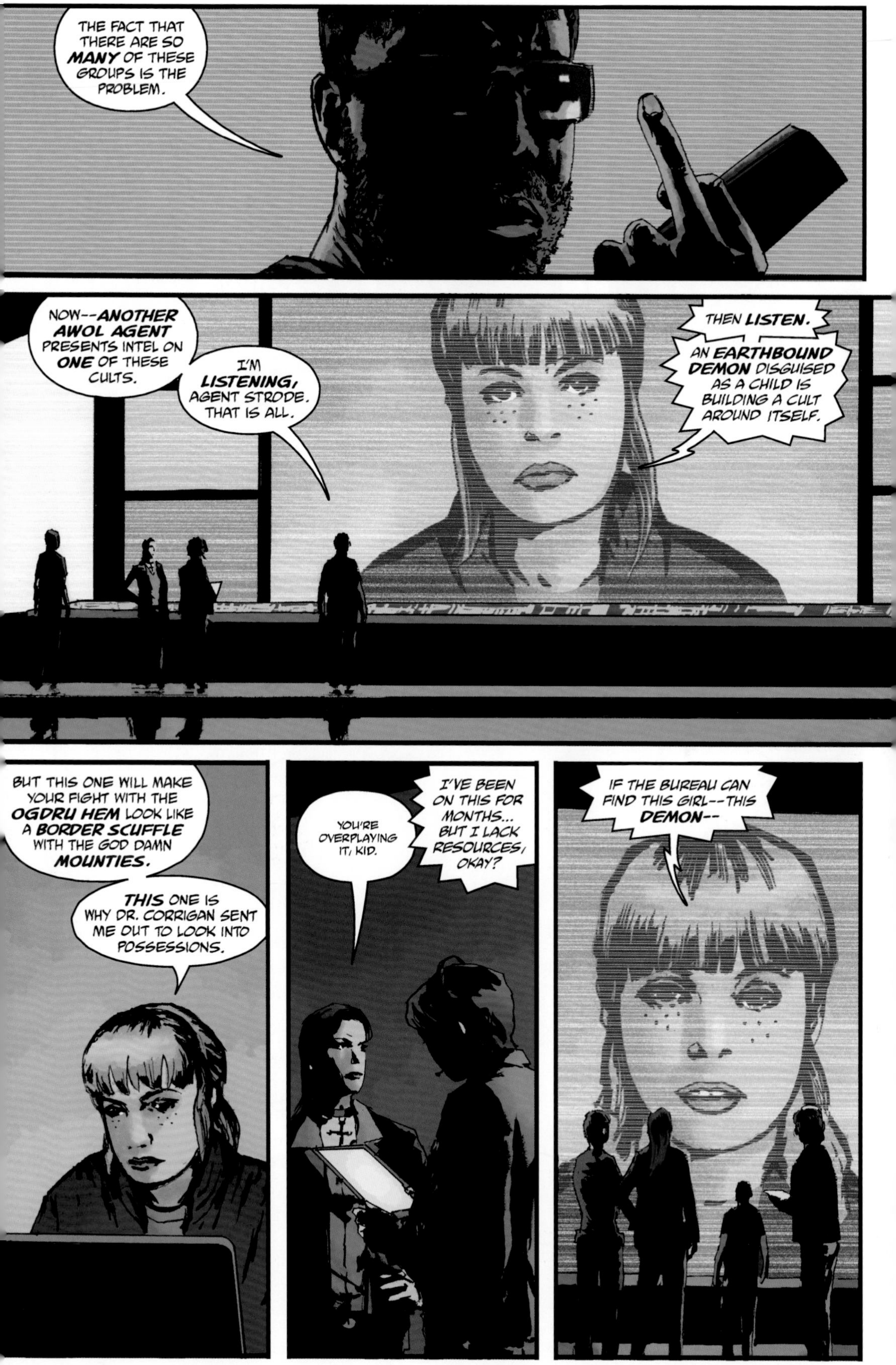
THE FACT THAT THERE ARE SO MANY OF THESE GROUPS IS THE PROBLEM.
NOW--ANOTHER AWOL AGENT PRESENTS INTEL ON ONE OF THESE CULTS.
I'M LISTENING, AGENT STRODE. THAT IS ALL.
THEN LISTEN.
AN EARTHBOUND DEMON DISGUISED AS A CHILD IS BUILDING A CULT AROUND ITSELF.
BUT THIS ONE WILL MAKE YOUR FIGHT WITH THE OGDRU HEM LOOK LIKE A BORDER SCUFFLE WITH THE GOD DAMN MOUNTIES.
THIS ONE IS WHY DR. CORRIGAN SENT ME OUT TO LOOK INTO POSSESSIONS.
YOU'RE OVERPLAYING IT, KID.
I'VE BEEN ON THIS FOR MONTHS... BUT I LACK RESOURCES, OKAY?
IF THE BUREAU CAN FIND THIS GIRL--THIS DEMON--

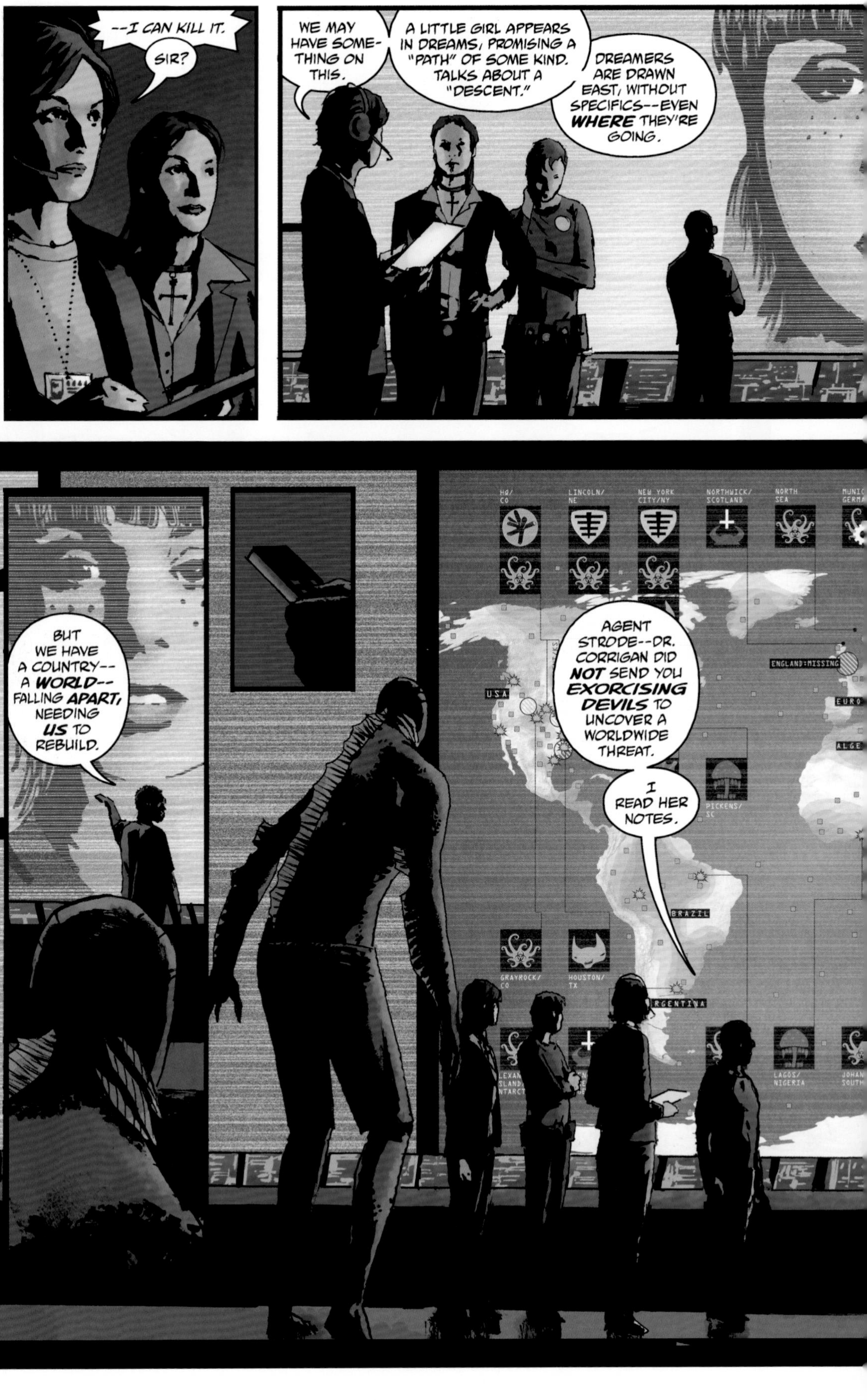
--I CAN KILL IT.
SIR?
WE MAY HAVE SOMETHING ON THIS.
A LITTLE GIRL APPEARS IN DREAMS, PROMISING A "PATH" OF SOME KIND. TALKS ABOUT A "DESCENT."
DREAMERS ARE DRAWN EAST, WITHOUT SPECIFICS--EVEN **WHERE** THEY'RE GOING.
HQ/CO
LINCOLN/NE
NEW YORK CITY/NY
NORTHWICK/SCOTLAND
NORTH SEA
USA
ENGLAND:MISSING
PICKENS/SC
BRAZIL
GRAYROCK/CO
HOUSTON/TX
LAGOS/NIGERIA
BUT WE HAVE A COUNTRY-- A **WORLD**-- FALLING **APART**, NEEDING **US** TO REBUILD.
AGENT STRODE--DR. CORRIGAN DID **NOT** SEND YOU ***EXORCISING DEVILS*** TO UNCOVER A WORLDWIDE THREAT.
I READ HER NOTES.

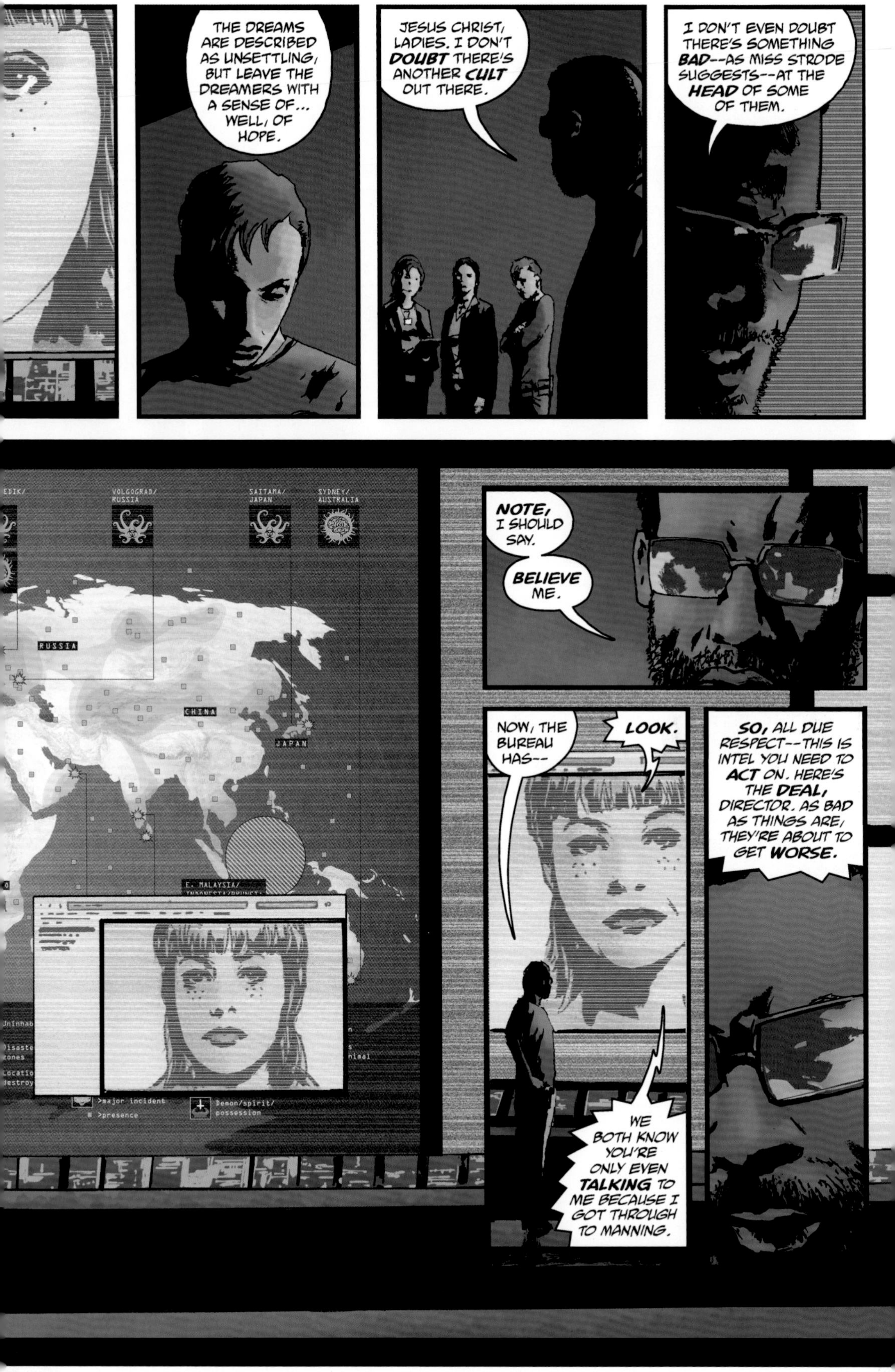
THE DREAMS ARE DESCRIBED AS UNSETTLING, BUT LEAVE THE DREAMERS WITH A SENSE OF... WELL, OF HOPE.
JESUS CHRIST, LADIES. I DON'T DOUBT THERE'S ANOTHER CULT OUT THERE.
I DON'T EVEN DOUBT THERE'S SOMETHING BAD--AS MISS STRODE SUGGESTS--AT THE HEAD OF SOME OF THEM.
VOLGOGRAD/ RUSSIA
SAITAMA/ JAPAN
SYDNEY/ AUSTRALIA
RUSSIA
CHINA
JAPAN
E. MALAYSIA/
>major incident
>presence
Demon/spirit/ possession
NOTE, I SHOULD SAY.
BELIEVE ME.
NOW, THE BUREAU HAS--
LOOK.
WE BOTH KNOW YOU'RE ONLY EVEN TALKING TO ME BECAUSE I GOT THROUGH TO MANNING.
SO, ALL DUE RESPECT--THIS IS INTEL YOU NEED TO ACT ON. HERE'S THE DEAL, DIRECTOR. AS BAD AS THINGS ARE, THEY'RE ABOUT TO GET WORSE.

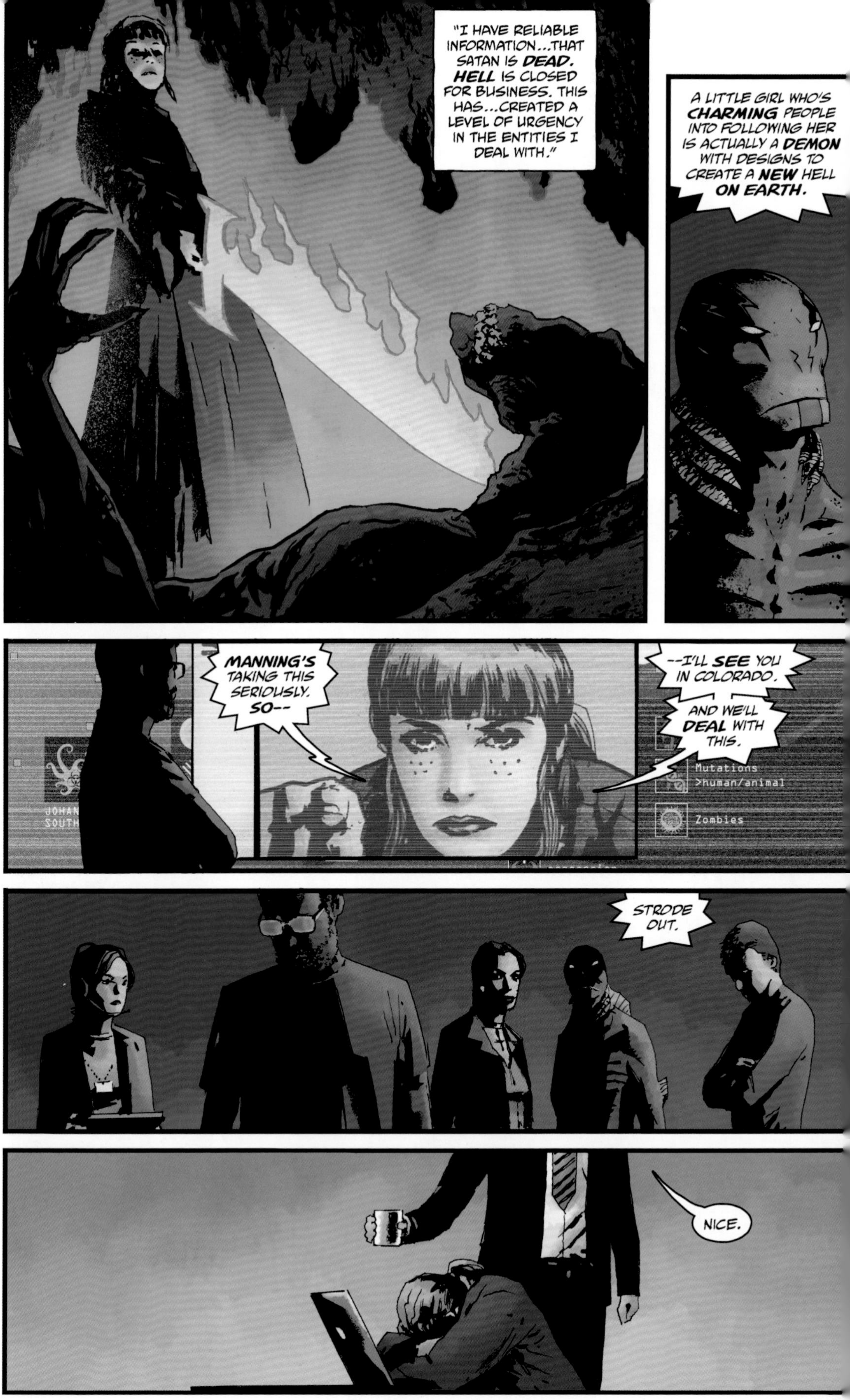
"I HAVE RELIABLE INFORMATION...THAT SATAN IS DEAD. HELL IS CLOSED FOR BUSINESS. THIS HAS...CREATED A LEVEL OF URGENCY IN THE ENTITIES I DEAL WITH."
A LITTLE GIRL WHO'S CHARMING PEOPLE INTO FOLLOWING HER IS ACTUALLY A DEMON WITH DESIGNS TO CREATE A NEW HELL ON EARTH.
MANNING'S TAKING THIS SERIOUSLY. SO--
--I'LL SEE YOU IN COLORADO.
AND WE'LL DEAL WITH THIS.
Mutations
>human/animal
Zombies
STRODE OUT.
NICE.

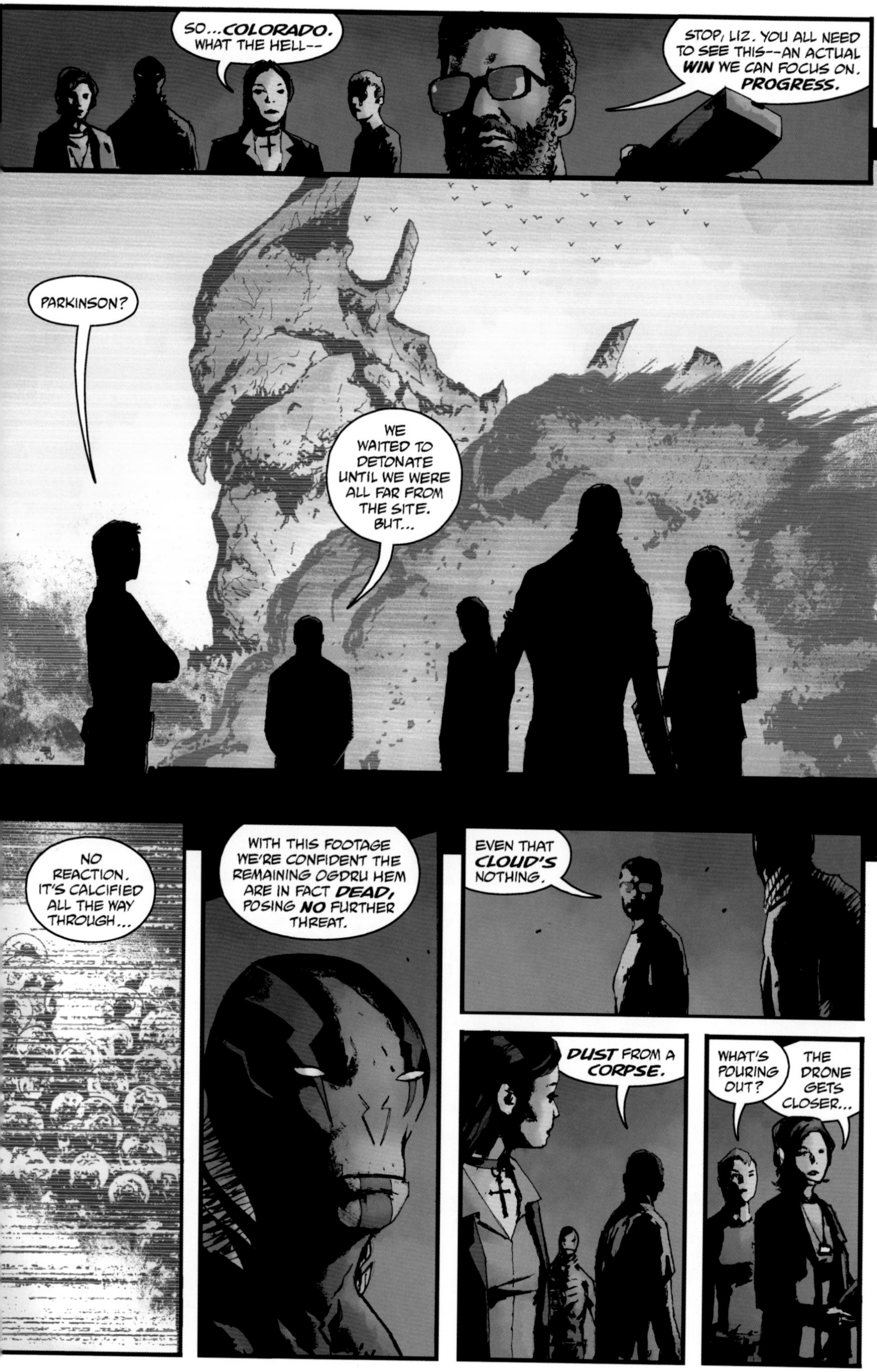
SO...COLORADO. WHAT THE HELL--
STOP, LIZ. YOU ALL NEED TO SEE THIS--AN ACTUAL WIN WE CAN FOCUS ON. PROGRESS.
PARKINSON?
WE WAITED TO DETONATE UNTIL WE WERE ALL FAR FROM THE SITE. BUT...
NO REACTION. IT'S CALCIFIED ALL THE WAY THROUGH...
WITH THIS FOOTAGE WE'RE CONFIDENT THE REMAINING OGDRU HEM ARE IN FACT DEAD, POSING NO FURTHER THREAT.
EVEN THAT CLOUD'S NOTHING.
DUST FROM A CORPSE.
WHAT'S POURING OUT?
THE DRONE GETS CLOSER...

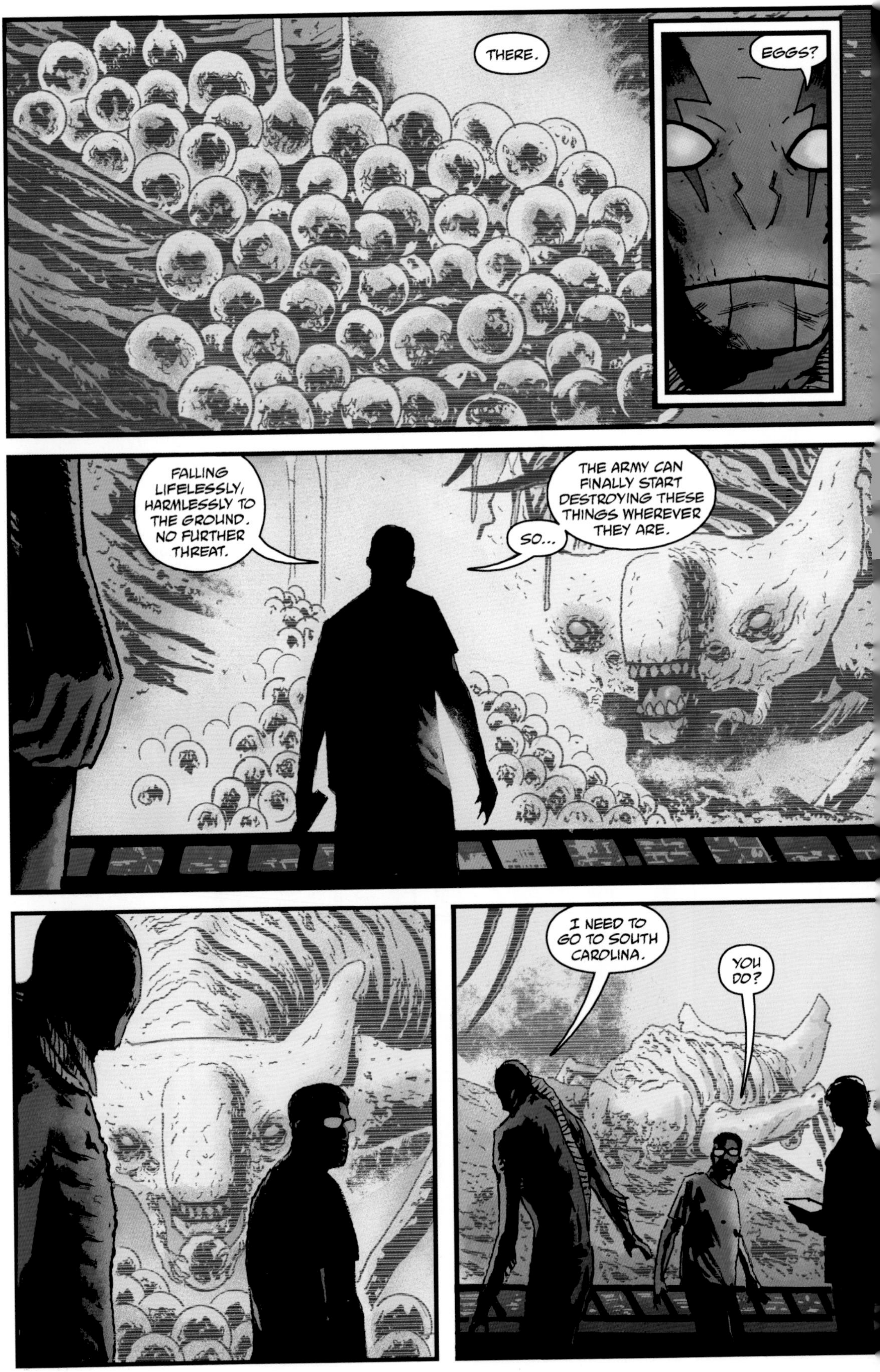
THERE.
EGGS?
FALLING LIFELESSLY, HARMLESSLY TO THE GROUND. NO FURTHER THREAT.
SO...
THE ARMY CAN FINALLY START DESTROYING THESE THINGS WHEREVER THEY ARE.
I NEED TO GO TO SOUTH CAROLINA.
YOU DO?

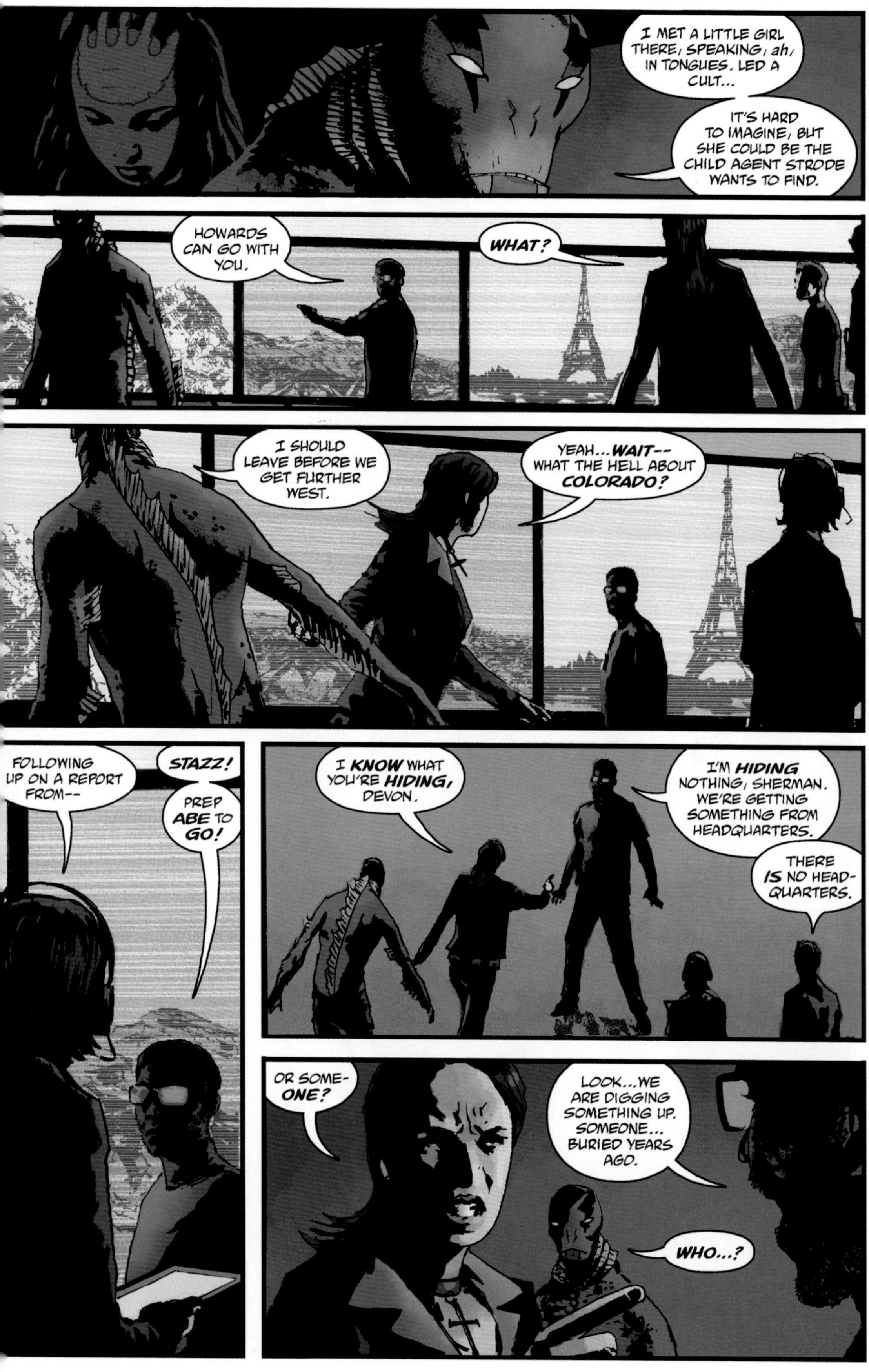
I MET A LITTLE GIRL THERE, SPEAKING, *ah*, IN TONGUES. LED A CULT...
IT'S HARD TO IMAGINE, BUT SHE COULD BE THE CHILD AGENT STRODE WANTS TO FIND.
HOWARDS CAN GO WITH YOU.
WHAT?
I SHOULD LEAVE BEFORE WE GET FURTHER WEST.
YEAH...**WAIT**-- WHAT THE HELL ABOUT **COLORADO?**
FOLLOWING UP ON A REPORT FROM--
STAZZ!
PREP **ABE** TO **GO!**
I **KNOW** WHAT YOU'RE **HIDING,** DEVON.
I'M **HIDING** NOTHING, SHERMAN. WE'RE GETTING SOMETHING FROM HEADQUARTERS.
THERE **IS** NO HEAD-QUARTERS.
OR SOME-**ONE?**
LOOK...WE ARE DIGGING SOMETHING UP. SOMEONE... BURIED YEARS AGO.
WHO...?

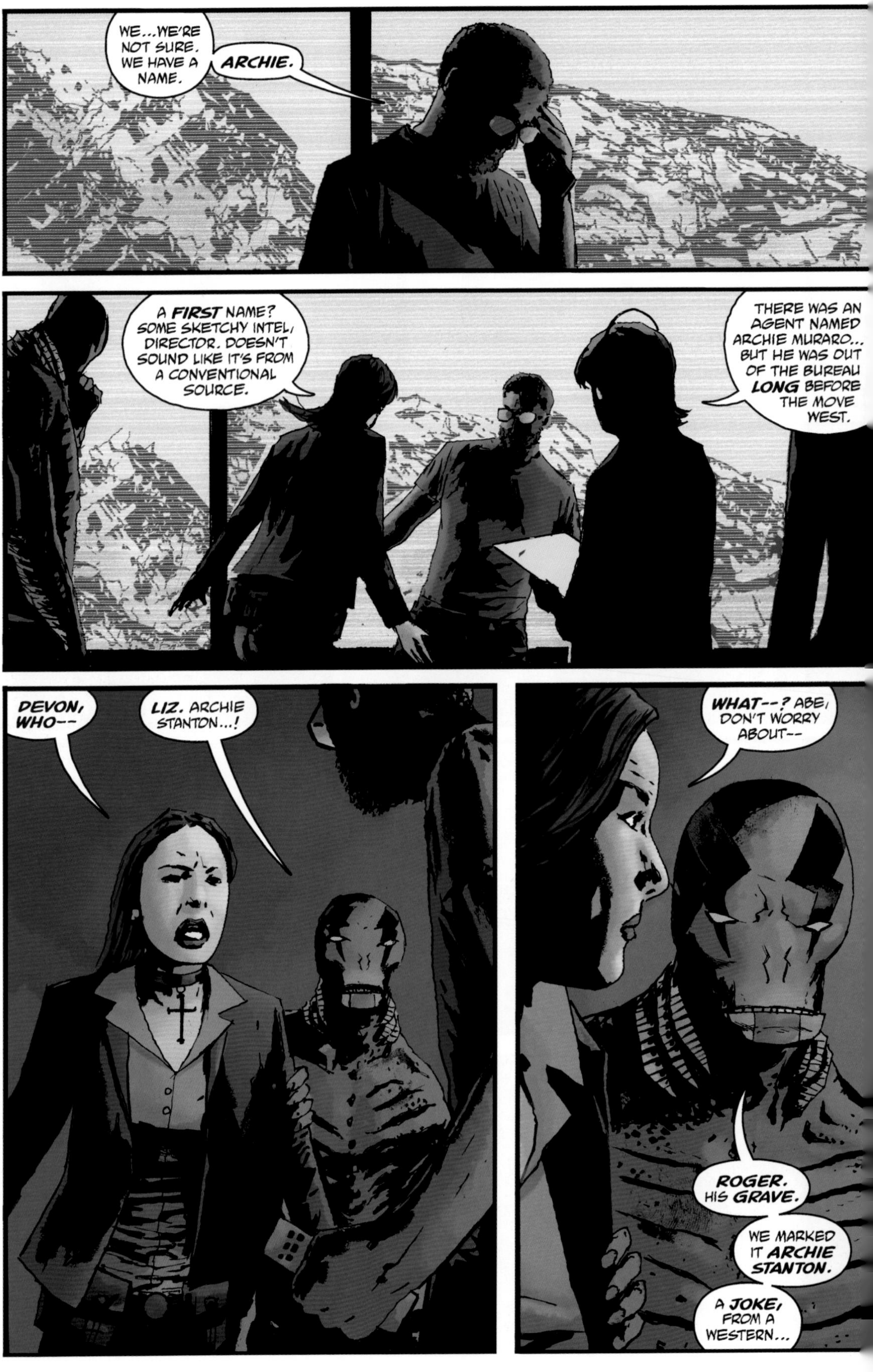
WE...WE'RE NOT SURE. WE HAVE A NAME.
ARCHIE.
A FIRST NAME? SOME SKETCHY INTEL, DIRECTOR. DOESN'T SOUND LIKE IT'S FROM A CONVENTIONAL SOURCE.
THERE WAS AN AGENT NAMED ARCHIE MURARO... BUT HE WAS OUT OF THE BUREAU LONG BEFORE THE MOVE WEST.
DEVON, WHO--
LIZ. ARCHIE STANTON...!
WHAT--? ABE, DON'T WORRY ABOUT--
ROGER. HIS GRAVE.
WE MARKED IT ARCHIE STANTON.
A JOKE, FROM A WESTERN...

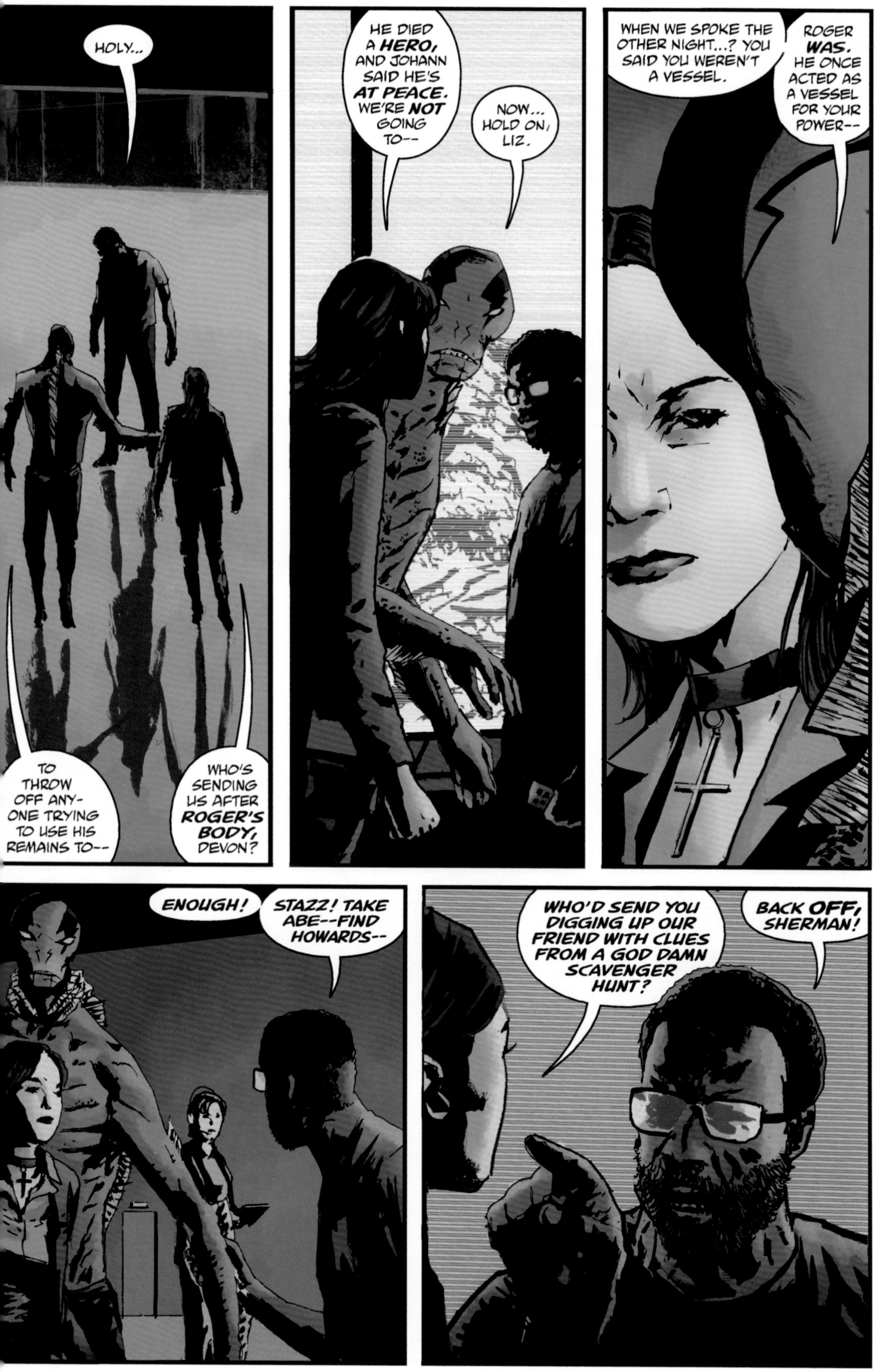
HOLY...
TO THROW OFF ANY-ONE TRYING TO USE HIS REMAINS TO--
WHO'S SENDING US AFTER ROGER'S BODY, DEVON?
HE DIED A HERO, AND JOHANN SAID HE'S AT PEACE. WE'RE NOT GOING TO--
NOW... HOLD ON, LIZ.
WHEN WE SPOKE THE OTHER NIGHT...? YOU SAID YOU WEREN'T A VESSEL.
ROGER WAS. HE ONCE ACTED AS A VESSEL FOR YOUR POWER--
ENOUGH!
STAZZ! TAKE ABE--FIND HOWARDS--
WHO'D SEND YOU DIGGING UP OUR FRIEND WITH CLUES FROM A GOD DAMN SCAVENGER HUNT?
BACK OFF, SHERMAN!

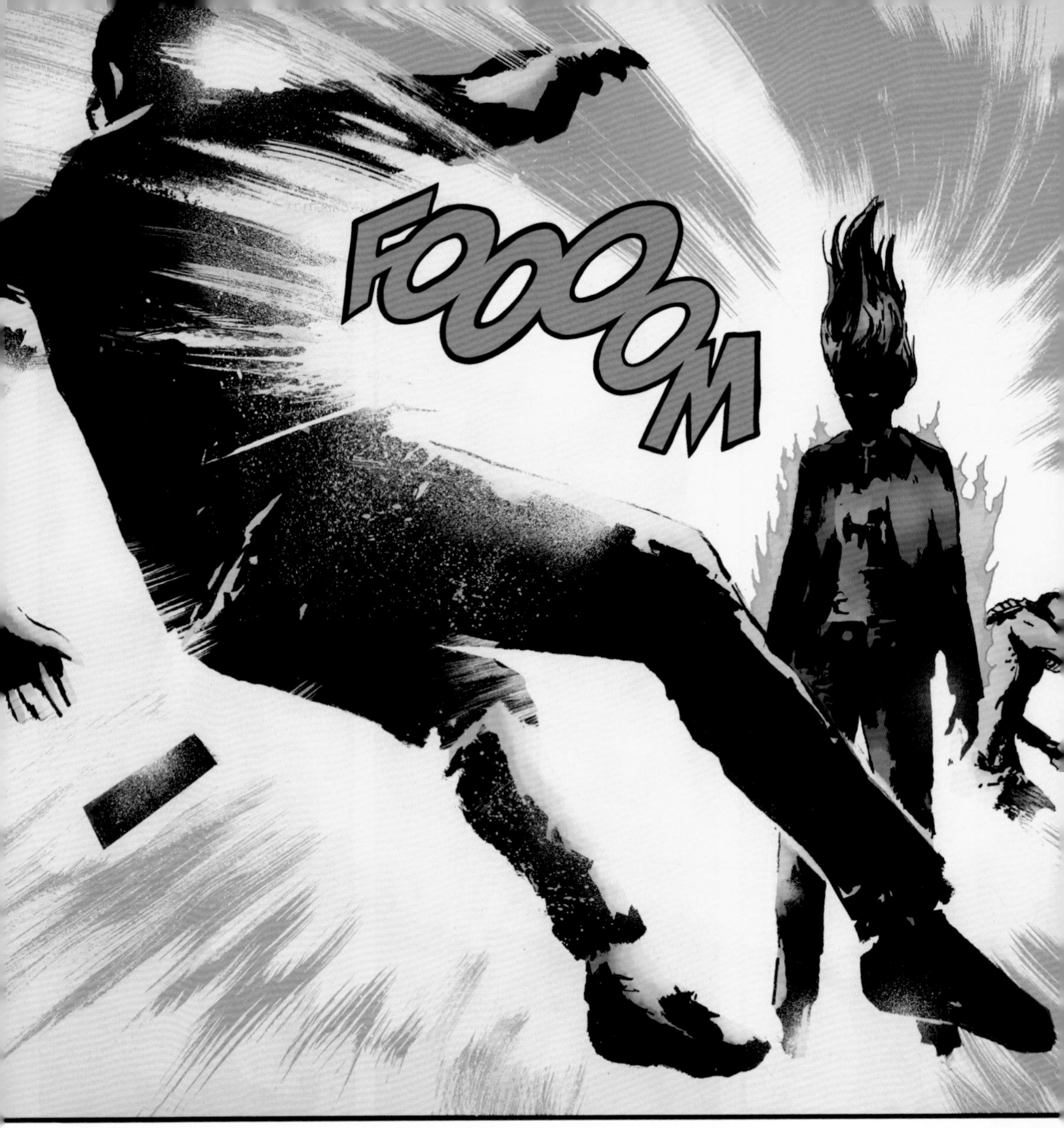
FOOOOM

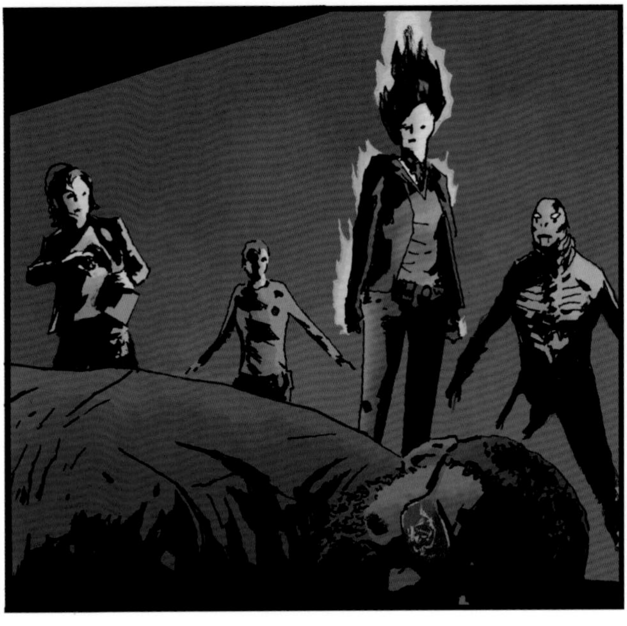

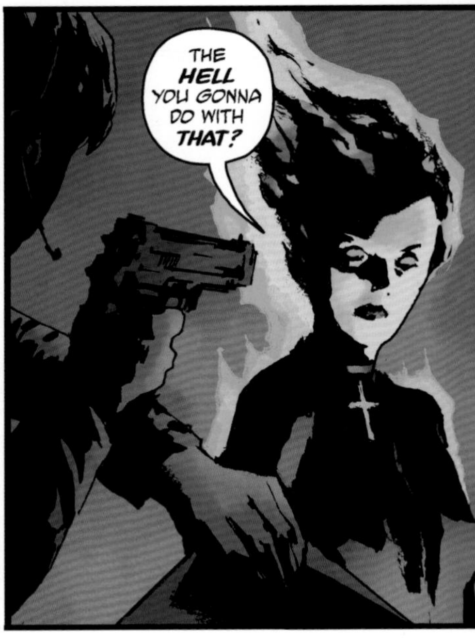
THE HELL YOU GONNA DO WITH THAT?

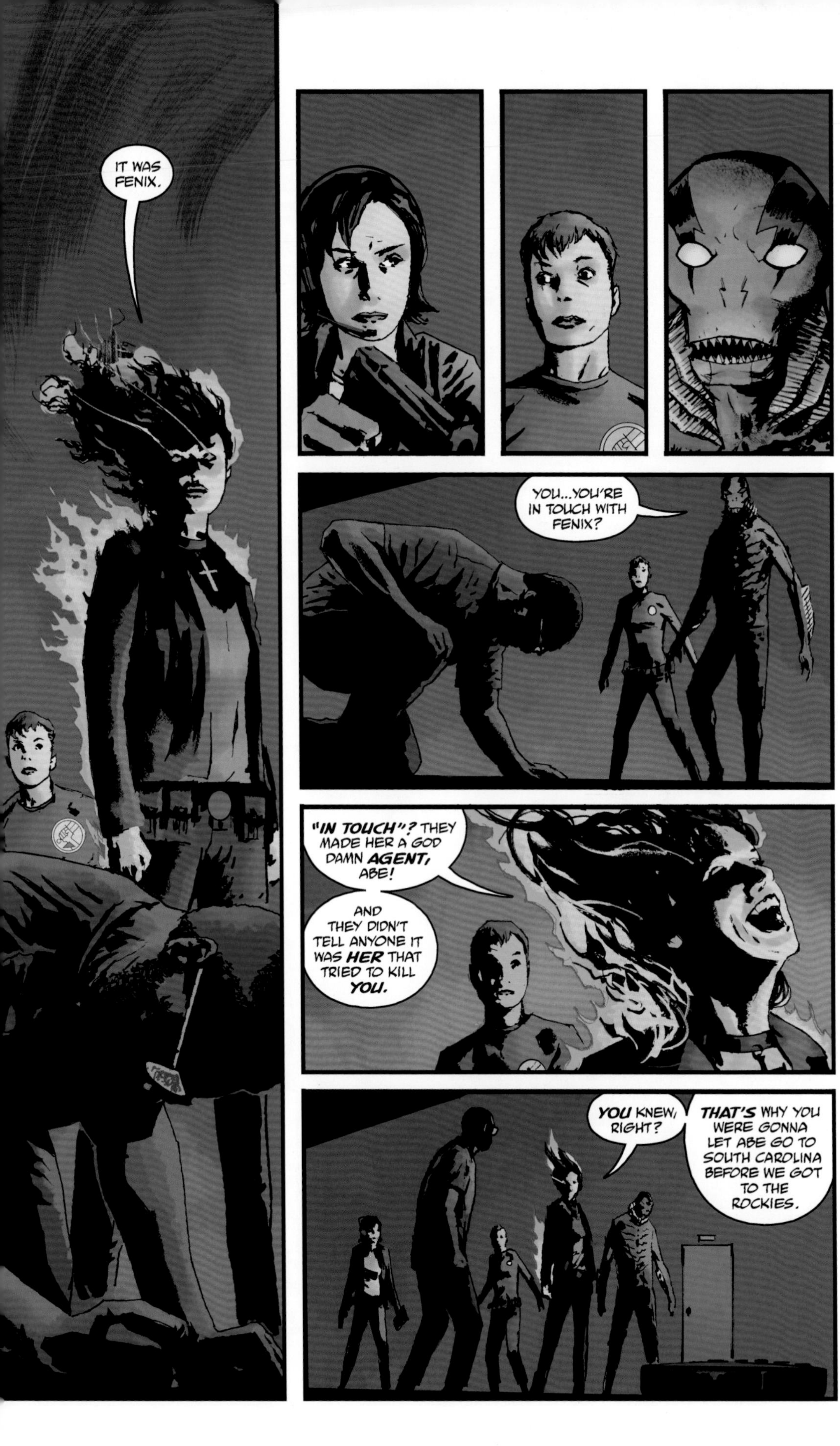
IT WAS FENIX.
YOU...YOU'RE IN TOUCH WITH FENIX?
"IN TOUCH"? THEY MADE HER A GOD DAMN AGENT, ABE!
AND THEY DIDN'T TELL ANYONE IT WAS HER THAT TRIED TO KILL YOU.
YOU KNEW, RIGHT?
THAT'S WHY YOU WERE GONNA LET ABE GO TO SOUTH CAROLINA BEFORE WE GOT TO THE ROCKIES.

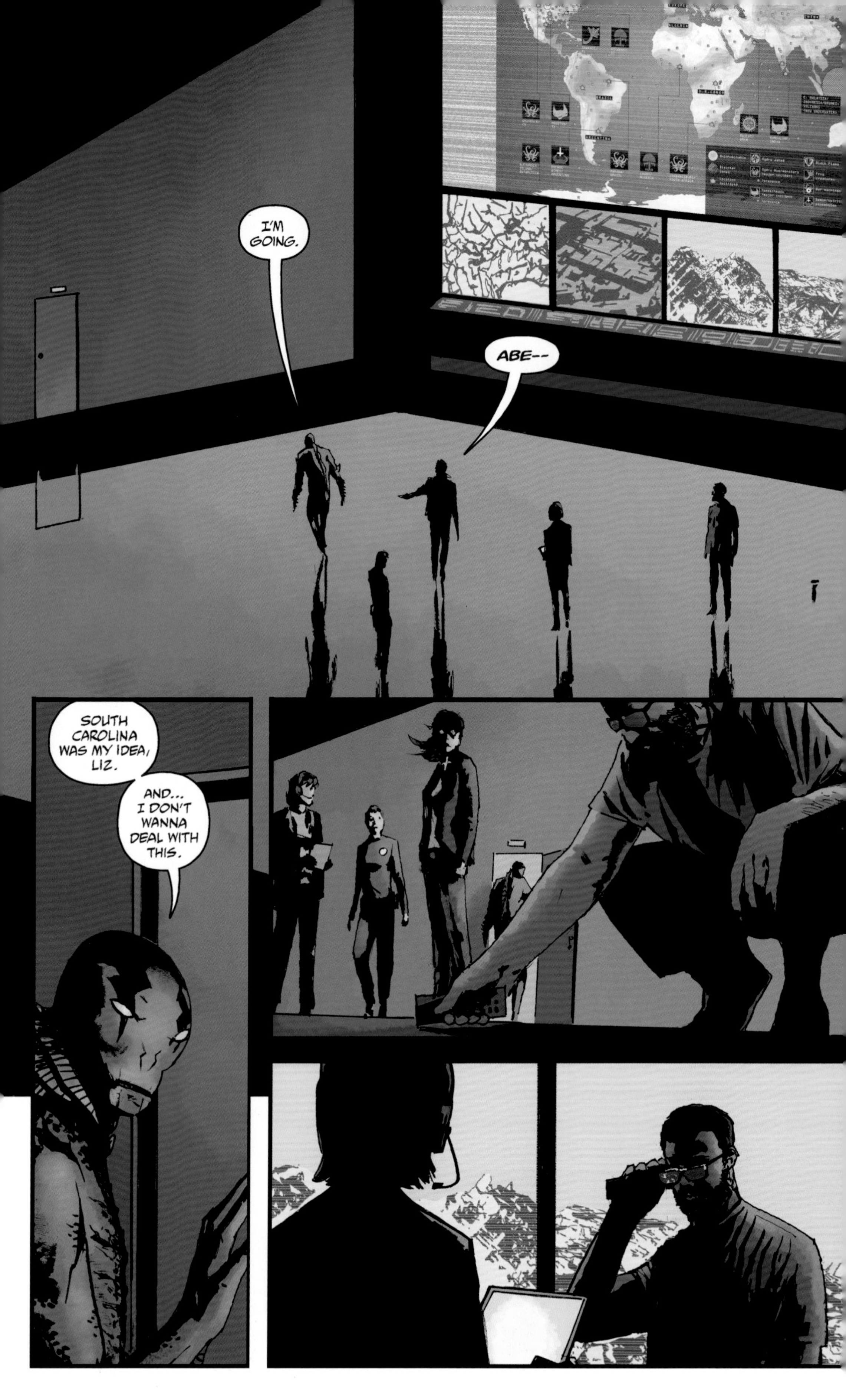
I'M GOING.
ABE--
SOUTH CAROLINA WAS MY IDEA, LIZ.
AND... I DON'T WANNA DEAL WITH THIS.

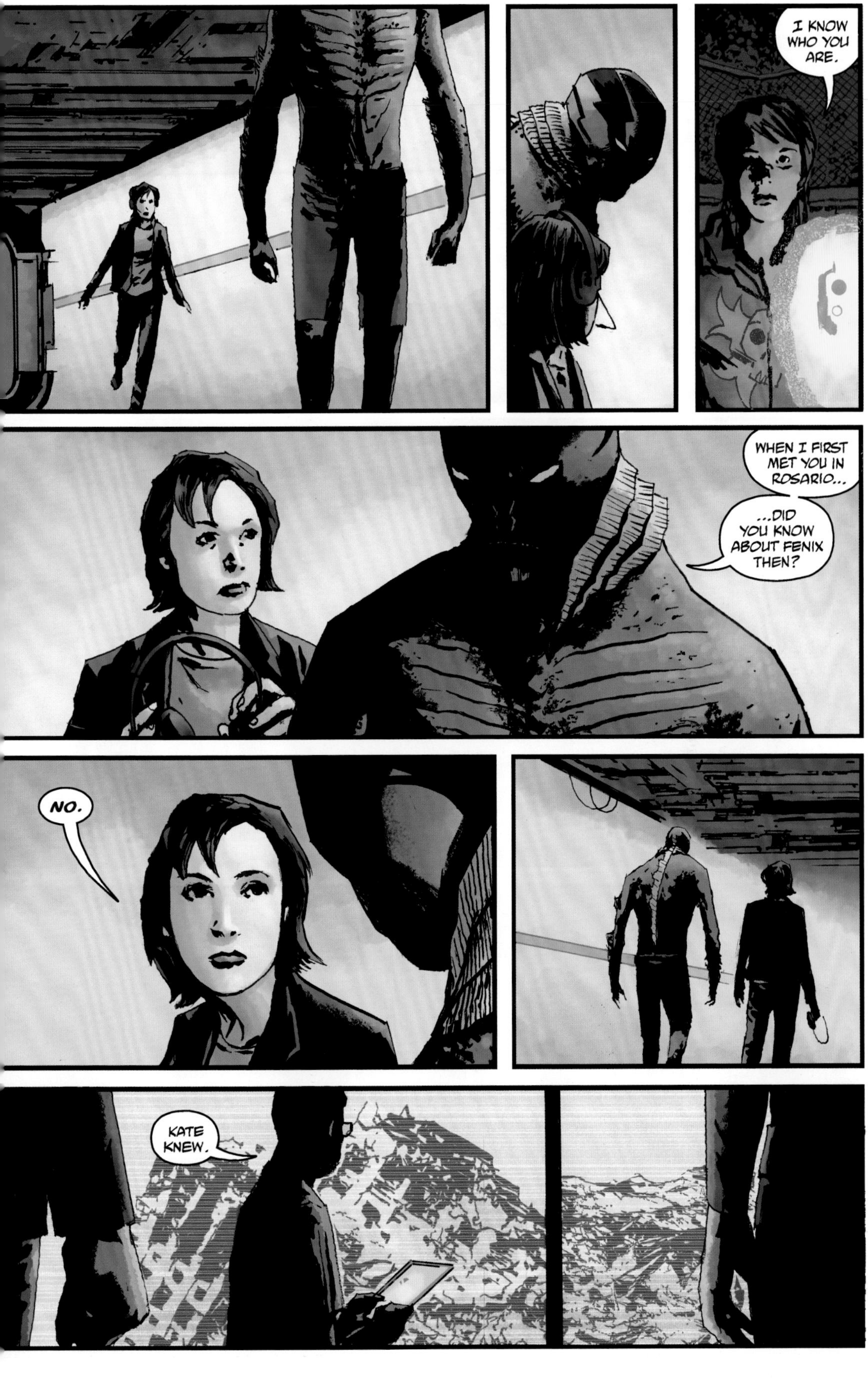
I KNOW WHO YOU ARE.
WHEN I FIRST MET YOU IN ROSARIO...
...DID YOU KNOW ABOUT FENIX THEN?
NO.
KATE KNEW.

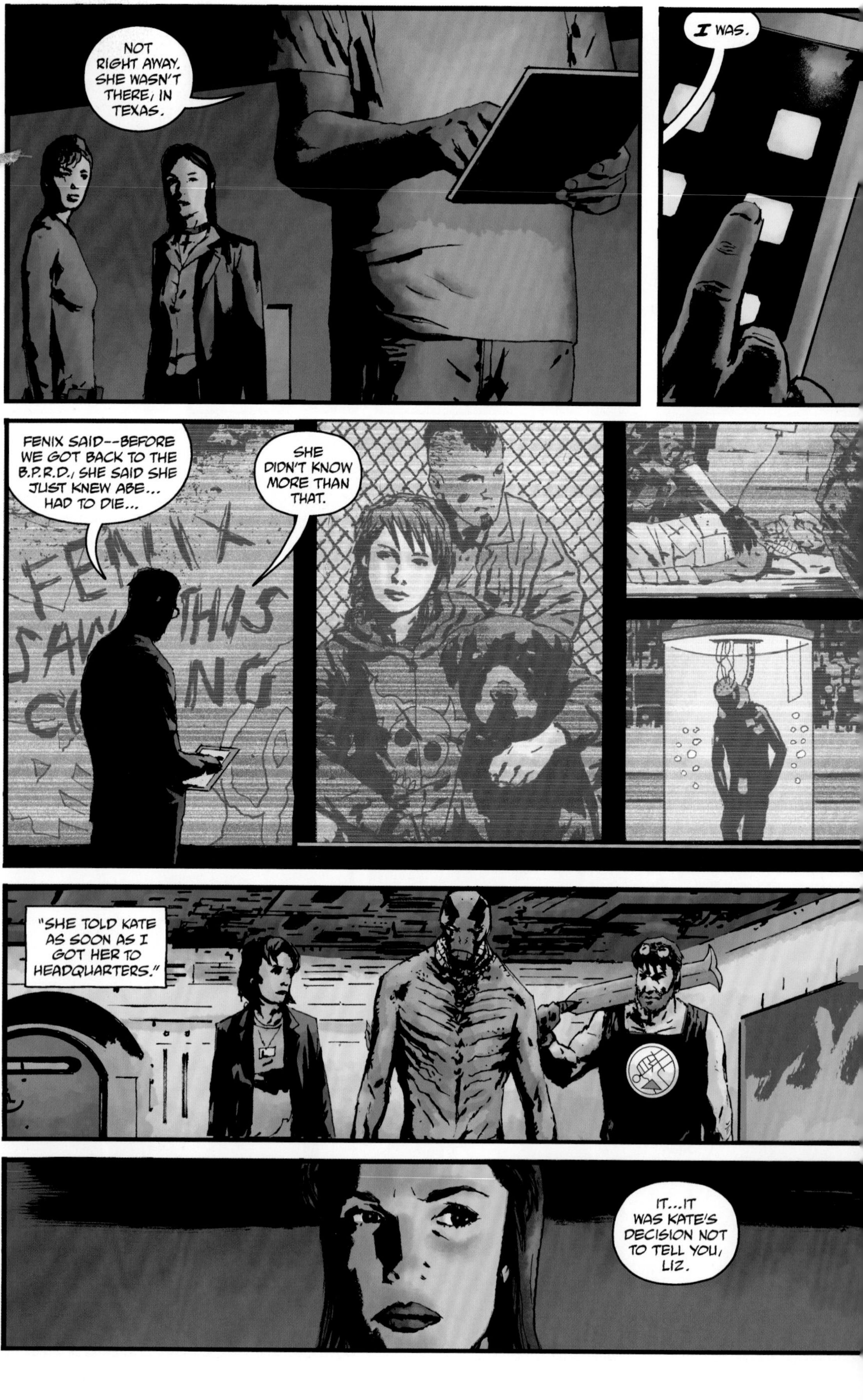
NOT RIGHT AWAY. SHE WASN'T THERE, IN TEXAS.
I WAS.
FENIX SAID--BEFORE WE GOT BACK TO THE B.P.R.D., SHE SAID SHE JUST KNEW ABE... HAD TO DIE...
SHE DIDN'T KNOW MORE THAN THAT.
"SHE TOLD KATE AS SOON AS I GOT HER TO HEADQUARTERS."
IT...IT WAS KATE'S DECISION NOT TO TELL YOU, LIZ.

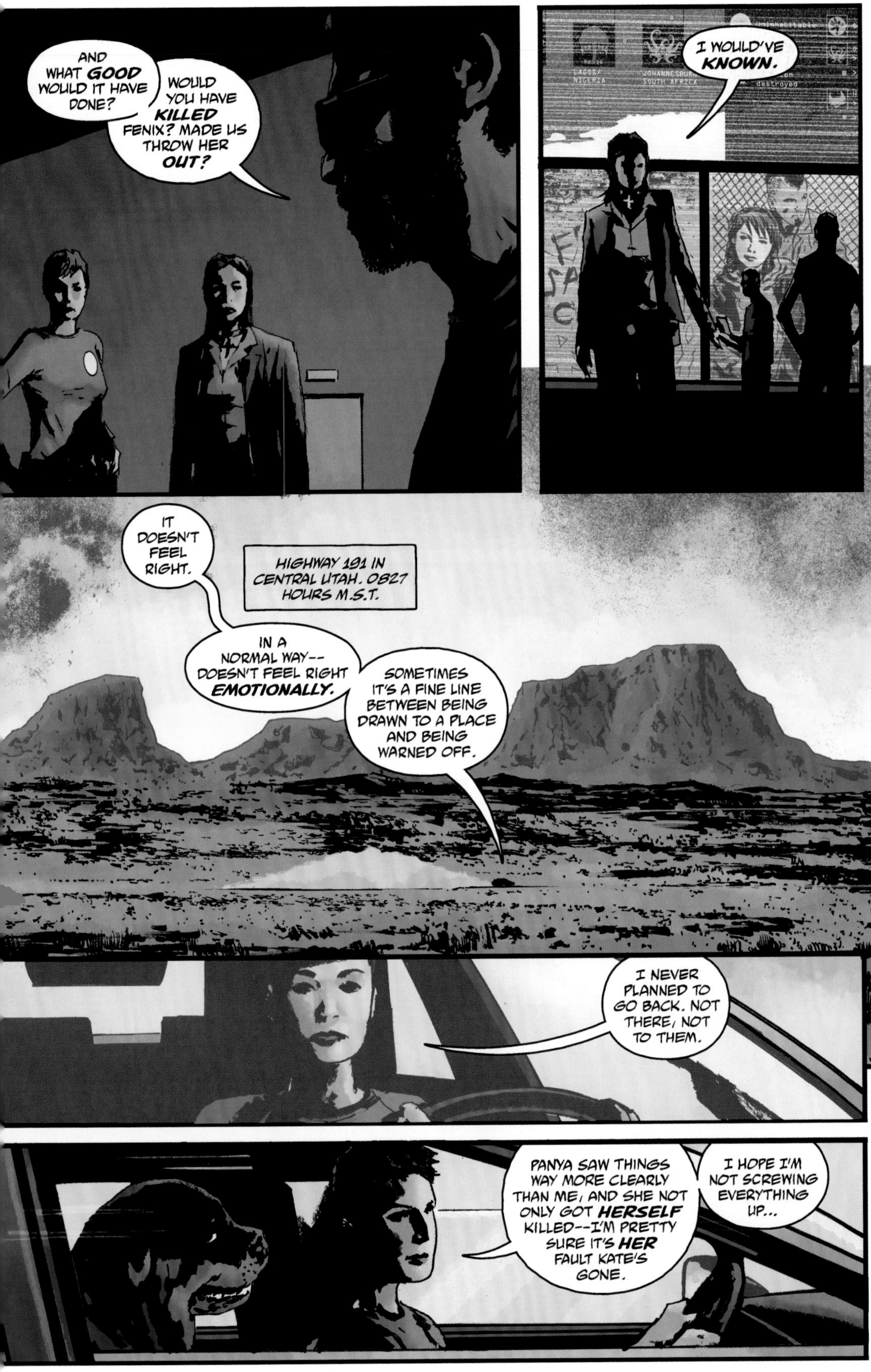
AND WHAT GOOD WOULD IT HAVE DONE?
WOULD YOU HAVE KILLED FENIX? MADE US THROW HER OUT?
I WOULD'VE KNOWN.
IT DOESN'T FEEL RIGHT.
HIGHWAY 191 IN CENTRAL UTAH. 0827 HOURS M.S.T.
IN A NORMAL WAY-- DOESN'T FEEL RIGHT EMOTIONALLY.
SOMETIMES IT'S A FINE LINE BETWEEN BEING DRAWN TO A PLACE AND BEING WARNED OFF.
I NEVER PLANNED TO GO BACK. NOT THERE, NOT TO THEM.
PANYA SAW THINGS WAY MORE CLEARLY THAN ME, AND SHE NOT ONLY GOT HERSELF KILLED--I'M PRETTY SURE IT'S HER FAULT KATE'S GONE.
I HOPE I'M NOT SCREWING EVERYTHING UP...

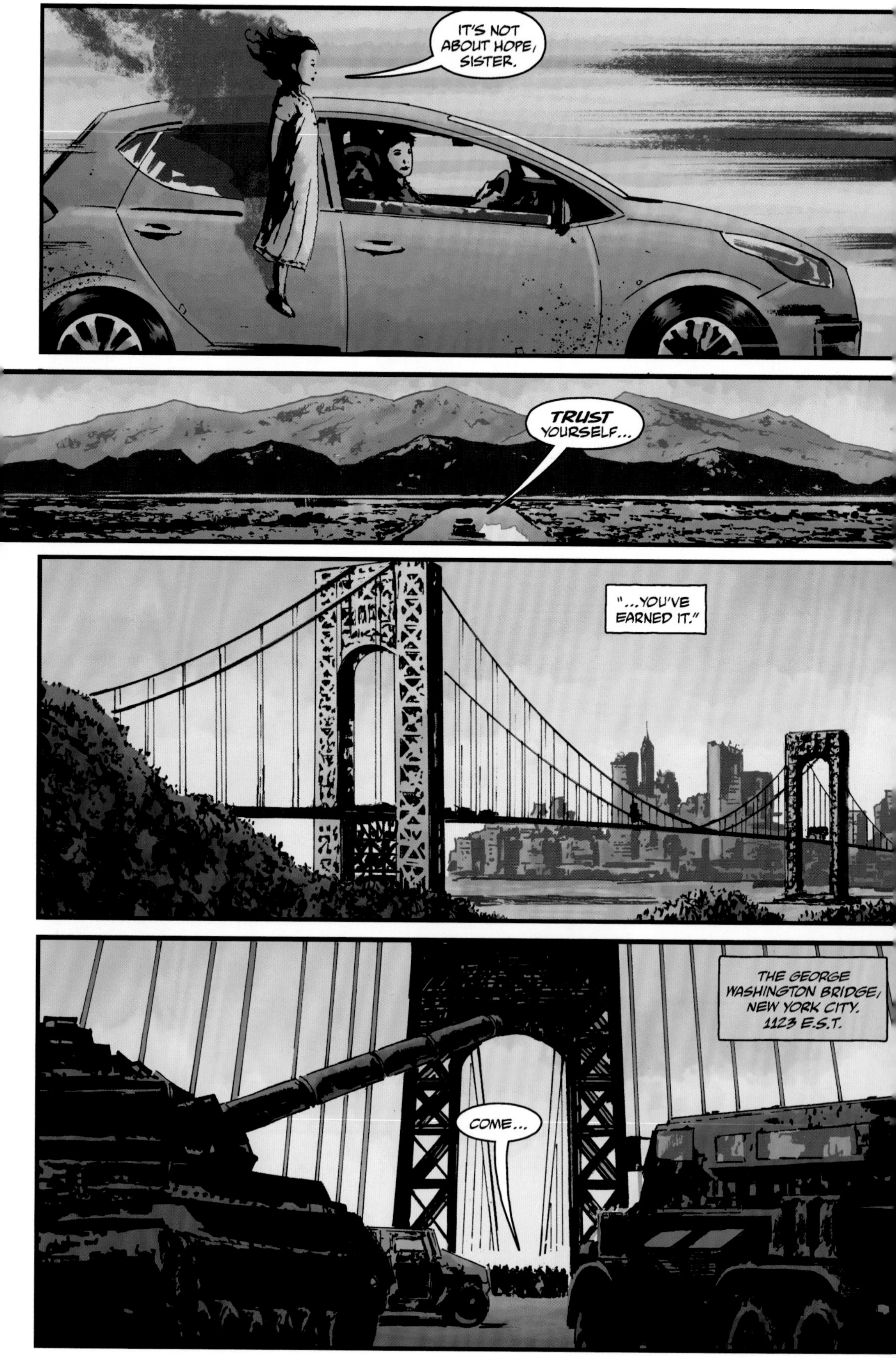
IT'S NOT ABOUT HOPE, SISTER.
TRUST YOURSELF...
"...YOU'VE EARNED IT."
THE GEORGE WASHINGTON BRIDGE, NEW YORK CITY. 1123 E.S.T.
COME...

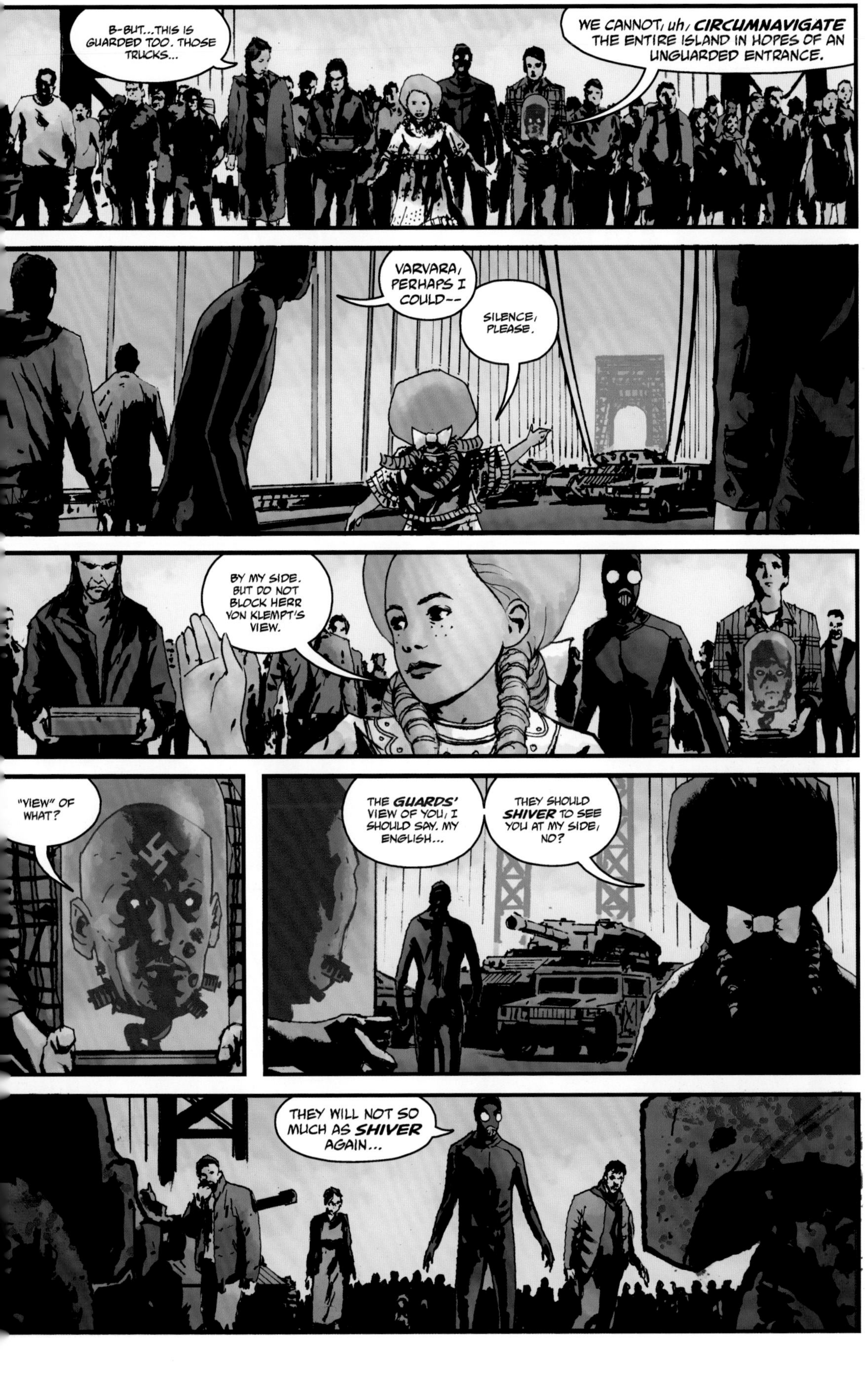
B-BUT...THIS IS GUARDED TOO. THOSE TRUCKS...
WE CANNOT, uh, CIRCUMNAVIGATE THE ENTIRE ISLAND IN HOPES OF AN UNGUARDED ENTRANCE.
VARVARA, PERHAPS I COULD--
SILENCE, PLEASE.
BY MY SIDE. BUT DO NOT BLOCK HERR VON KLEMPT'S VIEW.
"VIEW" OF WHAT?
THE GUARDS' VIEW OF YOU, I SHOULD SAY. MY ENGLISH...
THEY SHOULD SHIVER TO SEE YOU AT MY SIDE, NO?
THEY WILL NOT SO MUCH AS SHIVER AGAIN...

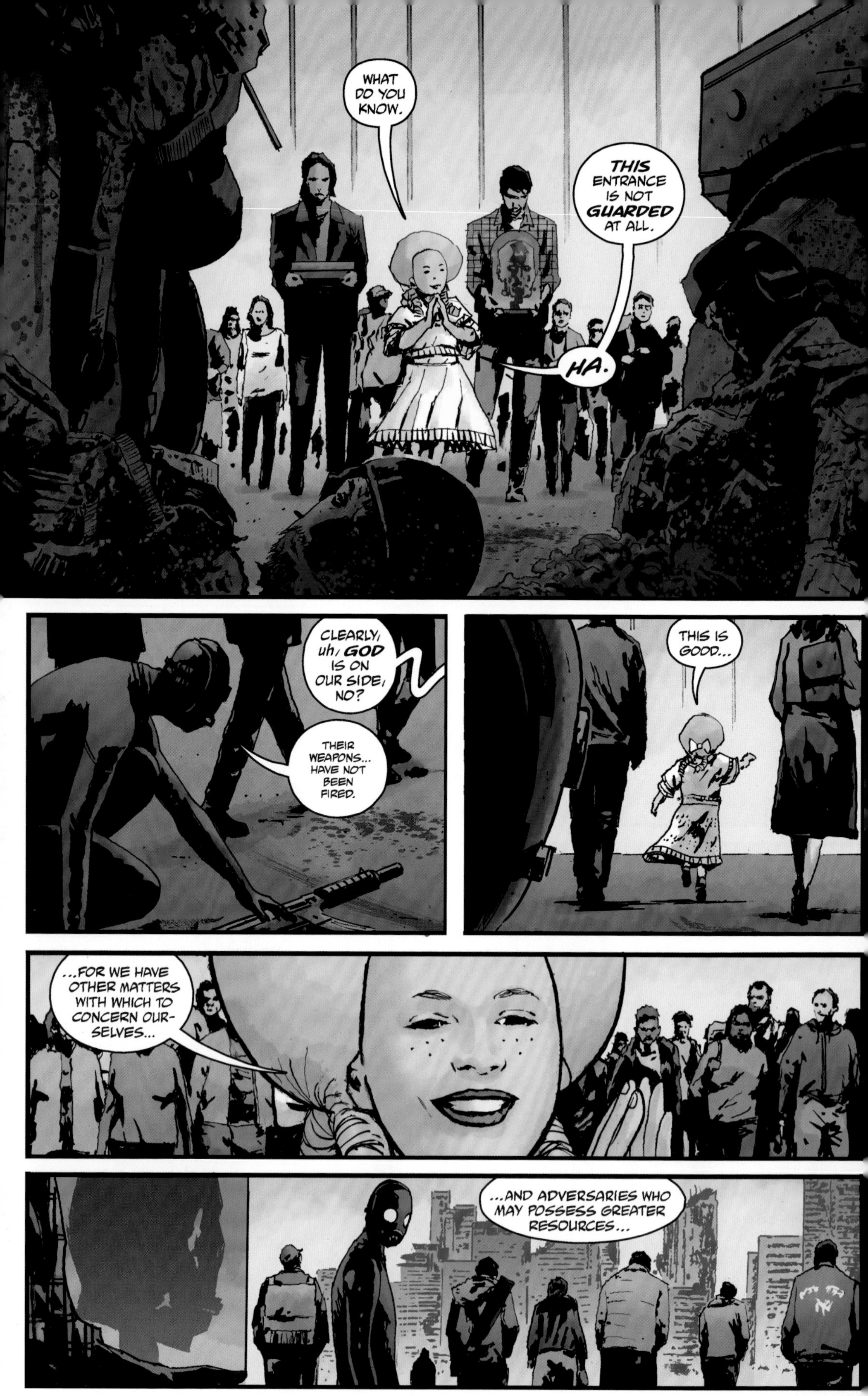
WHAT DO YOU KNOW.
THIS ENTRANCE IS NOT GUARDED AT ALL.
HA.
CLEARLY, uh, GOD IS ON OUR SIDE, NO?
THEIR WEAPONS... HAVE NOT BEEN FIRED.
THIS IS GOOD...
...FOR WE HAVE OTHER MATTERS WITH WHICH TO CONCERN OUR-SELVES...
...AND ADVERSARIES WHO MAY POSSESS GREATER RESOURCES...

CHAPTER FIVE

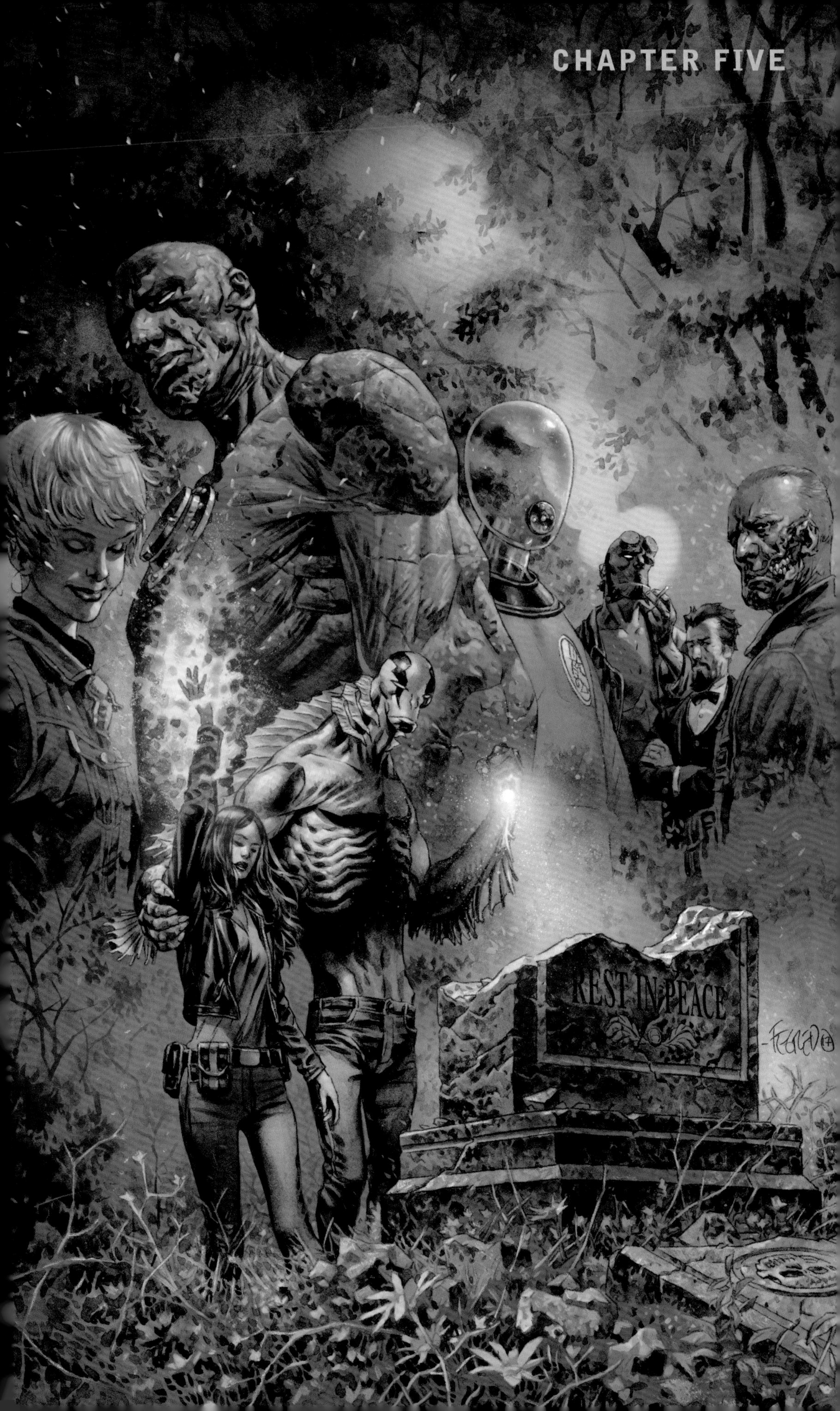
REST IN PEACE

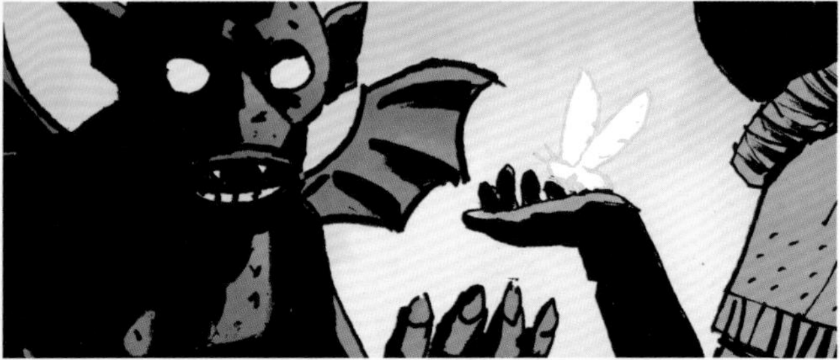

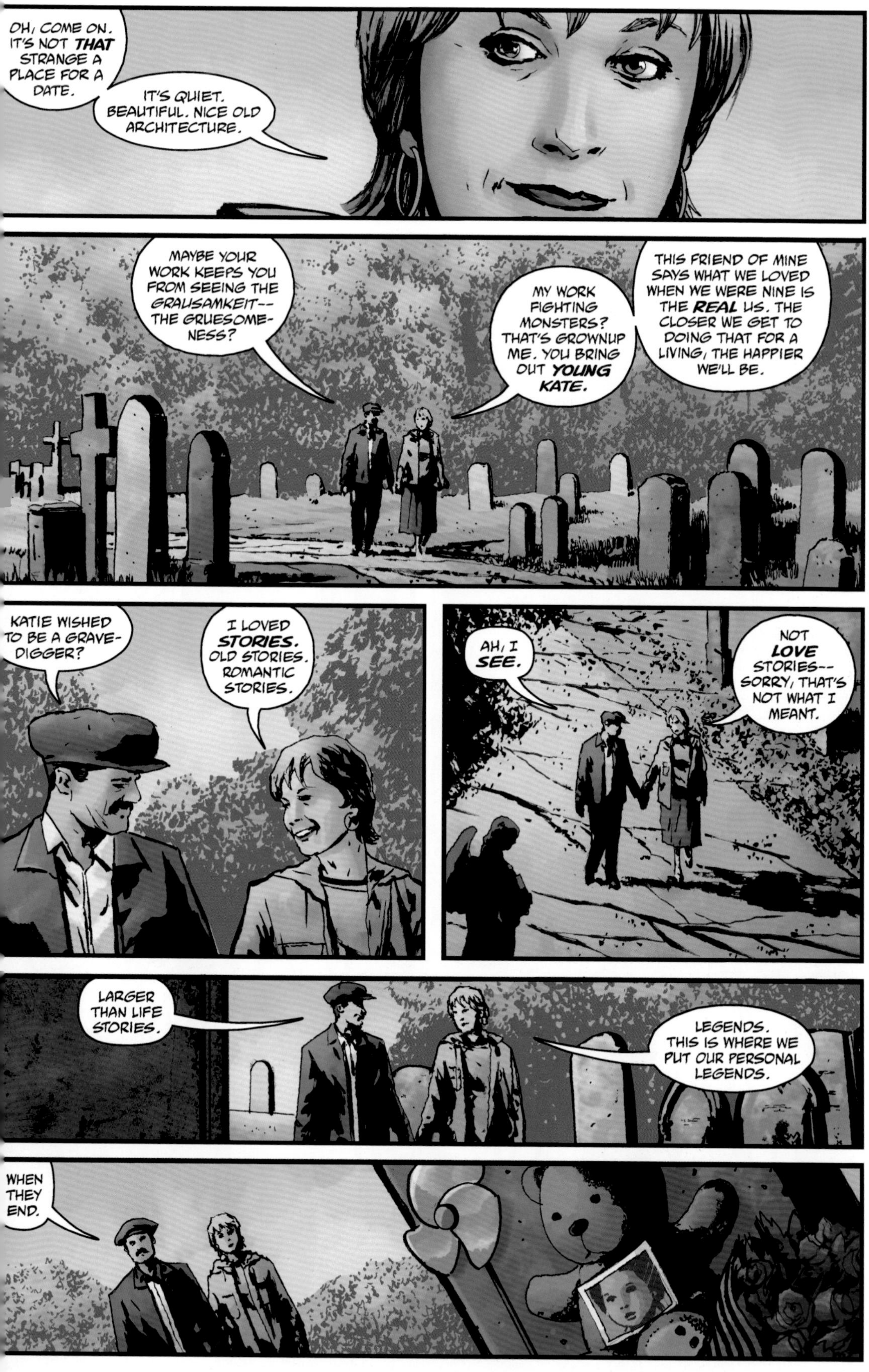

OH, COME ON. IT'S NOT **THAT** STRANGE A PLACE FOR A DATE.
IT'S QUIET. BEAUTIFUL. NICE OLD ARCHITECTURE.
MAYBE YOUR WORK KEEPS YOU FROM SEEING THE GRAUSAMKEIT-- THE GRUESOMENESS?
MY WORK FIGHTING MONSTERS? THAT'S GROWNUP ME. YOU BRING OUT **YOUNG KATE.**
THIS FRIEND OF MINE SAYS WHAT WE LOVED WHEN WE WERE NINE IS THE **REAL** US. THE CLOSER WE GET TO DOING THAT FOR A LIVING, THE HAPPIER WE'LL BE.
KATIE WISHED TO BE A GRAVE-DIGGER?
I LOVED **STORIES.** OLD STORIES. ROMANTIC STORIES.
AH, I **SEE.**
NOT **LOVE** STORIES-- SORRY, THAT'S NOT WHAT I MEANT.
LARGER THAN LIFE STORIES.
LEGENDS. THIS IS WHERE WE PUT OUR PERSONAL LEGENDS.
WHEN THEY END.

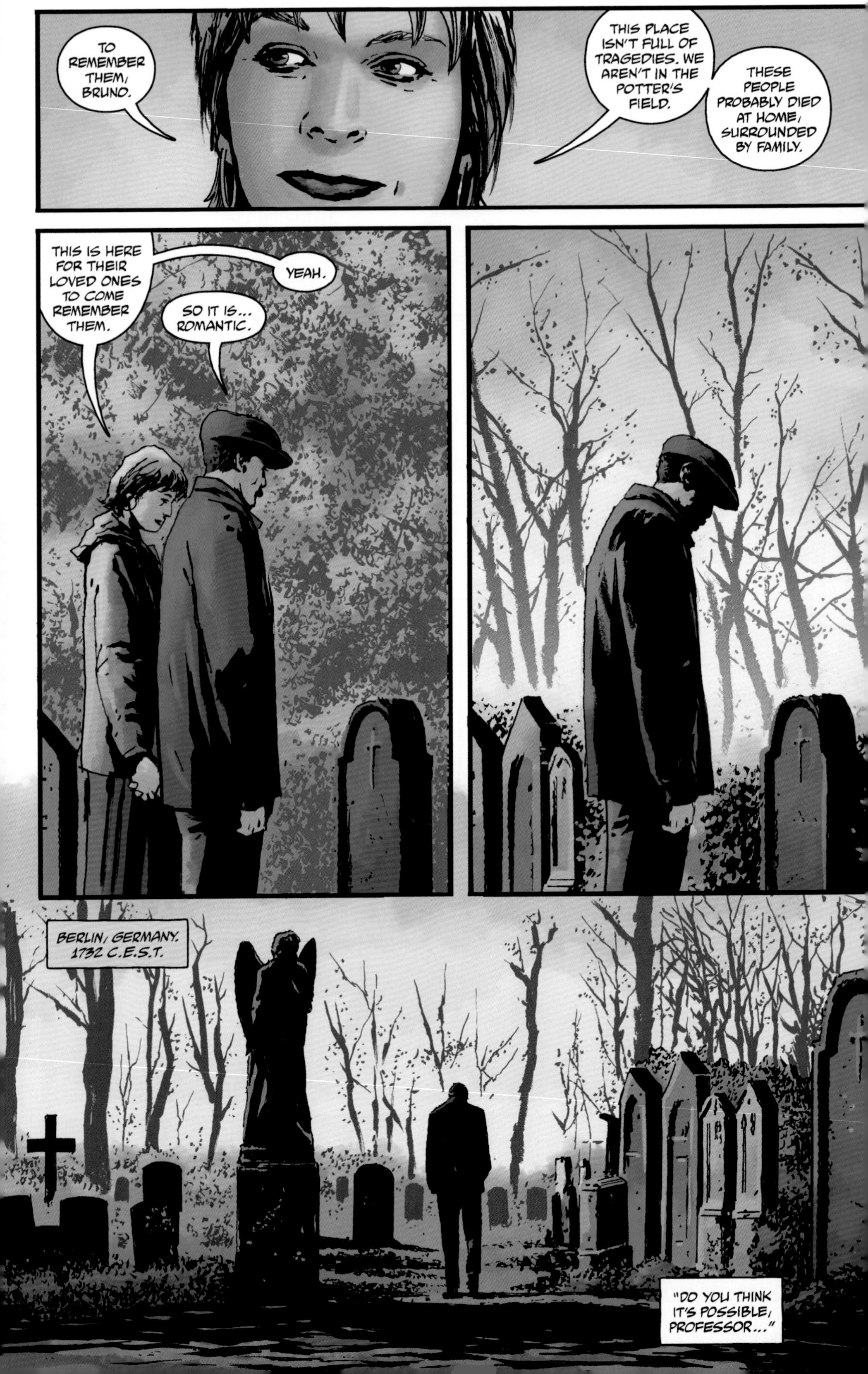

TO REMEMBER THEM, BRUNO.
THIS PLACE ISN'T FULL OF TRAGEDIES. WE AREN'T IN THE POTTER'S FIELD.
THESE PEOPLE PROBABLY DIED AT HOME, SURROUNDED BY FAMILY.
THIS IS HERE FOR THEIR LOVED ONES TO COME REMEMBER THEM.
YEAH.
SO IT IS... ROMANTIC.
BERLIN, GERMANY. 1732 C.E.S.T.
"DO YOU THINK IT'S POSSIBLE, PROFESSOR..."

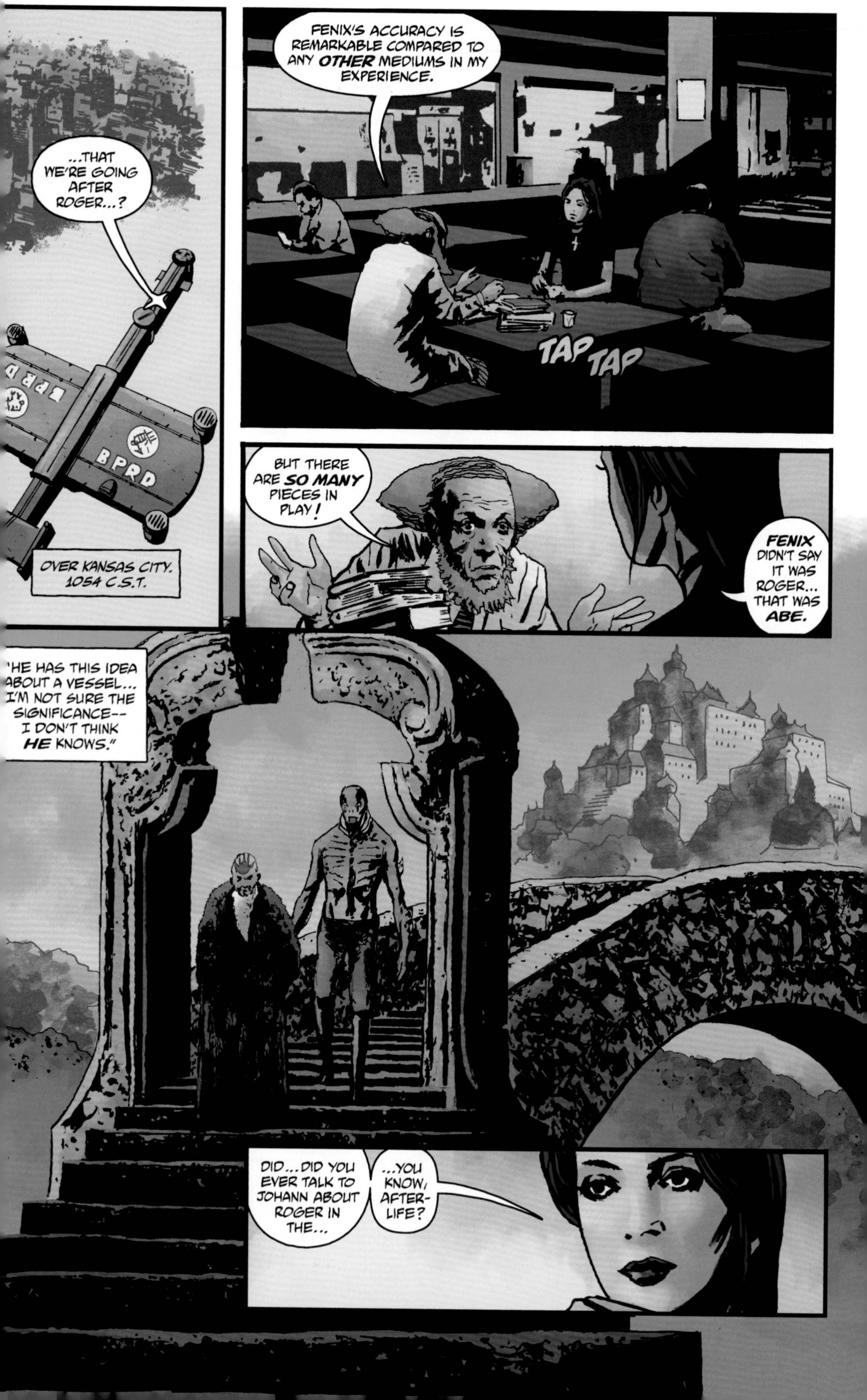
...THAT WE'RE GOING AFTER ROGER...?
BPRD
BPRD
OVER KANSAS CITY. 1054 C.S.T.
FENIX'S ACCURACY IS REMARKABLE COMPARED TO ANY OTHER MEDIUMS IN MY EXPERIENCE.
TAP TAP
BUT THERE ARE SO MANY PIECES IN PLAY!
FENIX DIDN'T SAY IT WAS ROGER... THAT WAS ABE.
"HE HAS THIS IDEA ABOUT A VESSEL... I'M NOT SURE THE SIGNIFICANCE-- I DON'T THINK HE KNOWS."
DID... DID YOU EVER TALK TO JOHANN ABOUT ROGER IN THE...
...YOU KNOW, AFTER-LIFE?

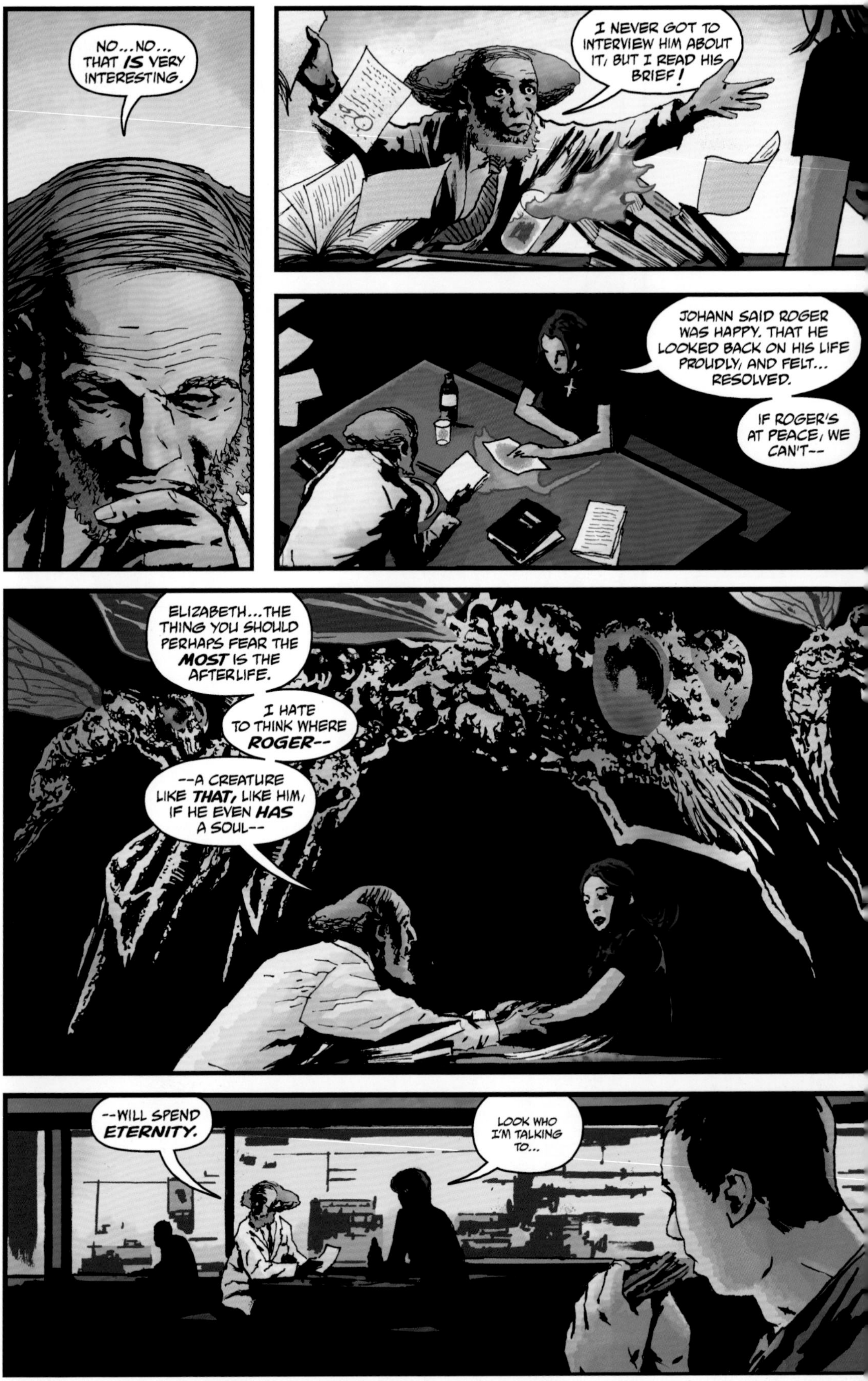
NO...NO... THAT IS VERY INTERESTING.
I NEVER GOT TO INTERVIEW HIM ABOUT IT, BUT I READ HIS BRIEF!
JOHANN SAID ROGER WAS HAPPY. THAT HE LOOKED BACK ON HIS LIFE PROUDLY, AND FELT... RESOLVED.
IF ROGER'S AT PEACE, WE CAN'T--
ELIZABETH...THE THING YOU SHOULD PERHAPS FEAR THE MOST IS THE AFTERLIFE.
I HATE TO THINK WHERE ROGER--
--A CREATURE LIKE THAT, LIKE HIM, IF HE EVEN HAS A SOUL--
--WILL SPEND ETERNITY.
LOOK WHO I'M TALKING TO...

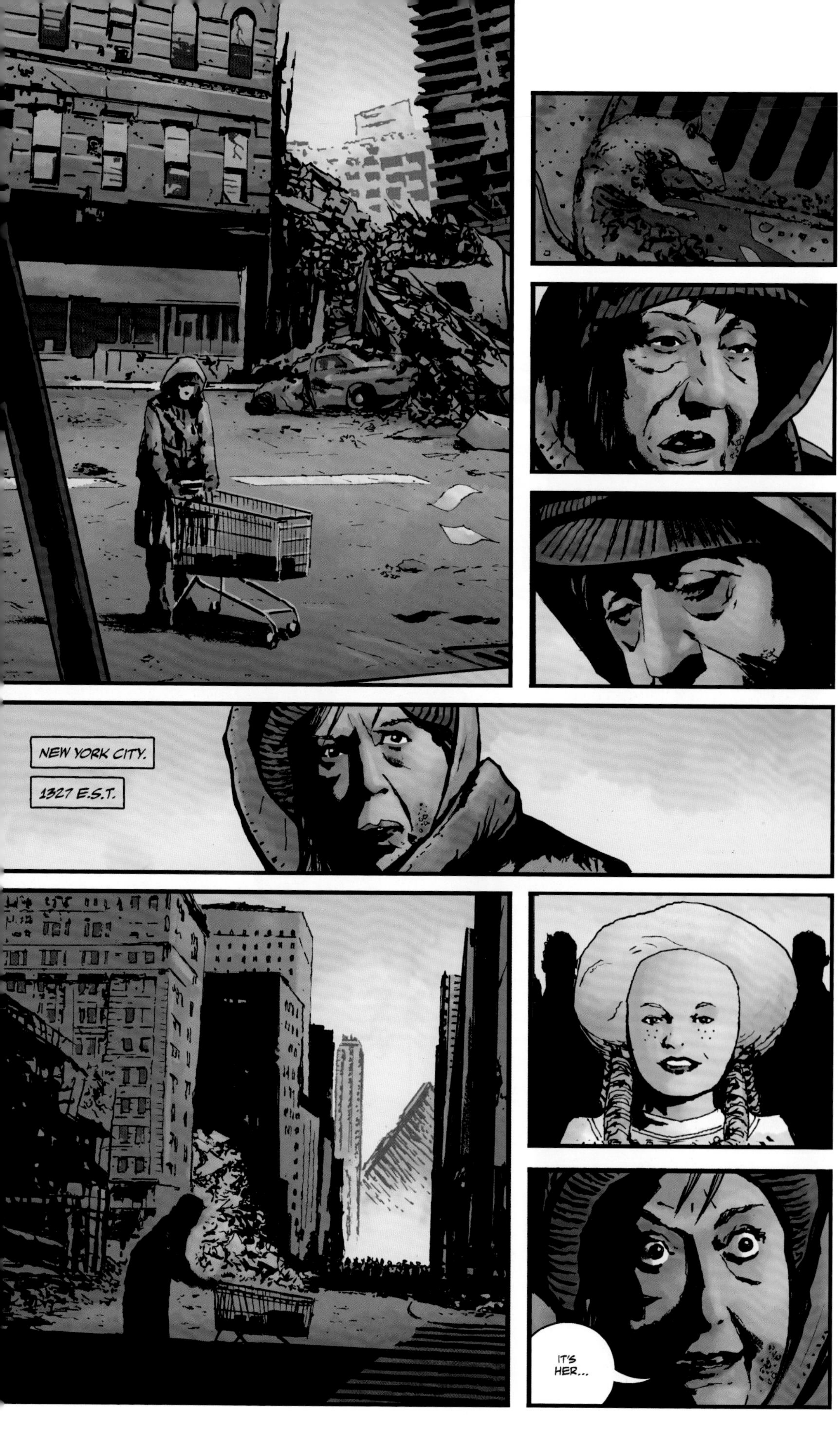
NEW YORK CITY.
1327 E.S.T.
IT'S HER...

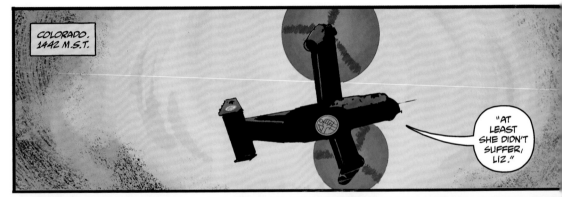

COLORADO.
1442 M.S.T.

"AT LEAST SHE DIDN'T SUFFER, LIZ."

HUH?

"HAPPENED REAL QUICK, LIZ."

I, uh, DON'T KNOW WHAT YOU...

THAT'S HOW *TIAN* TOLD ME ABOUT KATE...

"...SO YOU GOTTA APPRECIATE THE IRONY..."

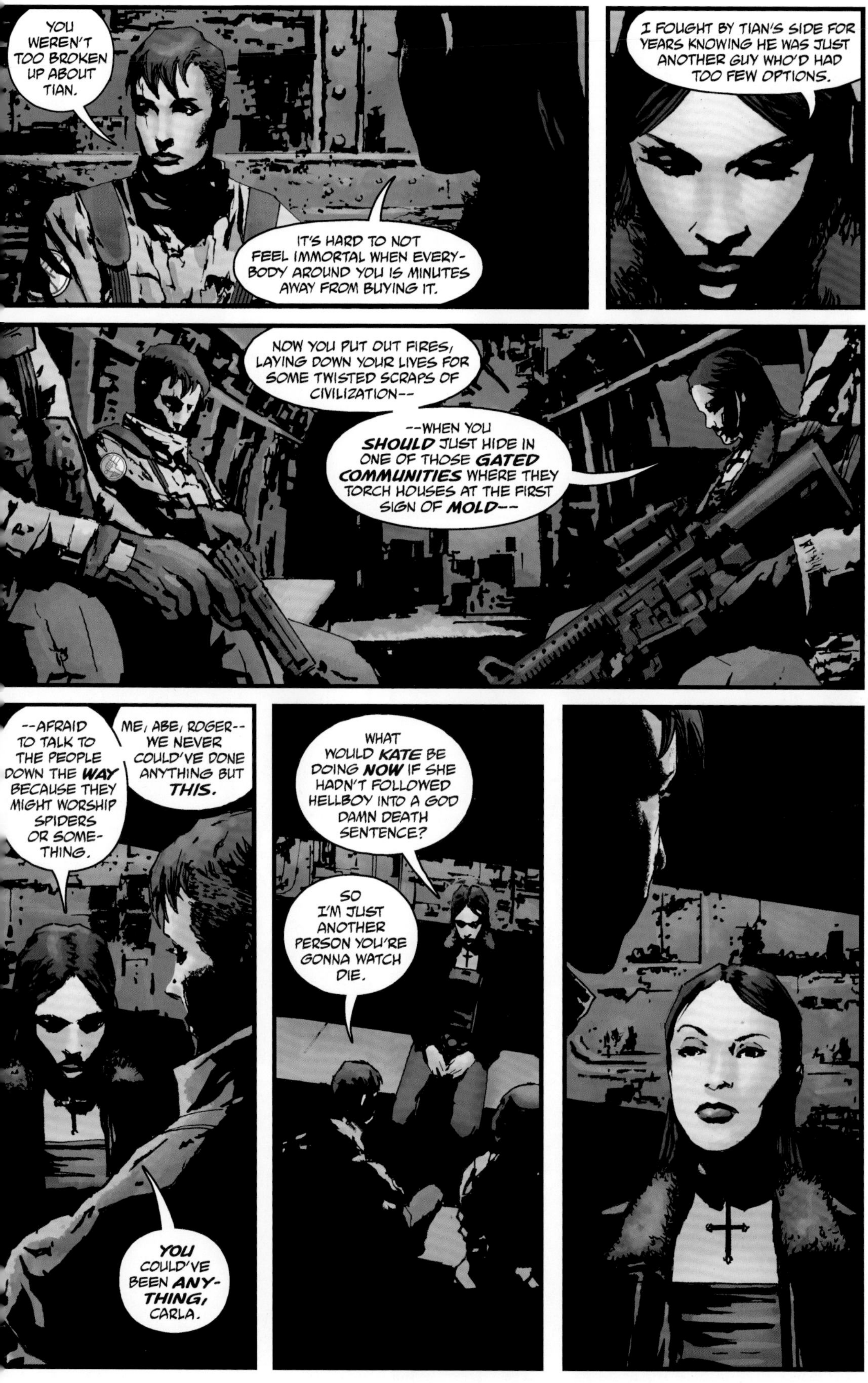

YOU WEREN'T TOO BROKEN UP ABOUT TIAN.
IT'S HARD TO NOT FEEL IMMORTAL WHEN EVERY-BODY AROUND YOU IS MINUTES AWAY FROM BUYING IT.
I FOUGHT BY TIAN'S SIDE FOR YEARS KNOWING HE WAS JUST ANOTHER GUY WHO'D HAD TOO FEW OPTIONS.
NOW YOU PUT OUT FIRES, LAYING DOWN YOUR LIVES FOR SOME TWISTED SCRAPS OF CIVILIZATION--
--WHEN YOU SHOULD JUST HIDE IN ONE OF THOSE GATED COMMUNITIES WHERE THEY TORCH HOUSES AT THE FIRST SIGN OF MOLD--
--AFRAID TO TALK TO THE PEOPLE DOWN THE WAY BECAUSE THEY MIGHT WORSHIP SPIDERS OR SOME-THING.
ME, ABE, ROGER-- WE NEVER COULD'VE DONE ANYTHING BUT THIS.
YOU COULD'VE BEEN ANY-THING, CARLA.
WHAT WOULD KATE BE DOING NOW IF SHE HADN'T FOLLOWED HELLBOY INTO A GOD DAMN DEATH SENTENCE?
SO I'M JUST ANOTHER PERSON YOU'RE GONNA WATCH DIE.

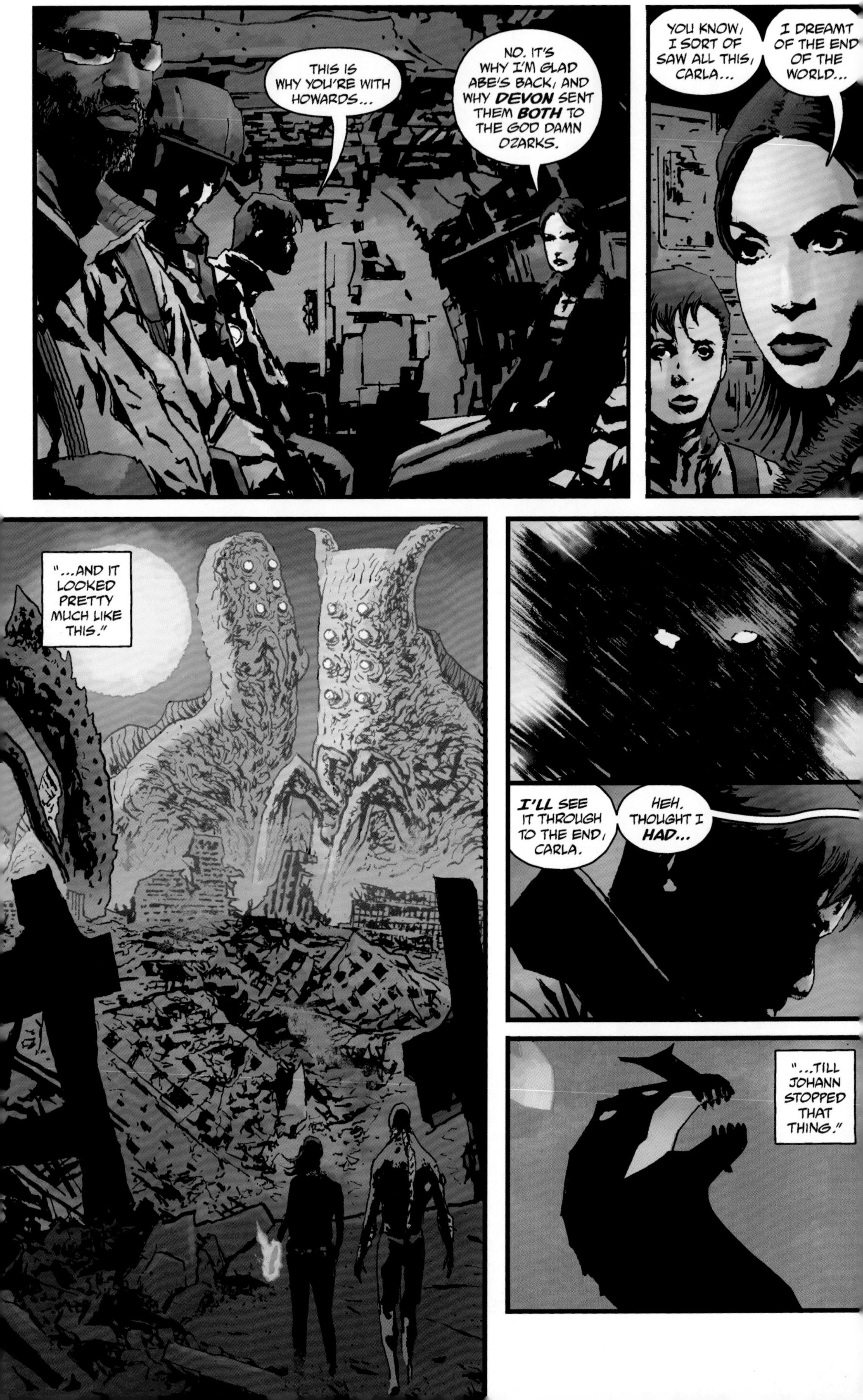
THIS IS WHY YOU'RE WITH HOWARDS...
NO. IT'S WHY I'M GLAD ABE'S BACK, AND WHY **DEVON** SENT THEM **BOTH** TO THE GOD DAMN OZARKS.
YOU KNOW, I SORT OF SAW ALL THIS, CARLA...
I DREAMT OF THE END OF THE WORLD...
"...AND IT LOOKED PRETTY MUCH LIKE THIS."
I'LL SEE IT THROUGH TO THE END, CARLA.
HEH. THOUGHT I **HAD...**
"...TILL JOHANN STOPPED THAT THING."

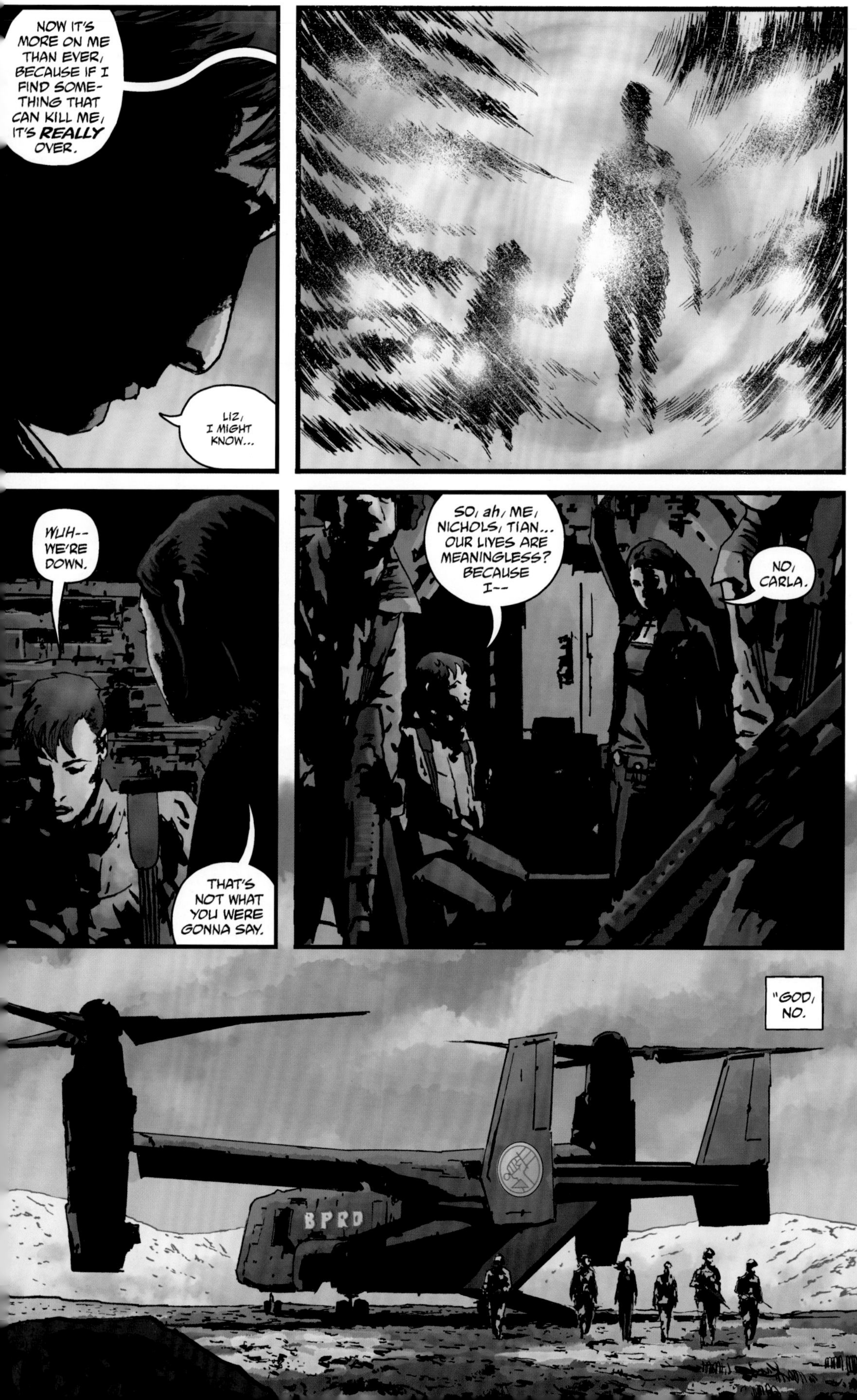
NOW IT'S MORE ON ME THAN EVER, BECAUSE IF I FIND SOME-THING THAT CAN KILL ME, IT'S *REALLY* OVER.
LIZ, I MIGHT KNOW...
WUH-- WE'RE DOWN.
THAT'S NOT WHAT YOU WERE GONNA SAY.
SO, ah, ME, NICHOLS, TIAN... OUR LIVES ARE MEANINGLESS? BECAUSE I--
NO, CARLA.
"GOD, NO.
BPRD

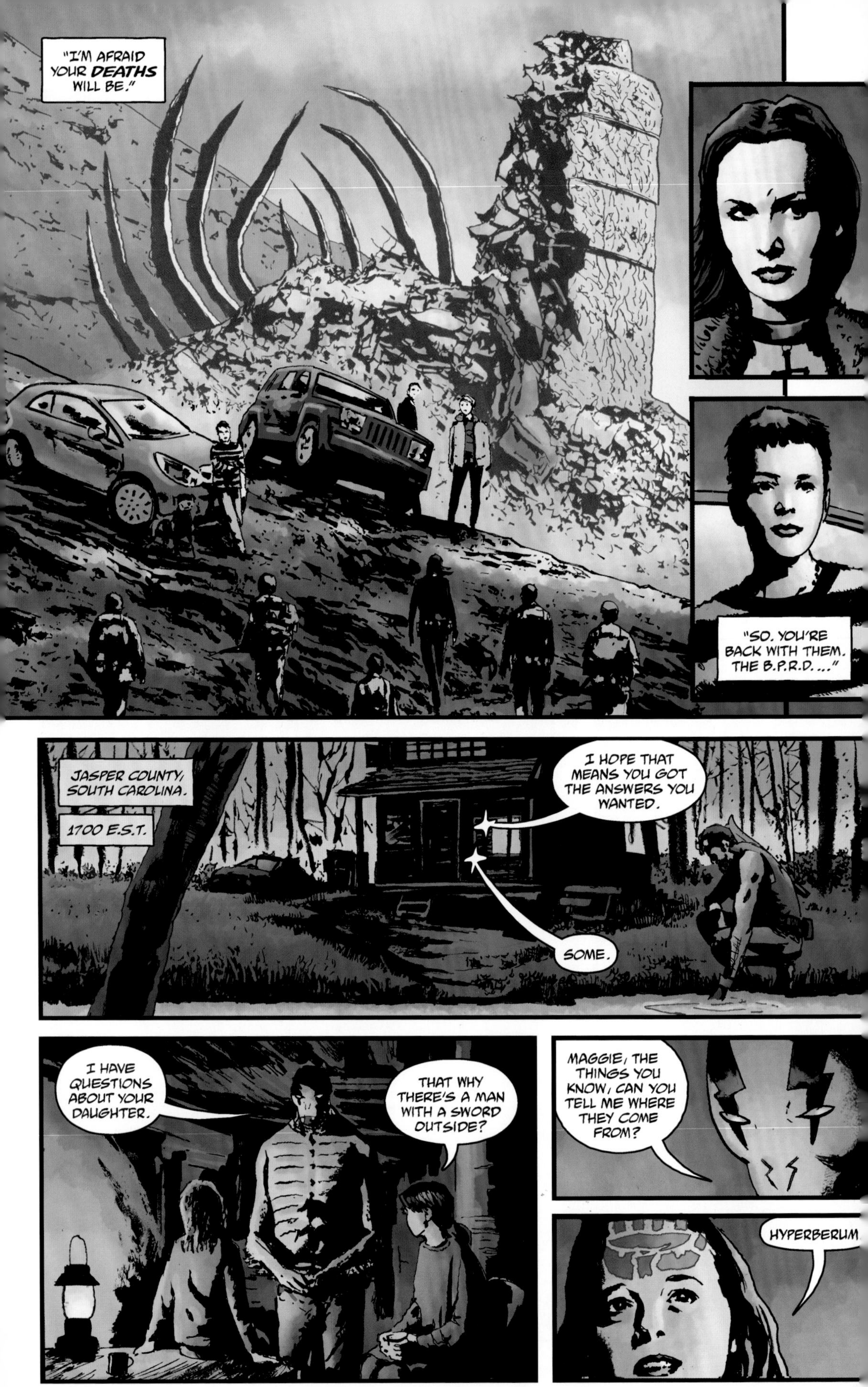
"I'M AFRAID YOUR DEATHS WILL BE."
"SO. YOU'RE BACK WITH THEM. THE B.P.R.D. ..."
JASPER COUNTY, SOUTH CAROLINA.
1700 E.S.T.
I HOPE THAT MEANS YOU GOT THE ANSWERS YOU WANTED.
SOME.
I HAVE QUESTIONS ABOUT YOUR DAUGHTER.
THAT WHY THERE'S A MAN WITH A SWORD OUTSIDE?
MAGGIE, THE THINGS YOU KNOW, CAN YOU TELL ME WHERE THEY COME FROM?
HYPERBERUM

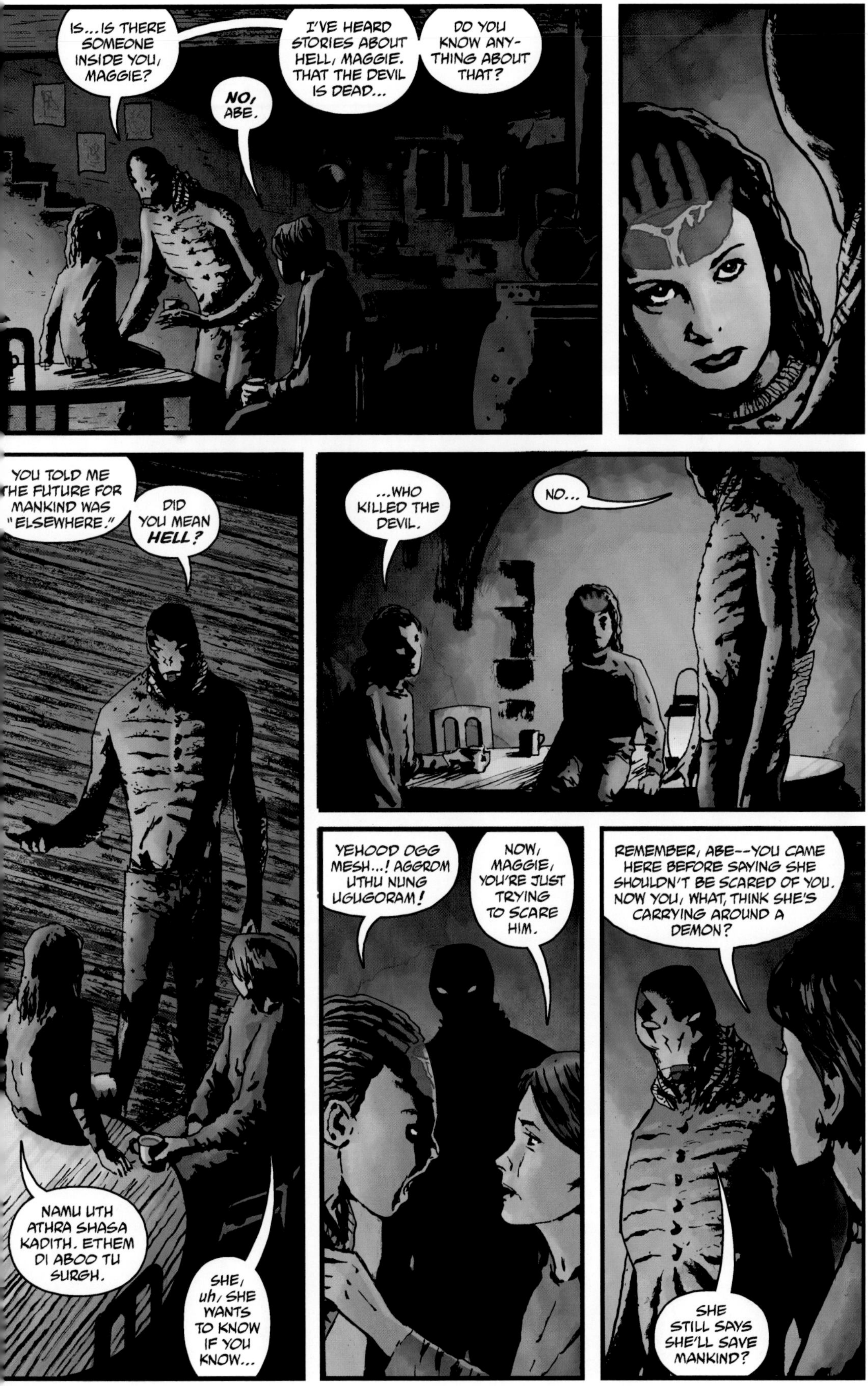

IS...IS THERE SOMEONE INSIDE YOU, MAGGIE?
NO, ABE.
I'VE HEARD STORIES ABOUT HELL, MAGGIE. THAT THE DEVIL IS DEAD...
DO YOU KNOW ANY-THING ABOUT THAT?
YOU TOLD ME THE FUTURE FOR MANKIND WAS "ELSEWHERE."
DID YOU MEAN HELL?
NAMU UTH ATHRA SHASA KADITH. ETHEM DI ABOO TU SURGH.
SHE, uh, SHE WANTS TO KNOW IF YOU KNOW...
...WHO KILLED THE DEVIL.
NO...
YEHOOD OGG MESH...! AGGROM UTHU NUNG UGUGORAM!
NOW, MAGGIE, YOU'RE JUST TRYING TO SCARE HIM.
REMEMBER, ABE--YOU CAME HERE BEFORE SAYING SHE SHOULDN'T BE SCARED OF YOU. NOW YOU, WHAT, THINK SHE'S CARRYING AROUND A DEMON?
SHE STILL SAYS SHE'LL SAVE MANKIND?

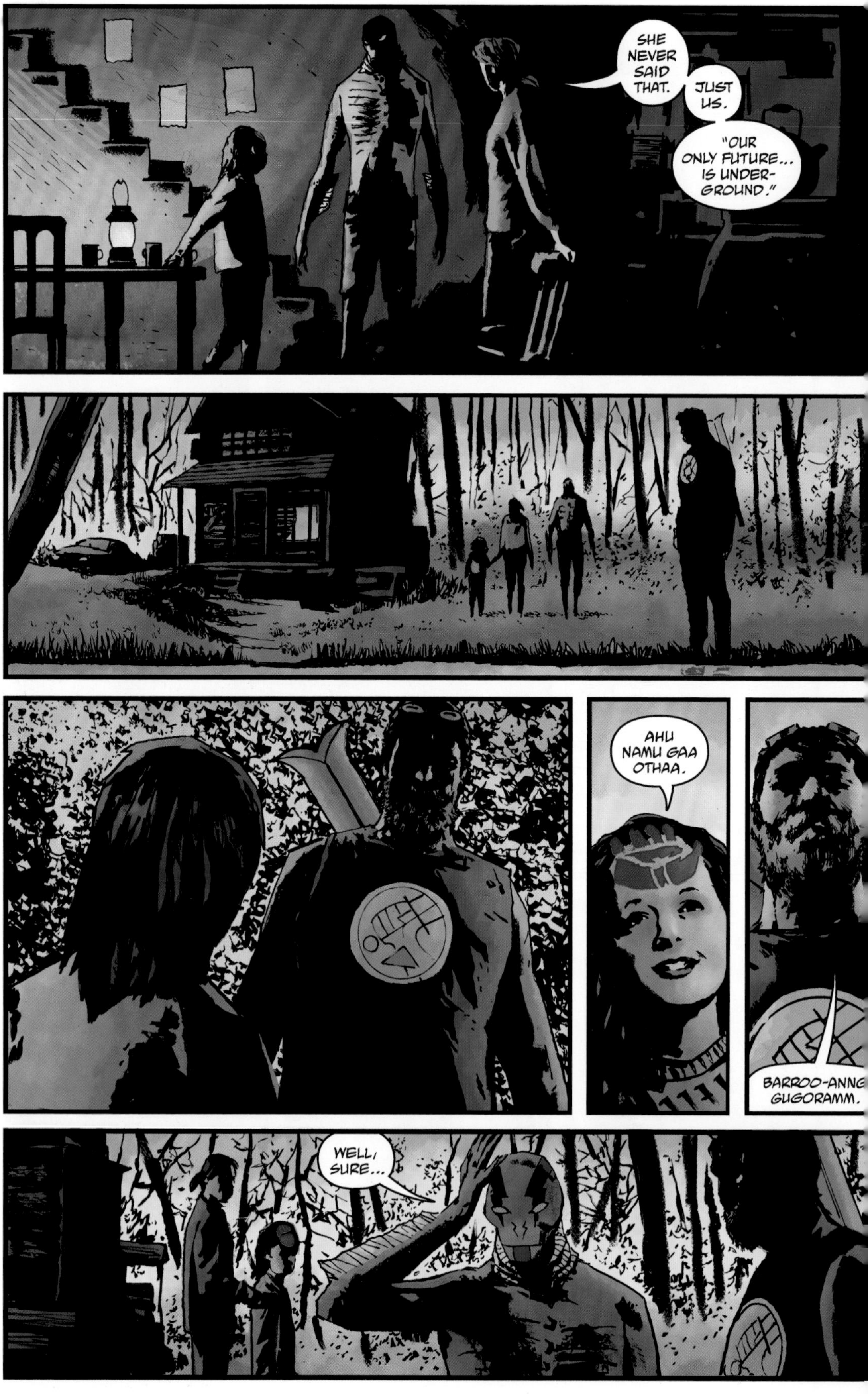
SHE NEVER SAID THAT.
JUST US.
"OUR ONLY FUTURE... IS UNDER-GROUND."
AHU NAMU GAA OTHAA.
BARROO-ANNG GUGORAMM.
WELL, SURE...

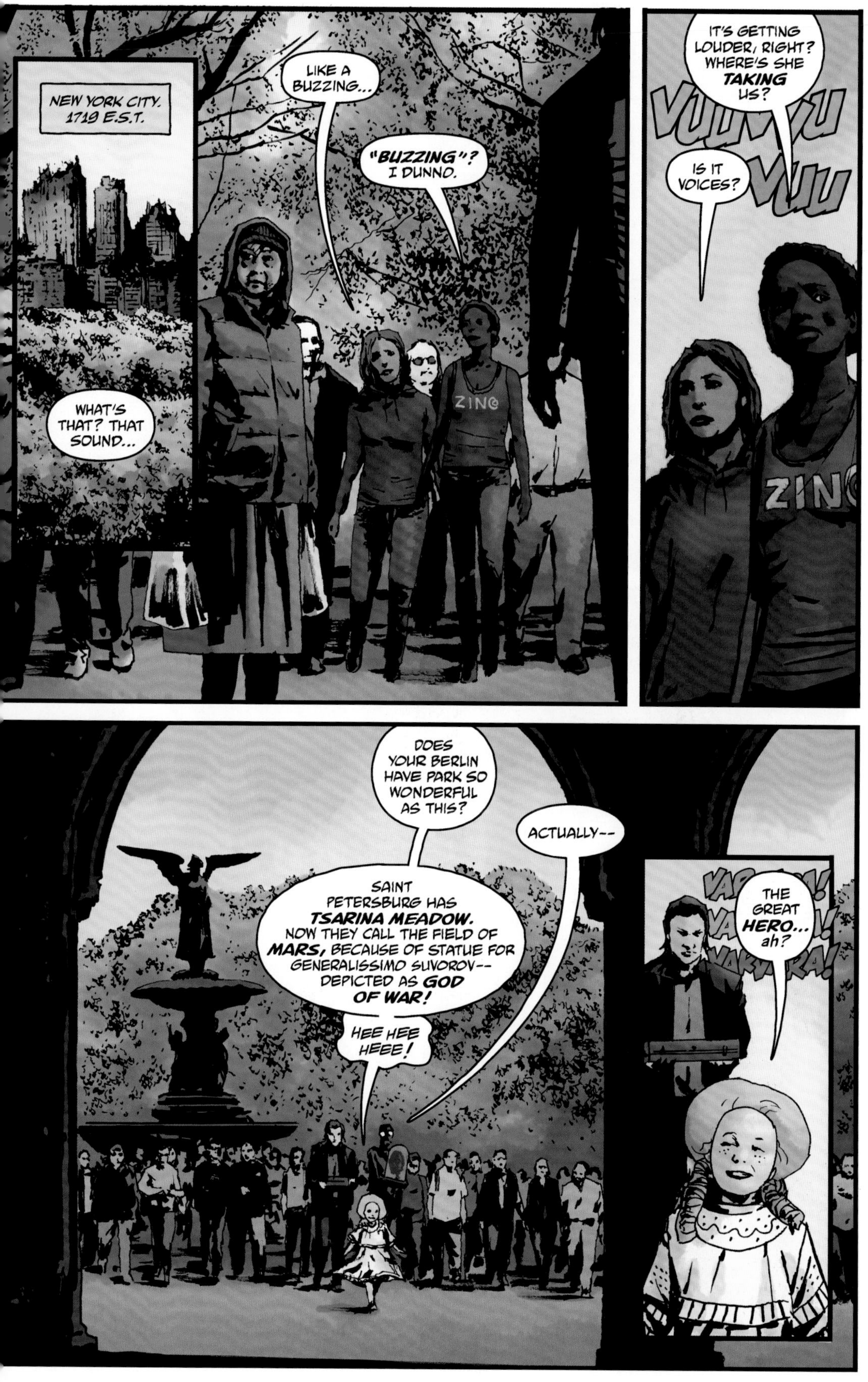
NEW YORK CITY. 1719 E.S.T.
WHAT'S THAT? THAT SOUND...
LIKE A BUZZING...
"BUZZING"? I DUNNO.
IT'S GETTING LOUDER, RIGHT? WHERE'S SHE TAKING US?
VUU
IS IT VOICES?
DOES YOUR BERLIN HAVE PARK SO WONDERFUL AS THIS?
ACTUALLY--
SAINT PETERSBURG HAS TSARINA MEADOW. NOW THEY CALL THE FIELD OF MARS, BECAUSE OF STATUE FOR GENERALISSIMO SUVOROV-- DEPICTED AS GOD OF WAR!
HEE HEE HEEE!
THE GREAT HERO... ah?

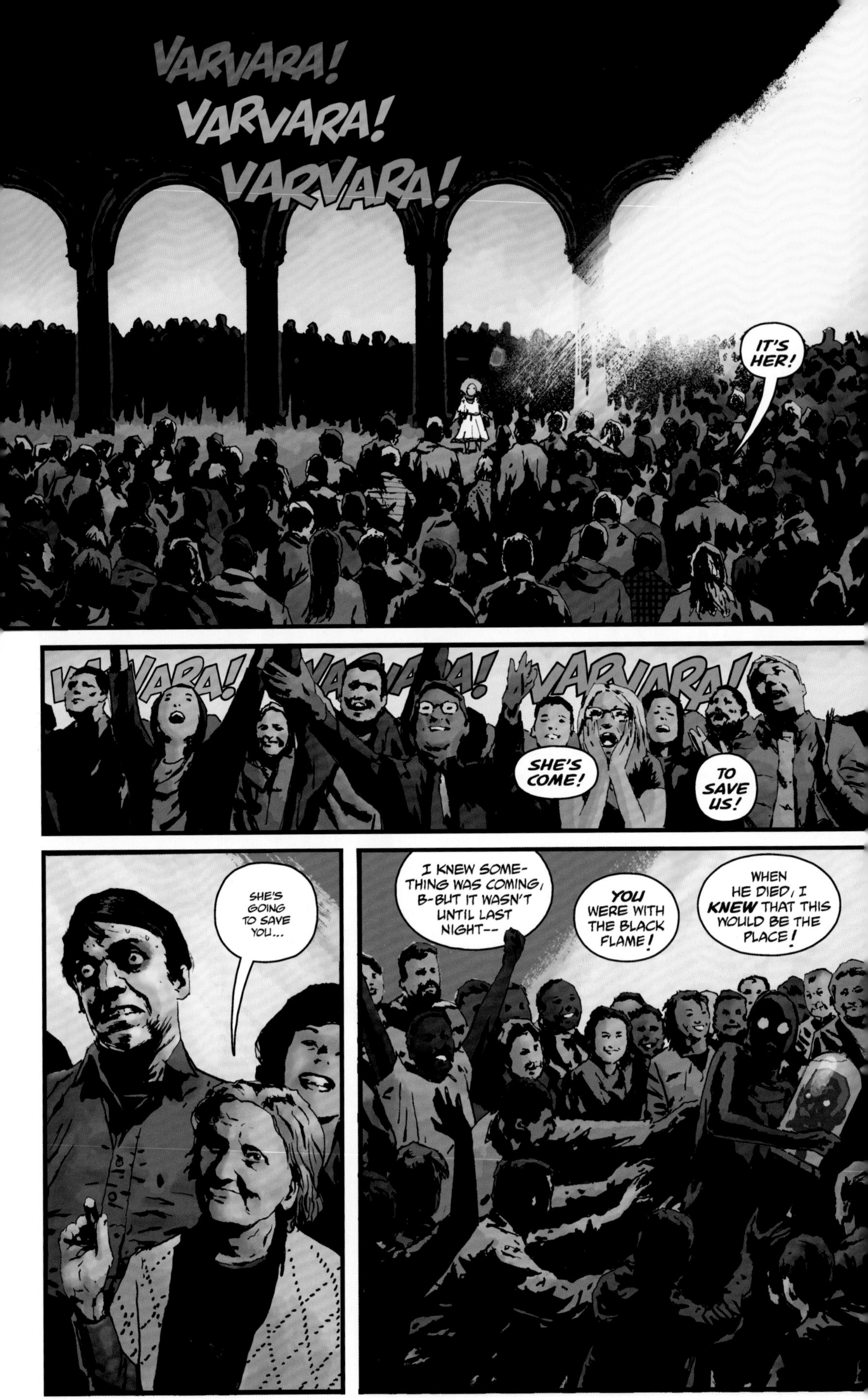
VARVARA!
VARVARA!
VARVARA!
IT'S HER!
SHE'S COME!
TO SAVE US!
SHE'S GOING TO SAVE YOU...
I KNEW SOMETHING WAS COMING, B-BUT IT WASN'T UNTIL LAST NIGHT--
YOU WERE WITH THE BLACK FLAME!
WHEN HE DIED, I KNEW THAT THIS WOULD BE THE PLACE!

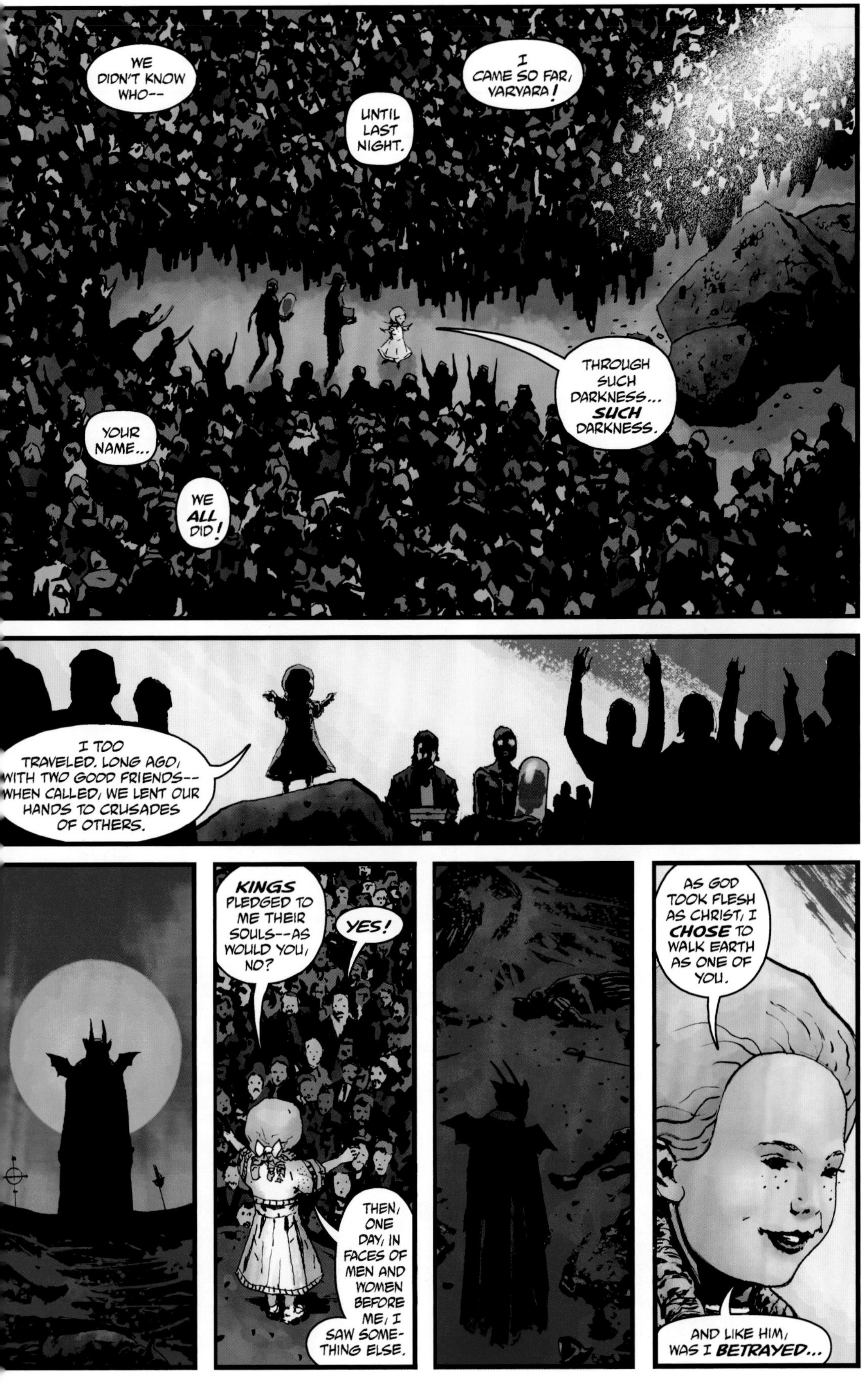
WE DIDN'T KNOW WHO--
UNTIL LAST NIGHT.
I CAME SO FAR, VARYARA!
THROUGH SUCH DARKNESS... SUCH DARKNESS.
YOUR NAME...
WE ALL DID!
I TOO TRAVELED. LONG AGO, WITH TWO GOOD FRIENDS--WHEN CALLED, WE LENT OUR HANDS TO CRUSADES OF OTHERS.
KINGS PLEDGED TO ME THEIR SOULS--AS WOULD YOU, NO?
YES!
THEN, ONE DAY, IN FACES OF MEN AND WOMEN BEFORE ME, I SAW SOME-THING ELSE.
AS GOD TOOK FLESH AS CHRIST, I CHOSE TO WALK EARTH AS ONE OF YOU.
AND LIKE HIM, WAS I BETRAYED...

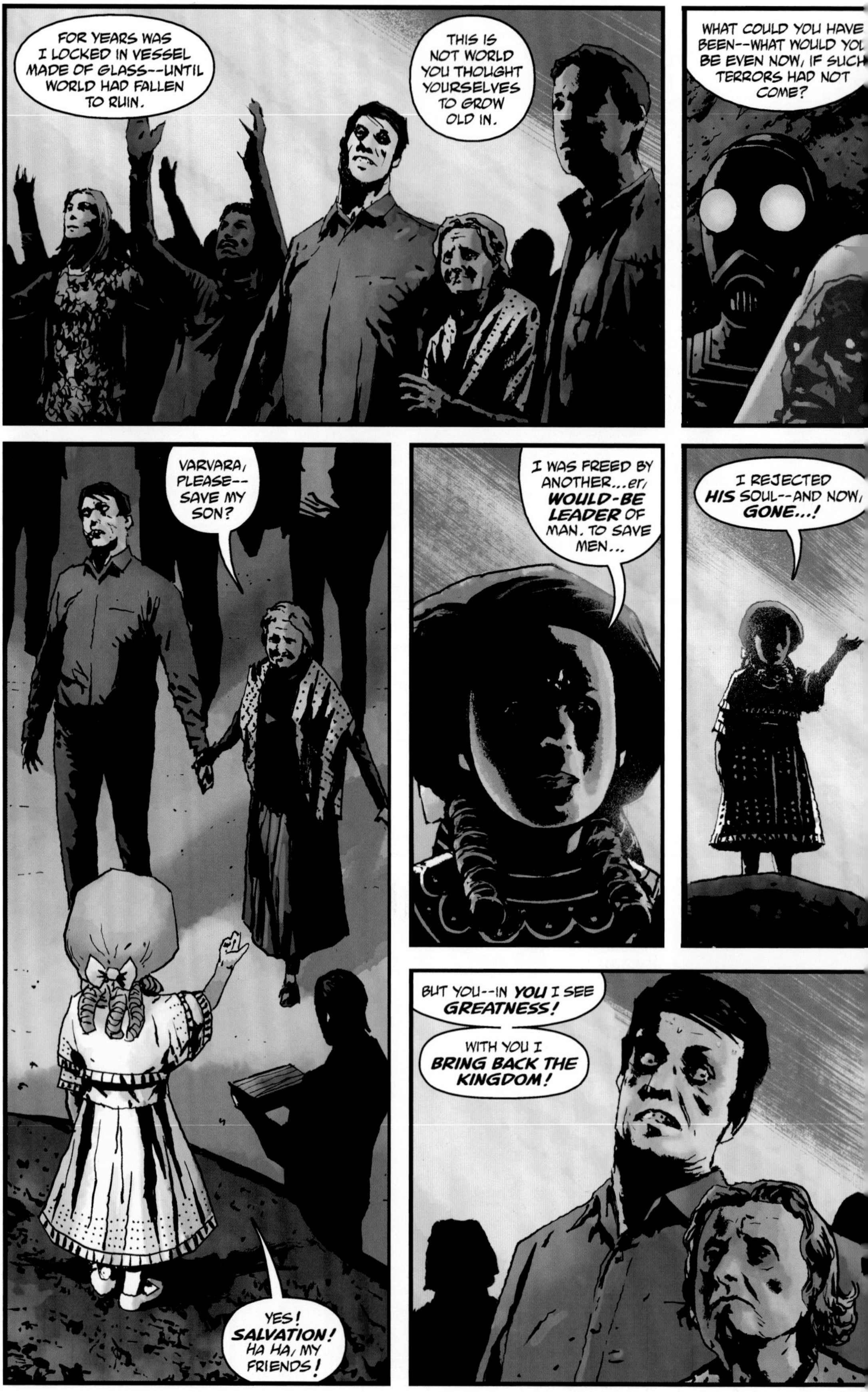
FOR YEARS WAS I LOCKED IN VESSEL MADE OF GLASS--UNTIL WORLD HAD FALLEN TO RUIN.
THIS IS NOT WORLD YOU THOUGHT YOURSELVES TO GROW OLD IN.
WHAT COULD YOU HAVE BEEN--WHAT WOULD YOU BE EVEN NOW, IF SUCH TERRORS HAD NOT COME?
VARVARA, PLEASE-- SAVE MY SON?
YES! SALVATION! HA HA, MY FRIENDS!
I WAS FREED BY ANOTHER...er, WOULD-BE LEADER OF MAN. TO SAVE MEN...
I REJECTED HIS SOUL--AND NOW, GONE...!
BUT YOU--IN YOU I SEE GREATNESS!
WITH YOU I BRING BACK THE KINGDOM!

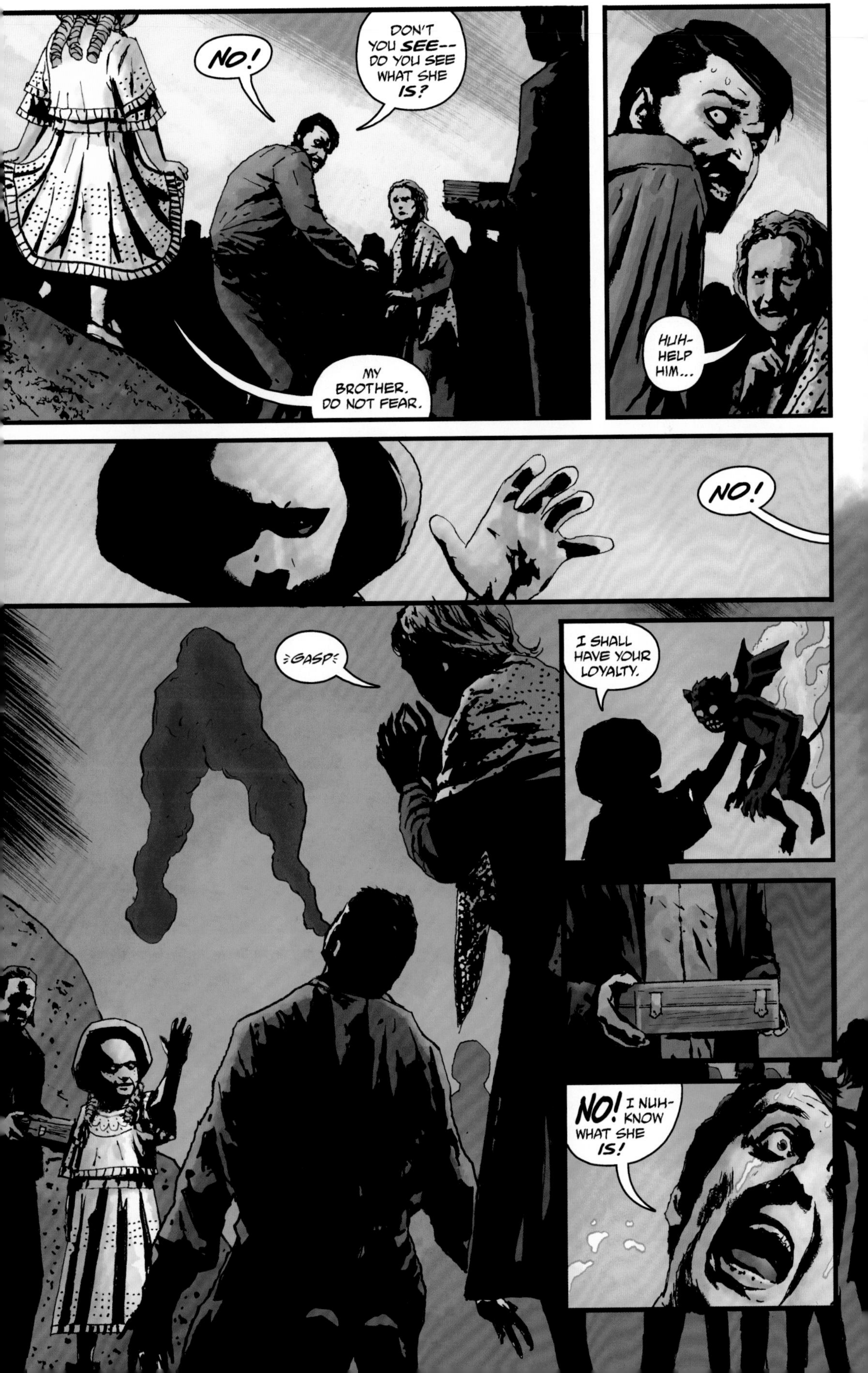

NO!
DON'T YOU SEE-- DO YOU SEE WHAT SHE IS?
MY BROTHER. DO NOT FEAR.
HUH- HELP HIM...
NO!
GASP
I SHALL HAVE YOUR LOYALTY.
NO! I NUH-KNOW WHAT SHE IS!

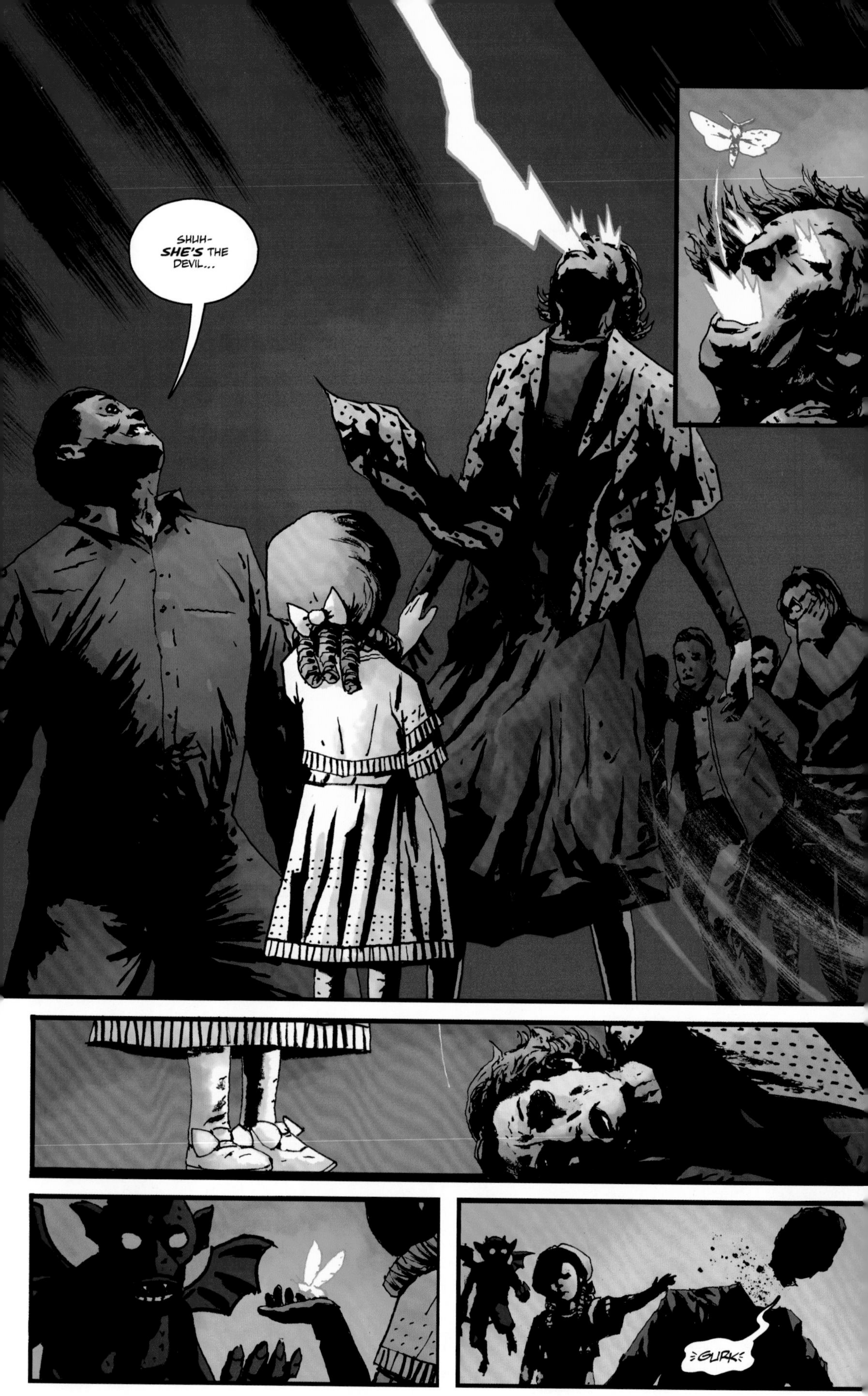
SHUH-
SHE'S THE DEVIL...
GURK

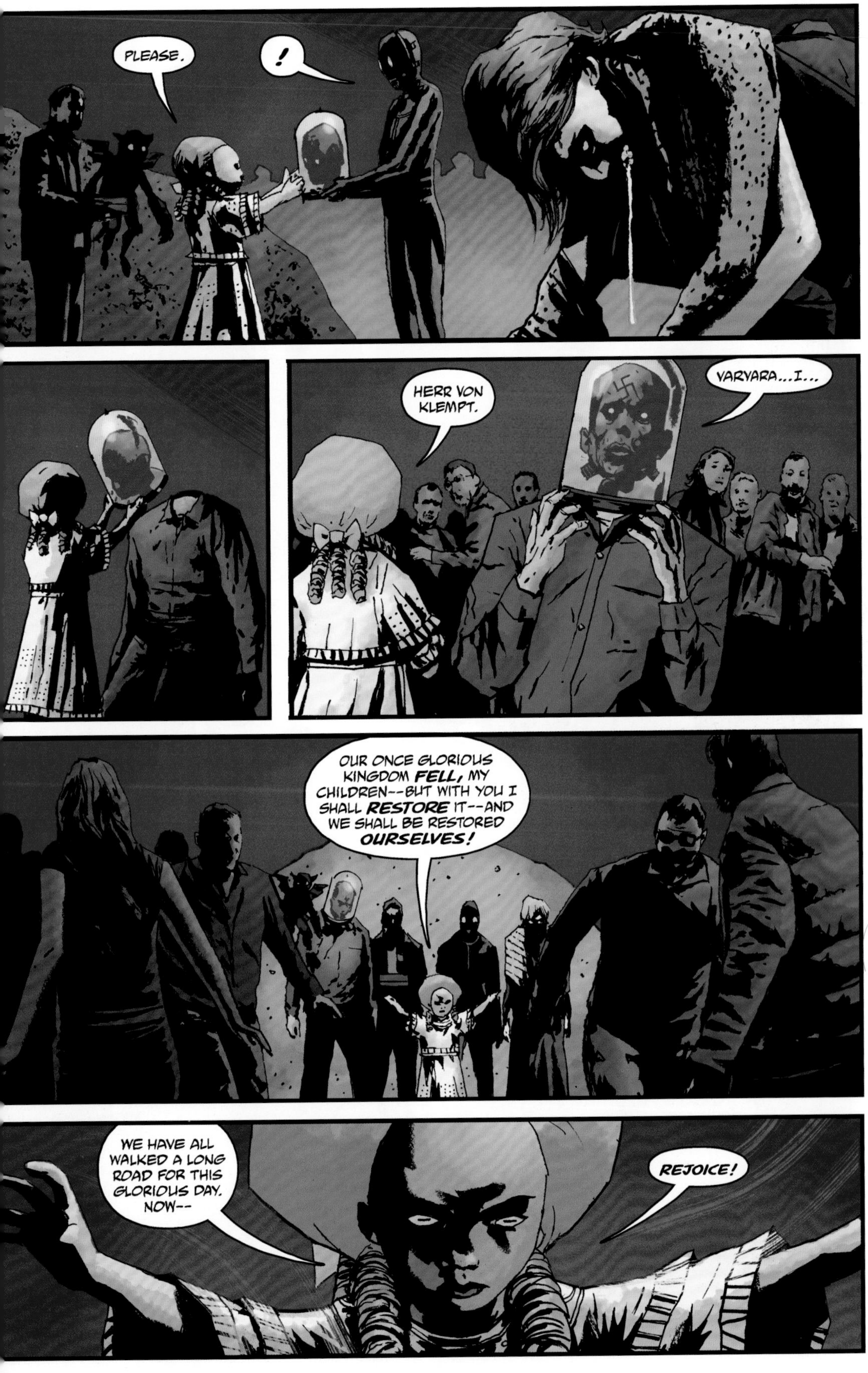
PLEASE.
!
HERR VON KLEMPT.
VARVARA...I...
OUR ONCE GLORIOUS KINGDOM **FELL,** MY CHILDREN--BUT WITH YOU I SHALL **RESTORE** IT--AND WE SHALL BE RESTORED **OURSELVES!**
WE HAVE ALL WALKED A LONG ROAD FOR THIS GLORIOUS DAY. NOW--
REJOICE!

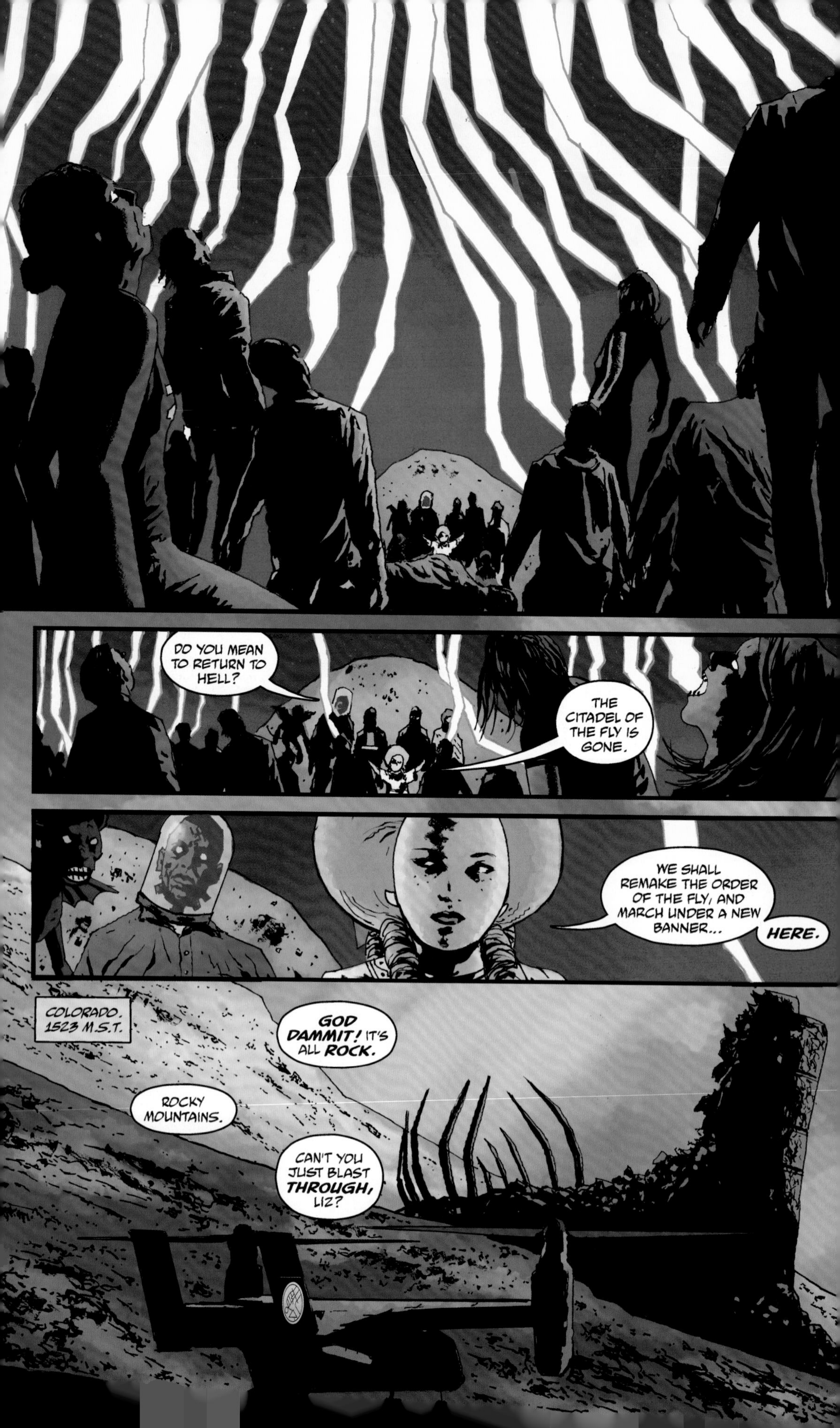

DO YOU MEAN TO RETURN TO HELL?
THE CITADEL OF THE FLY IS GONE.
WE SHALL REMAKE THE ORDER OF THE FLY, AND MARCH UNDER A NEW BANNER... HERE.
COLORADO. 1523 M.S.T.
GOD DAMMIT! IT'S ALL ROCK.
ROCKY MOUNTAINS.
CAN'T YOU JUST BLAST THROUGH, LIZ?

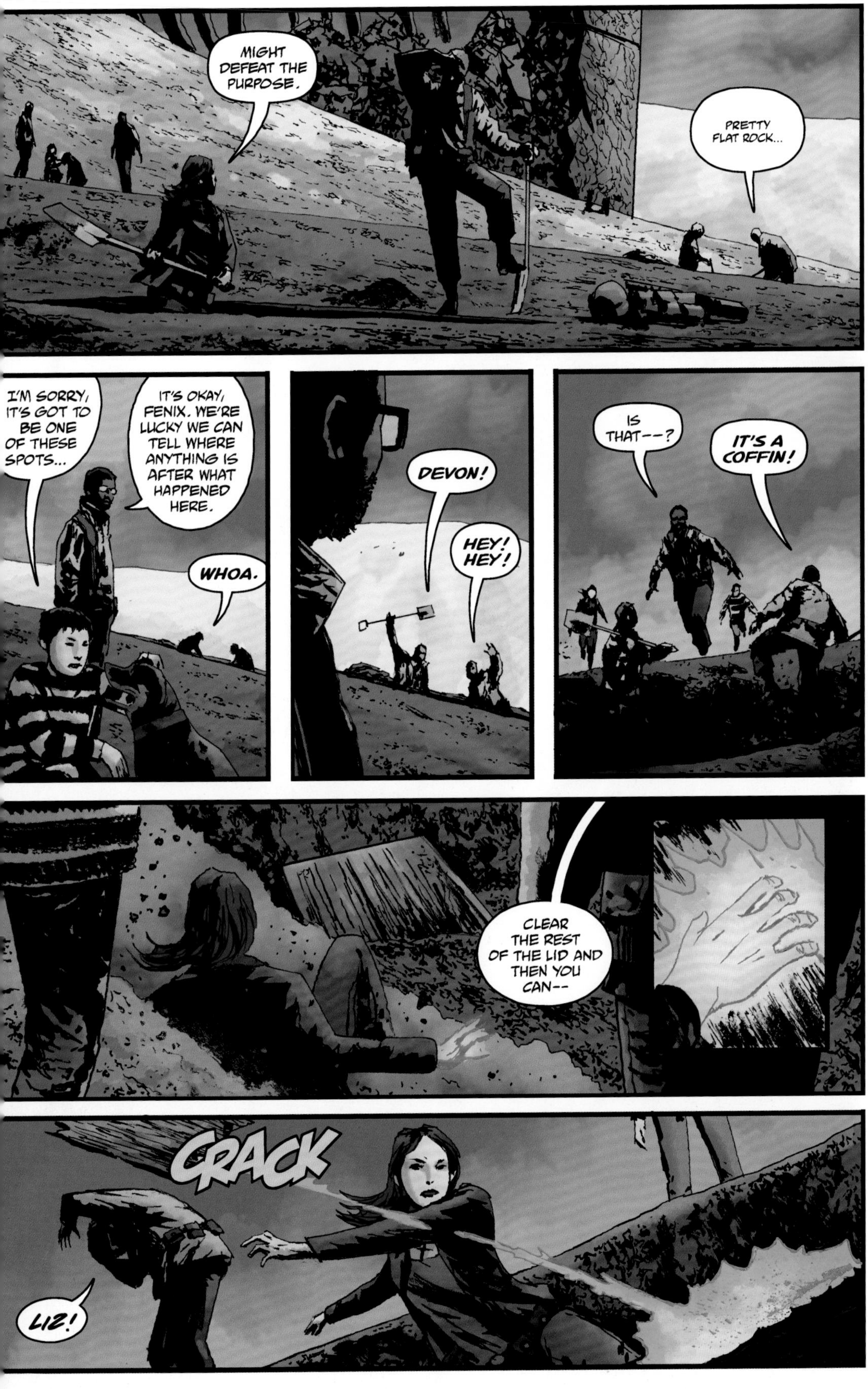

MIGHT DEFEAT THE PURPOSE.
PRETTY FLAT ROCK...
I'M SORRY, IT'S GOT TO BE ONE OF THESE SPOTS...
IT'S OKAY, FENIX. WE'RE LUCKY WE CAN TELL WHERE ANYTHING IS AFTER WHAT HAPPENED HERE.
WHOA.
DEVON!
HEY! HEY!
IS THAT--?
IT'S A COFFIN!
CLEAR THE REST OF THE LID AND THEN YOU CAN--
CRACK
LIZ!

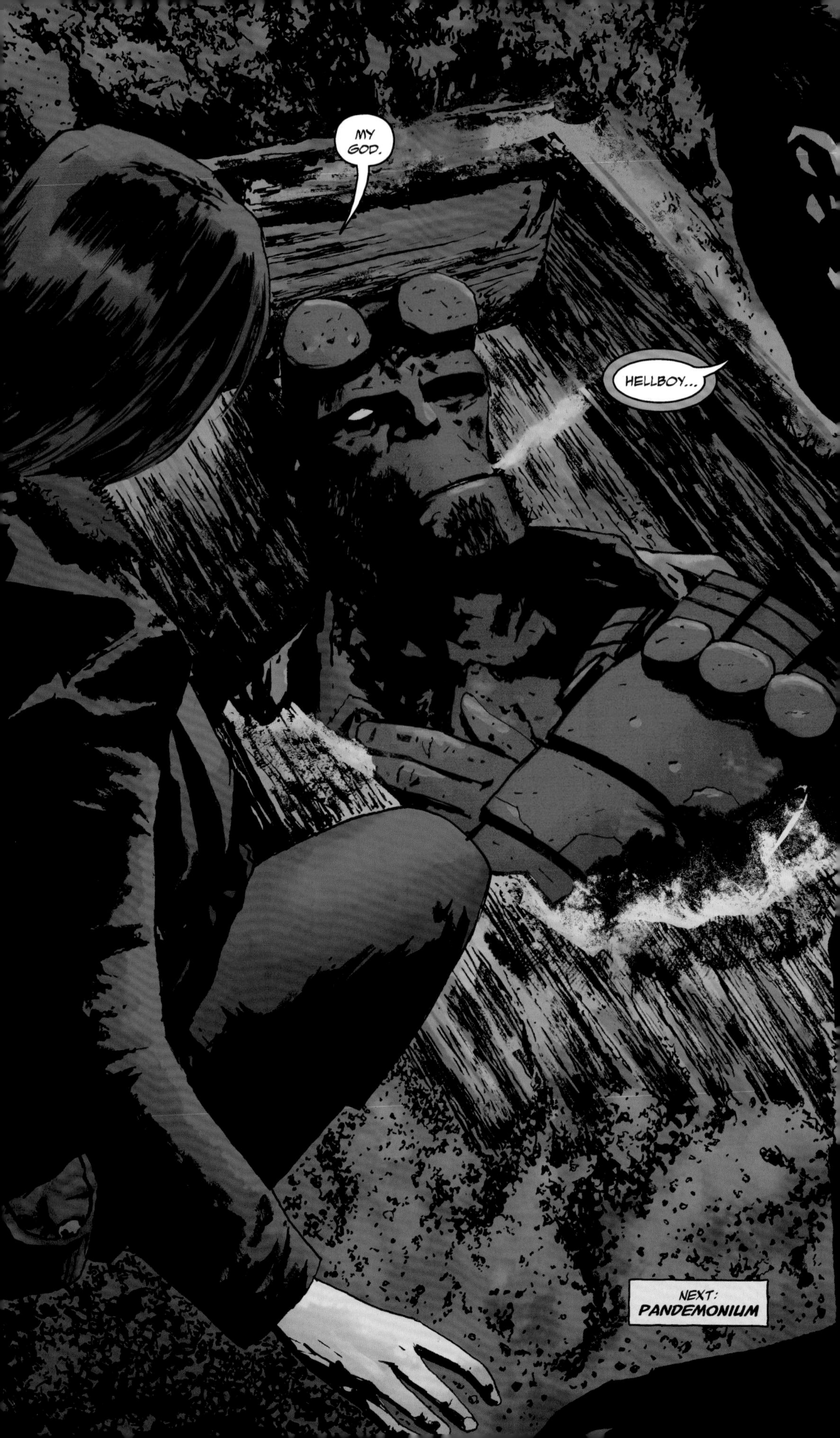

MY GOD.
HELLBOY...
NEXT: PANDEMONIUM

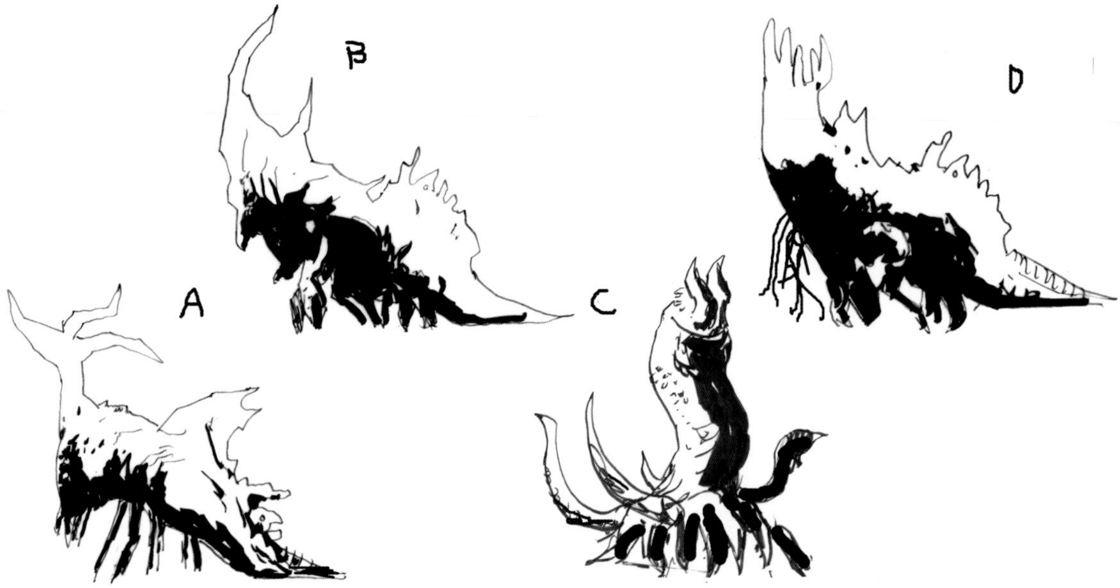
B
D
A
C

B.P.R.D.

SKETCHBOOK

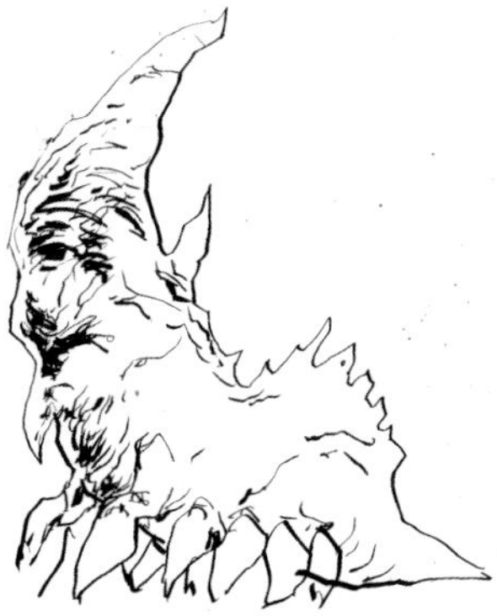

Notes by Laurence Campbell, Duncan Fegredo, and Katii O'Brien.

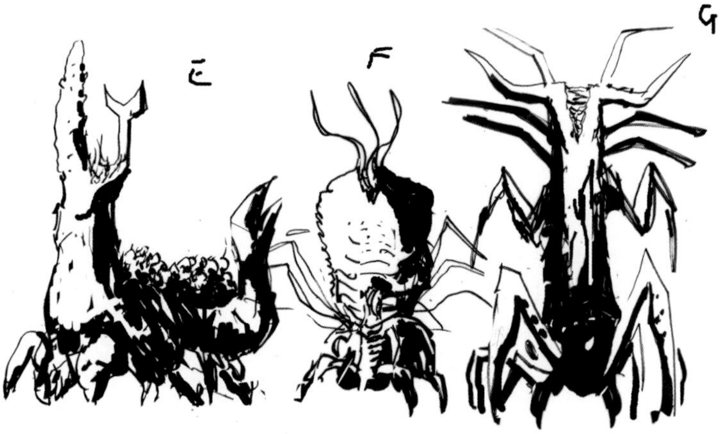
G
E
F

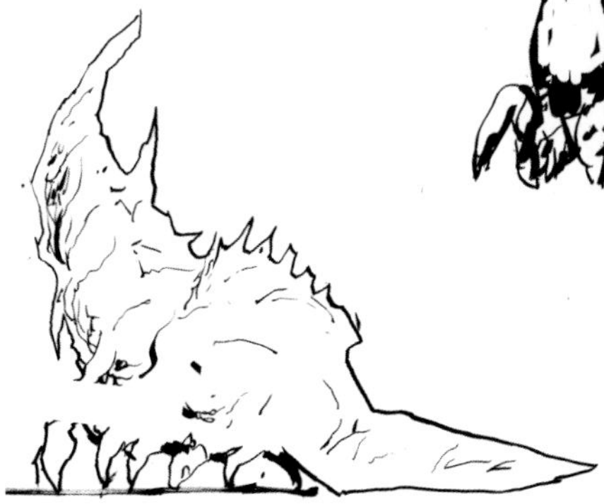

Laurence Campbell: Rough designs for Hem at the start of the first issue. I wanted something new, but fitted in with what has been done in the past. Iconic in shape, which could be recognized from a distance.

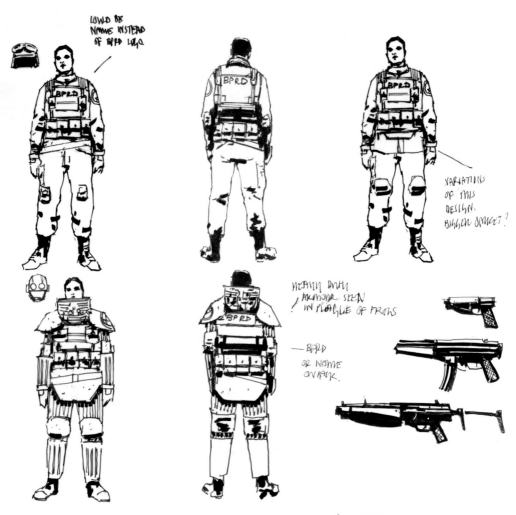

COULD BE NAME INSTEAD OF BPRD LOGO

BPRD

BPRD

BPRD

VARIATION OF THIS DESIGN. BIGGER JACKET?

HEAVY DUTY ARMOUR SEEN IN PLAGUE OF FROGS

BPRD OR NAME ON BACK.

Above: Rough design for the B.P.R.D. heavy-duty armor, which is based on Guy Davis's design from Liz's vision of the future in *Plague of Frogs*.

Right: Design for Nichols heavy-duty gun, which has an influence from Jack Kirby-type technology.

FENIX

FLAK JACKET

CROP HAIR

OLD HOODIE

MAGENTA OR BLUE HAIR?

NOSE PIERCING

NO HAIR CLIMPLE. SHOULD STAND OUT.

RED SHIRT

BLACK LEGGINGS

Above: Fenix designs. I wanted to change Fenix a little with a haircut and a change of look. The B.P.R.D. experience has changed her.

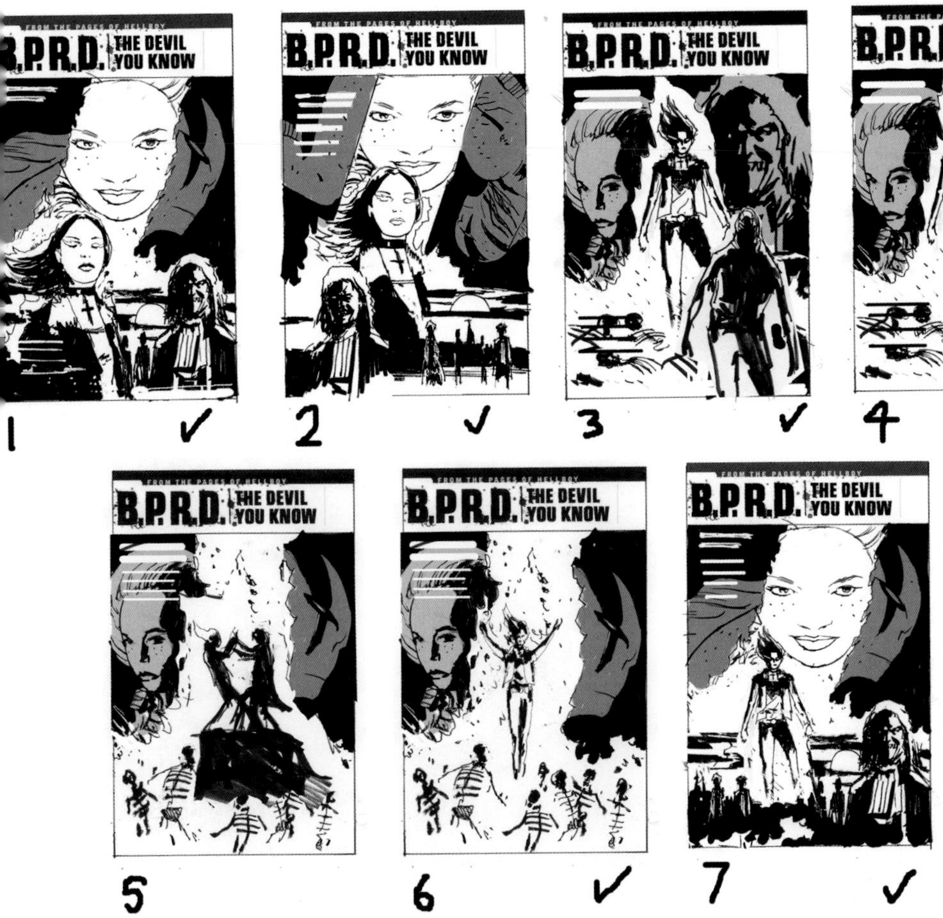
FROM THE PAGES OF HELLBOY
B.P.R.D. THE DEVIL YOU KNOW
1
2
3
4
5
6
7

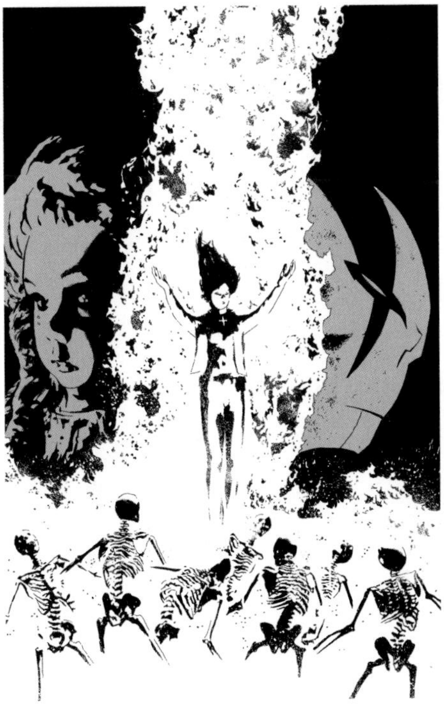

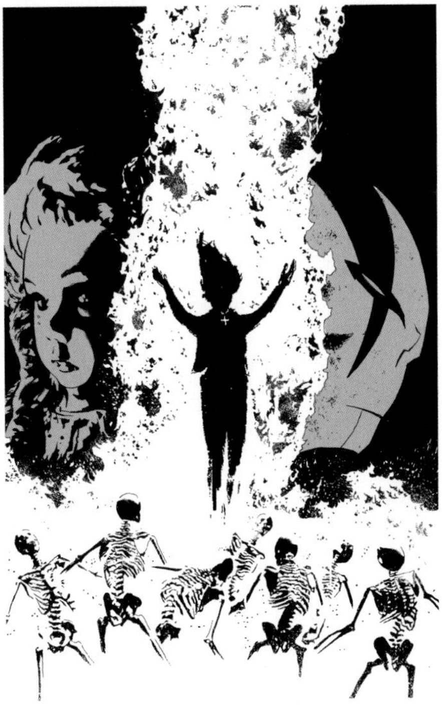

Rough ideas for the trade cover. Number 6 was picked, but once drawn up I felt Liz was lost in the overall image and worked better as a silhouette. Dave helped to sort this out in coloring and did an amazing job with the final image. Creating this cover made me realize how much I enjoy drawing skeletons.

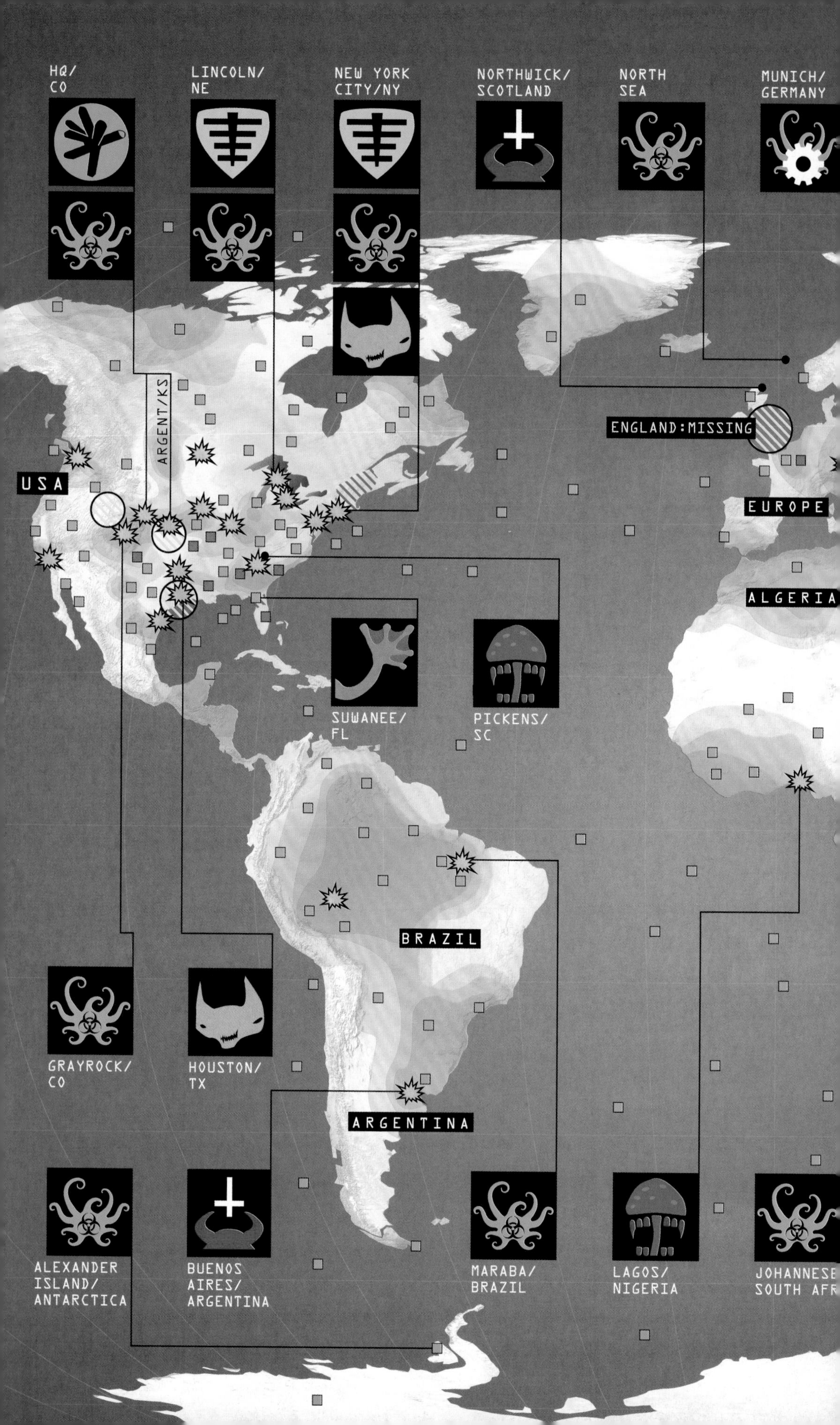
HQ/
CO
LINCOLN/
NE
NEW YORK
CITY/NY
NORTHWICK/
SCOTLAND
NORTH
SEA
MUNICH/
GERMANY
ARGENT/KS
ENGLAND:MISSING
USA
EUROPE
ALGERIA
SUWANEE/
FL
PICKENS/
SC
BRAZIL
GRAYROCK/
CO
HOUSTON/
TX
ARGENTINA
ALEXANDER
ISLAND/
ANTARCTICA
BUENOS
AIRES/
ARGENTINA
MARABA/
BRAZIL
LAGOS/
NIGERIA
JOHANNESE
SOUTH AFR

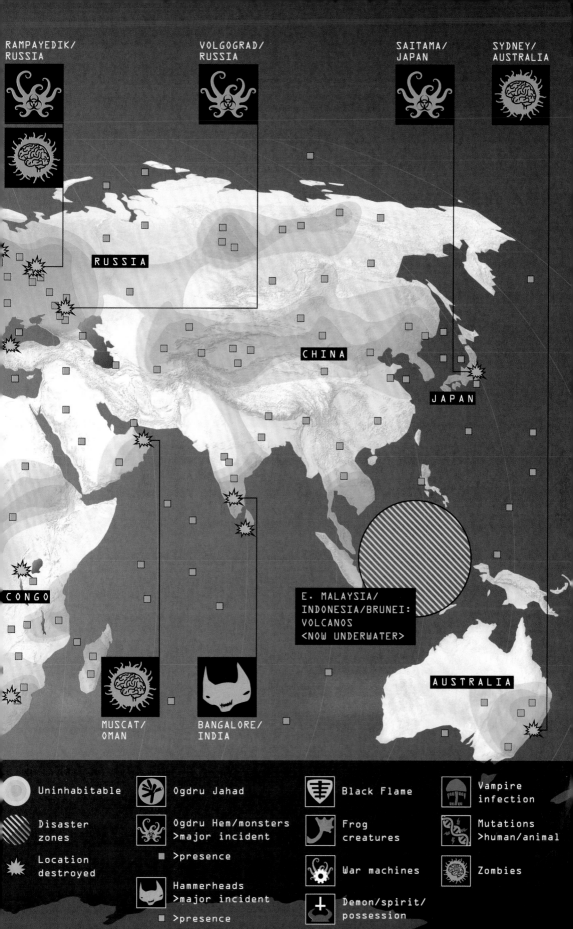

RAMPAYEDIK/
RUSSIA

VOLGOGRAD/
RUSSIA

SAITAMA/
JAPAN

SYDNEY/
AUSTRALIA

RUSSIA

CHINA

JAPAN

CONGO

E. MALAYSIA/
INDONESIA/BRUNEI:
VOLCANOS
<NOW UNDERWATER>

AUSTRALIA

MUSCAT/
OMAN

BANGALORE/
INDIA

Uninhabitable

Ogdru Jahad

Black Flame

Vampire
infection

Disaster
zones

Ogdru Hem/monsters
>major incident

>presence

Frog
creatures

Mutations
>human/animal

Location
destroyed

Hammerheads
>major incident

>presence

War machines

Zombies

Demon/spirit/
possession

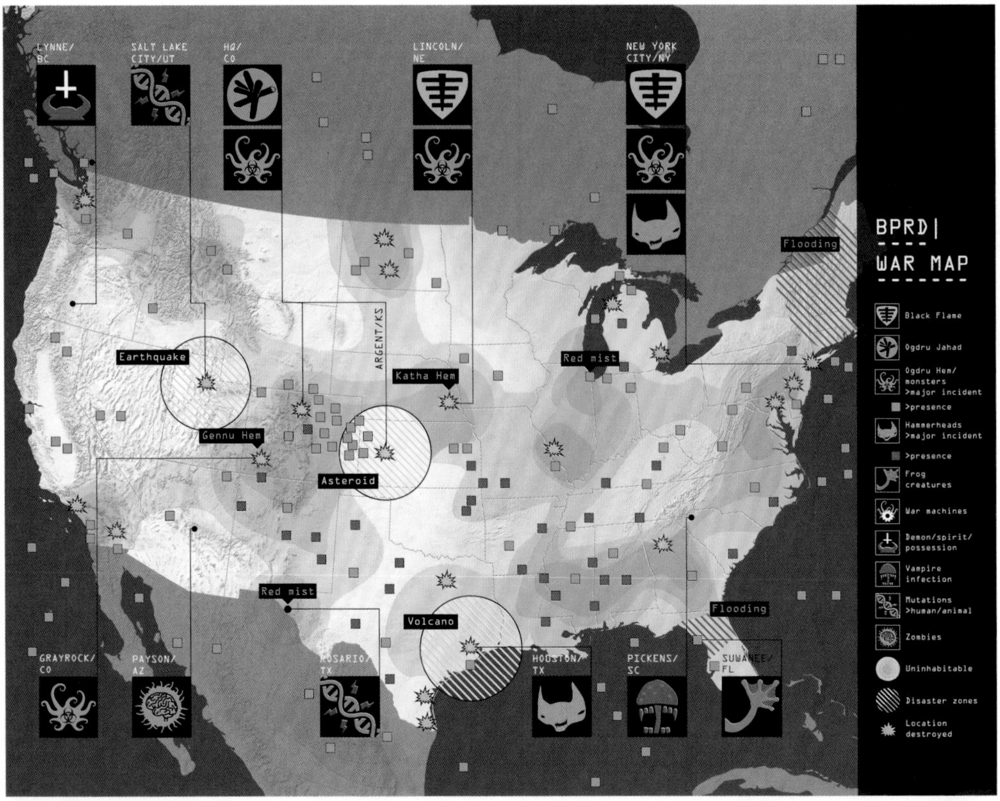
LYNNE/ BC
SALT LAKE CITY/UT
HQ/ CO
LINCOLN/ NE
NEW YORK CITY/NY
BPRD | WAR MAP
Black Flame
Ogdru Jahad
Ogdru Hem/ monsters >major incident
>presence
Hammerheads >major incident
>presence
Frog creatures
War machines
Demon/spirit/ possession
Vampire infection
Mutations >human/animal
Zombies
Uninhabitable
Disaster zones
Location destroyed
Flooding
Earthquake
ARGENT/KS
Katha Hem
Red mist
Gennu Hem
Asteroid
Red mist
Volcano
Flooding
GRAYROCK/ CO
PAYSON/ AZ
ROSARIO/ TX
HOUSTON/ TX
PICKENS/ SC
SUWANEE/ FL

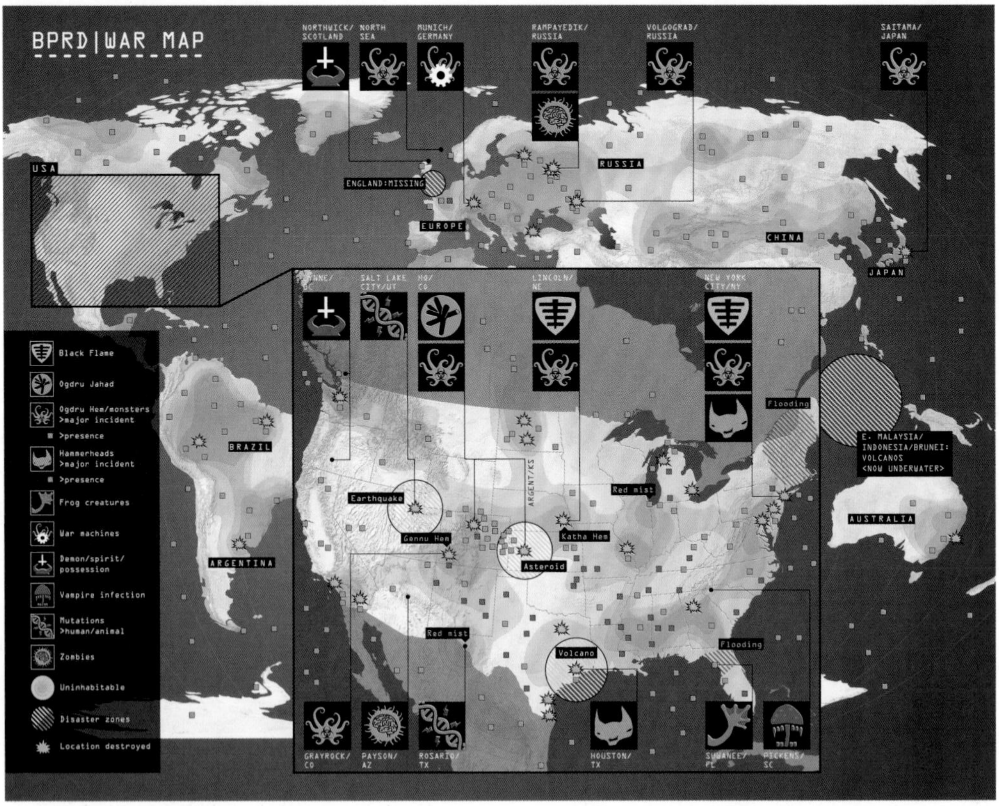
BPRD | WAR MAP
NORTHWICK/ SCOTLAND
NORTH SEA
MUNICH/ GERMANY
RAMPAYEDIK/ RUSSIA
VOLGOGRAD/ RUSSIA
SAITAMA/ JAPAN
USA
ENGLAND:MISSING
RUSSIA
EUROPE
CHINA
JAPAN
LYNNE/ BC
SALT LAKE CITY/UT
HQ/ CO
LINCOLN/ NE
NEW YORK CITY/NY
Black Flame
Ogdru Jahad
Ogdru Hem/monsters >major incident
>presence
Hammerheads >major incident
>presence
Frog creatures
War machines
Demon/spirit/ possession
Vampire infection
Mutations >human/animal
Zombies
Uninhabitable
Disaster zones
Location destroyed
Flooding
E. MALAYSIA/ INDONESIA/BRUNEI: VOLCANOS <NOW UNDERWATER>
BRAZIL
ARGENTINA
Earthquake
Gennu Hem
ARGENT/KS
Asteroid
Katha Hem
Red mist
AUSTRALIA
Red mist
Volcano
Flooding
GRAYROCK/ CO
PAYSON/ AZ
ROSARIO/ TX
HOUSTON/ TX
SUWANEE/ FL
PICKENS/ SC

Katii O'Brien: We asked Chris Campbell, who designs maps and data visualizations for the *Financial Times* in London, to create three versions of this "monster map" to show the destruction the B.P.R.D. is up against. The world map (*previous pages*) ran in #4, the two other versions are above.

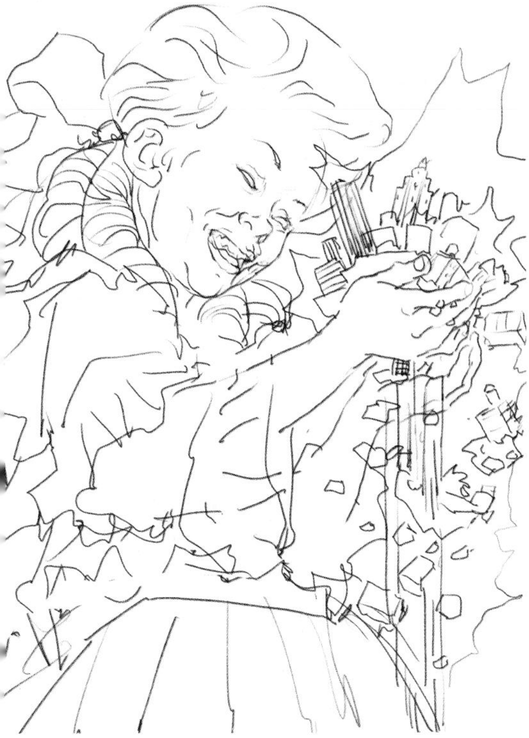

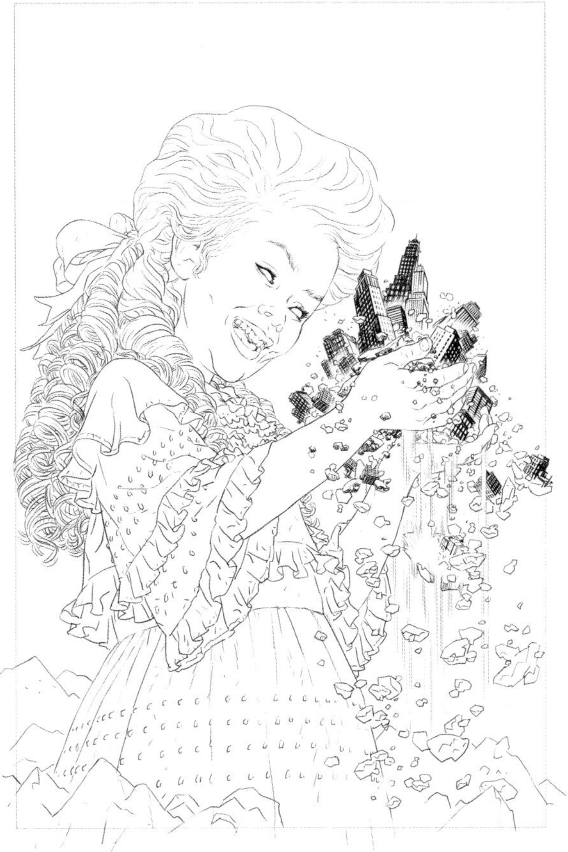

Duncan Fegredo: In the cover for #1 (*above*), Varvara is literally creating Hell on Earth.

For #2 (*below*) the essential idea was there from the start, but improved greatly by the burning zombie as a framing device. If in doubt, add a fiery reanimated corpse.

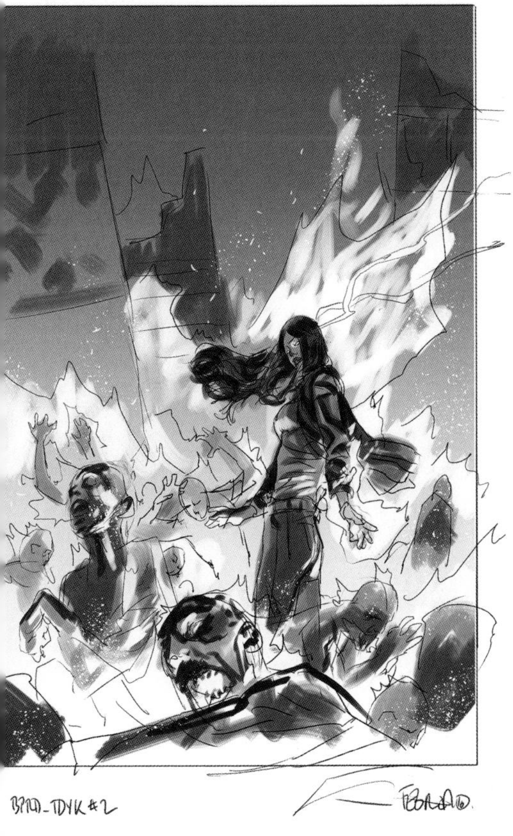
BPRD_TDYK #2

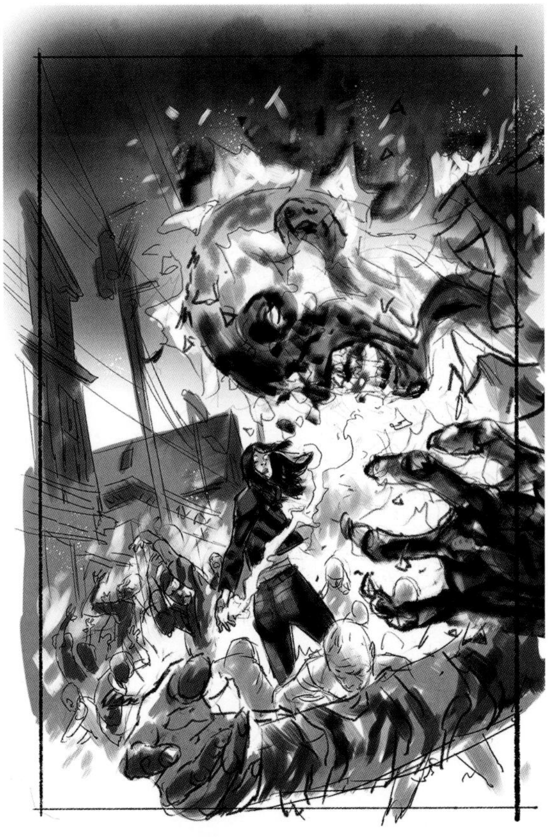

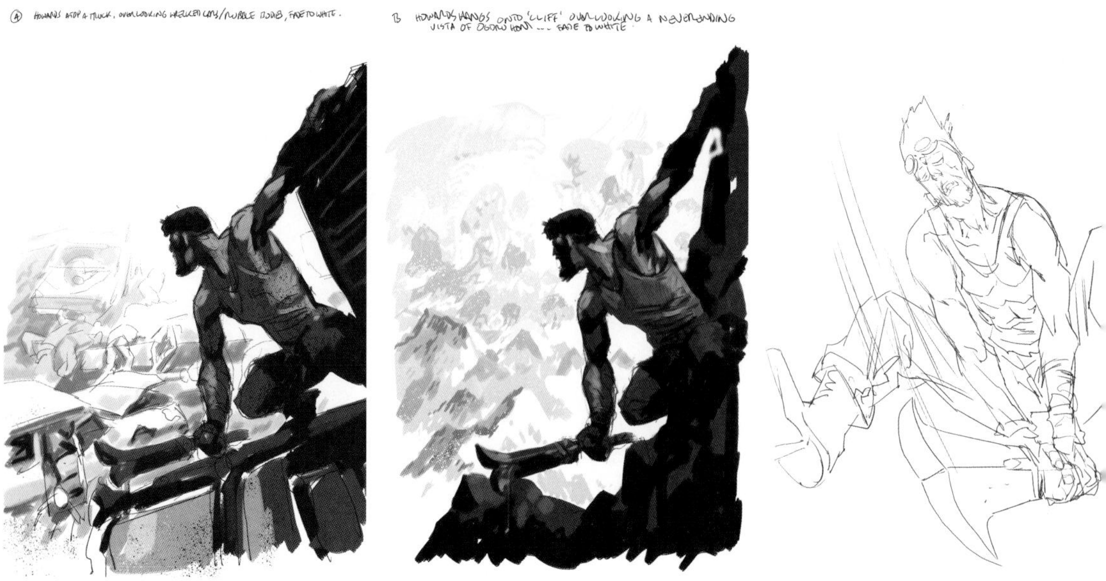
(A) HOWARDS ATOP A TRUCK, OVERLOOKING WRECKED CARS/RUBBLE BODIES, FADE TO WHITE.
B HOWARDS HANGS ONTO 'CLIFF' OVERLOOKING A NEVERENDING VISTA OF OGDRU HEM ... FADE TO WHITE.

#3 (*above*): Thank goodness the simpler idea won out or I'd still be painting burnt out cars even now.

On #4 (*below*): It was a lot of fun to paint this version of Abe, in particular to misleadingly present him as a classic monster in the shadows.

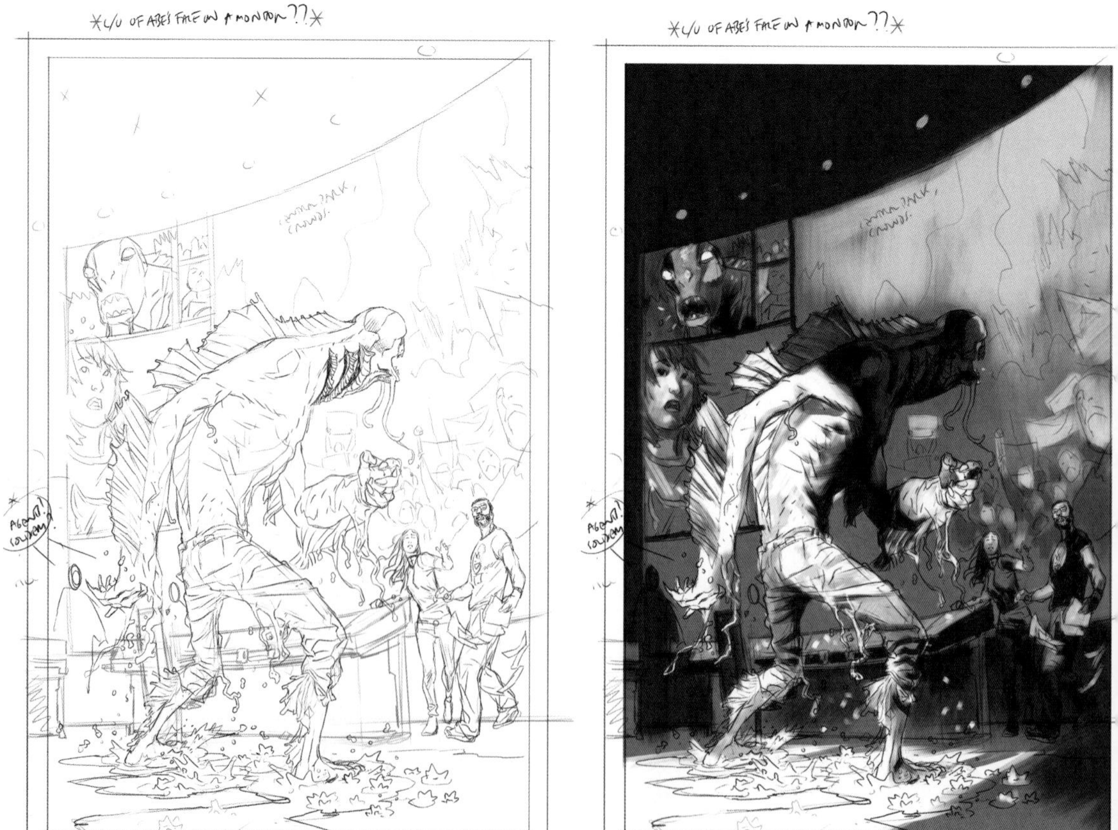
C/U OF ABE'S FACE ON A MONITOR??
TRAIL OF WATER... MAKES NO SENSE BUT IT'S A NICE GRAPHIC DEVICE!
C/U OF ABE'S FACE ON A MONITOR??
TRAIL OF WATER... MAKES NO SENSE BUT IT'S A NICE GRAPHIC DEVICE!

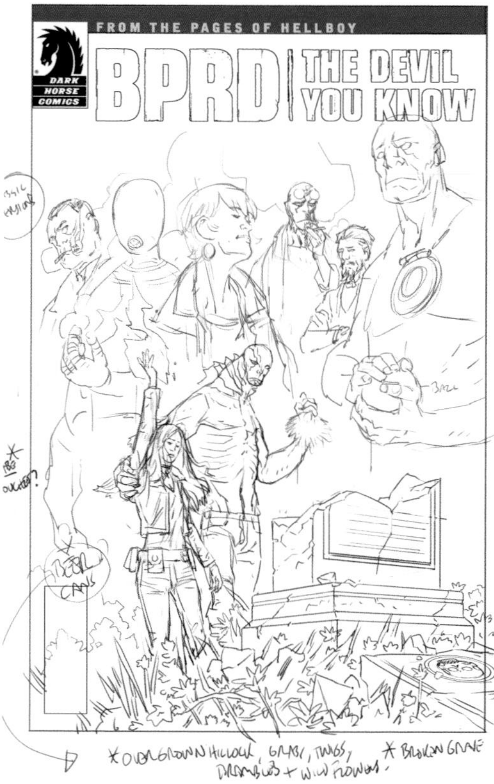
FROM THE PAGES OF HELLBOY
DARK HORSE COMICS
BPRD
THE DEVIL YOU KNOW

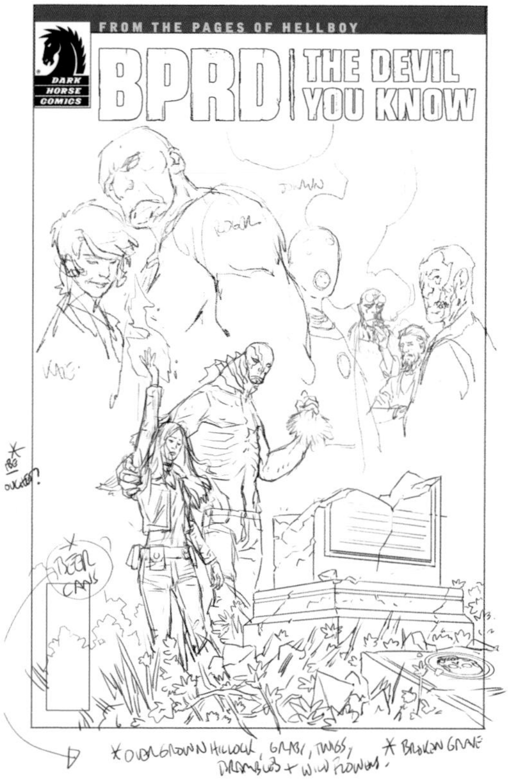
FROM THE PAGES OF HELLBOY
DARK HORSE COMICS
BPRD
THE DEVIL YOU KNOW

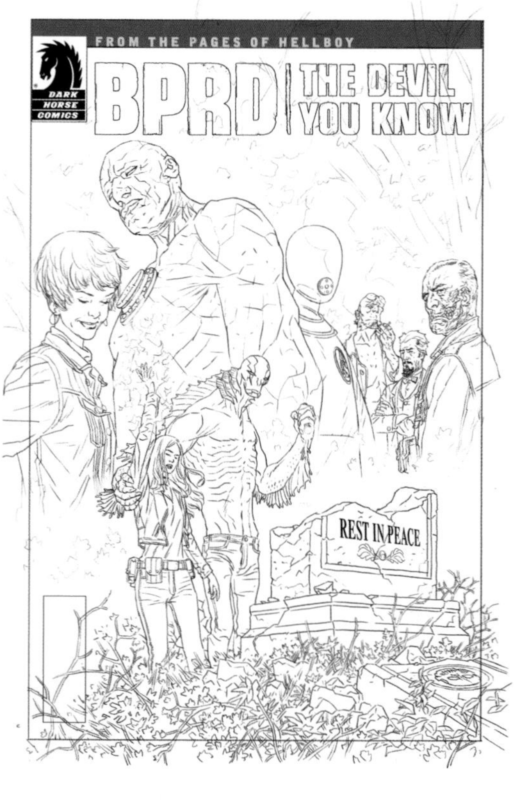
FROM THE PAGES OF HELLBOY
DARK HORSE COMICS
BPRD
THE DEVIL YOU KNOW
REST IN PEACE

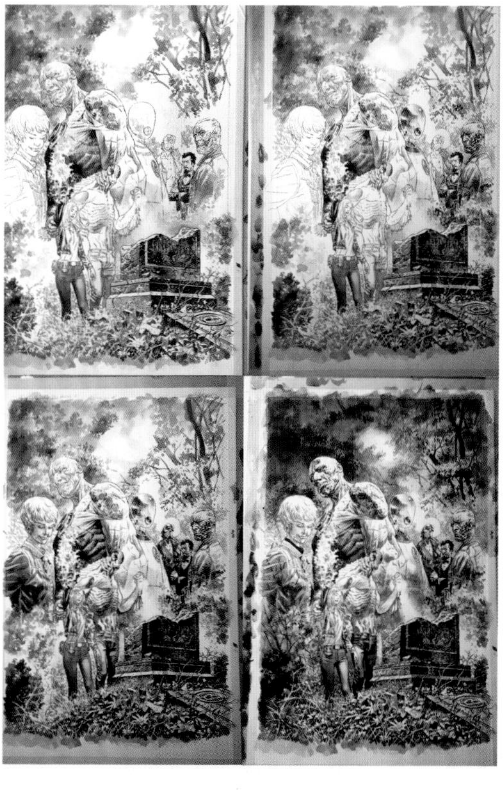

On #5 (*above*): The last time I painted a cover like this, only Hellboy was dead. Well, at least he has company now. Poor, poor B.P.R.D.

Katii O'Brien (*following pages*): Mignola's variant for *The Devil You Know* #1 and Tim Sale's cover for the *Hellboy Winter Special* 2016, followed by Sale's story that ran in that issue.

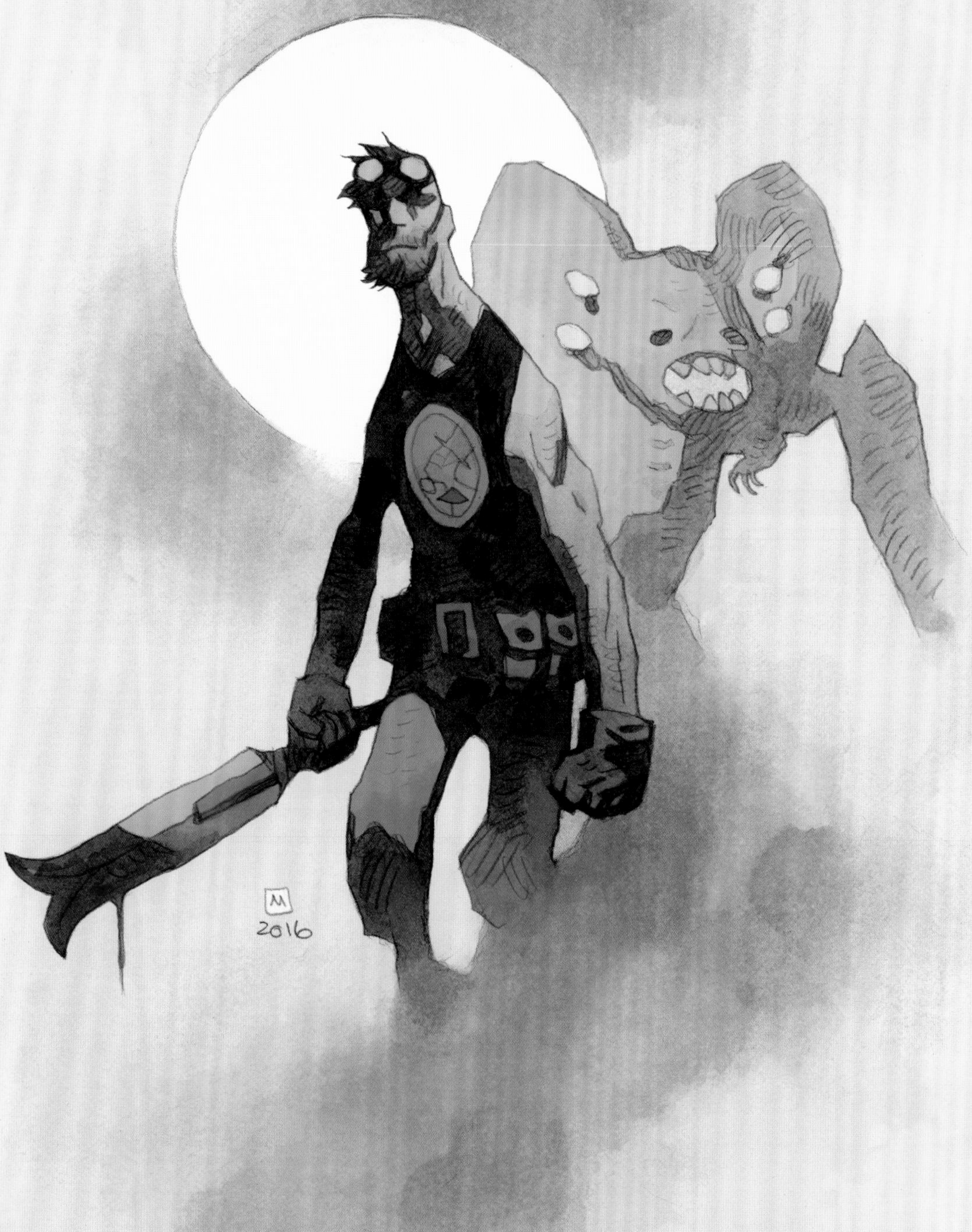
M
2016

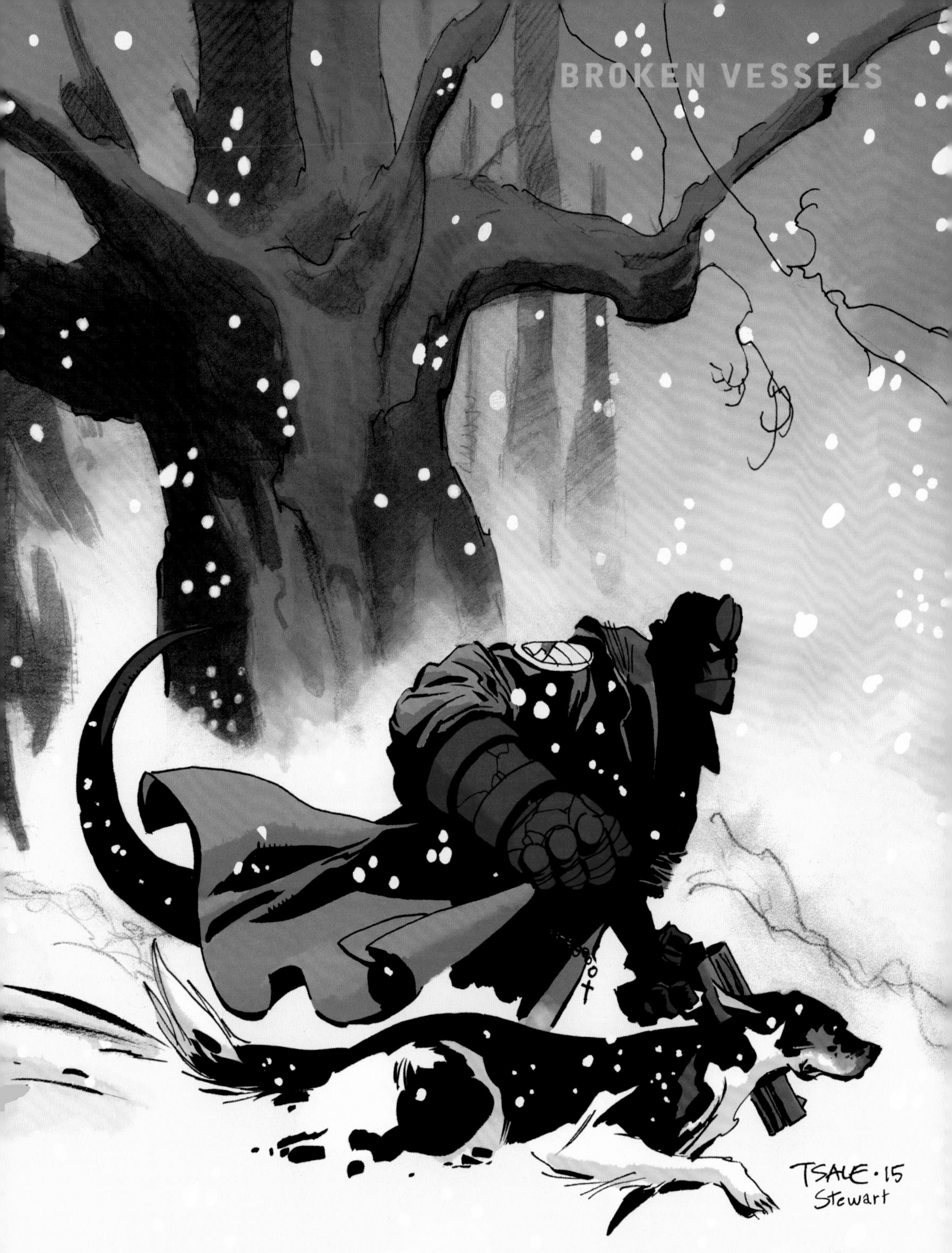
TSALE·15
Stewart

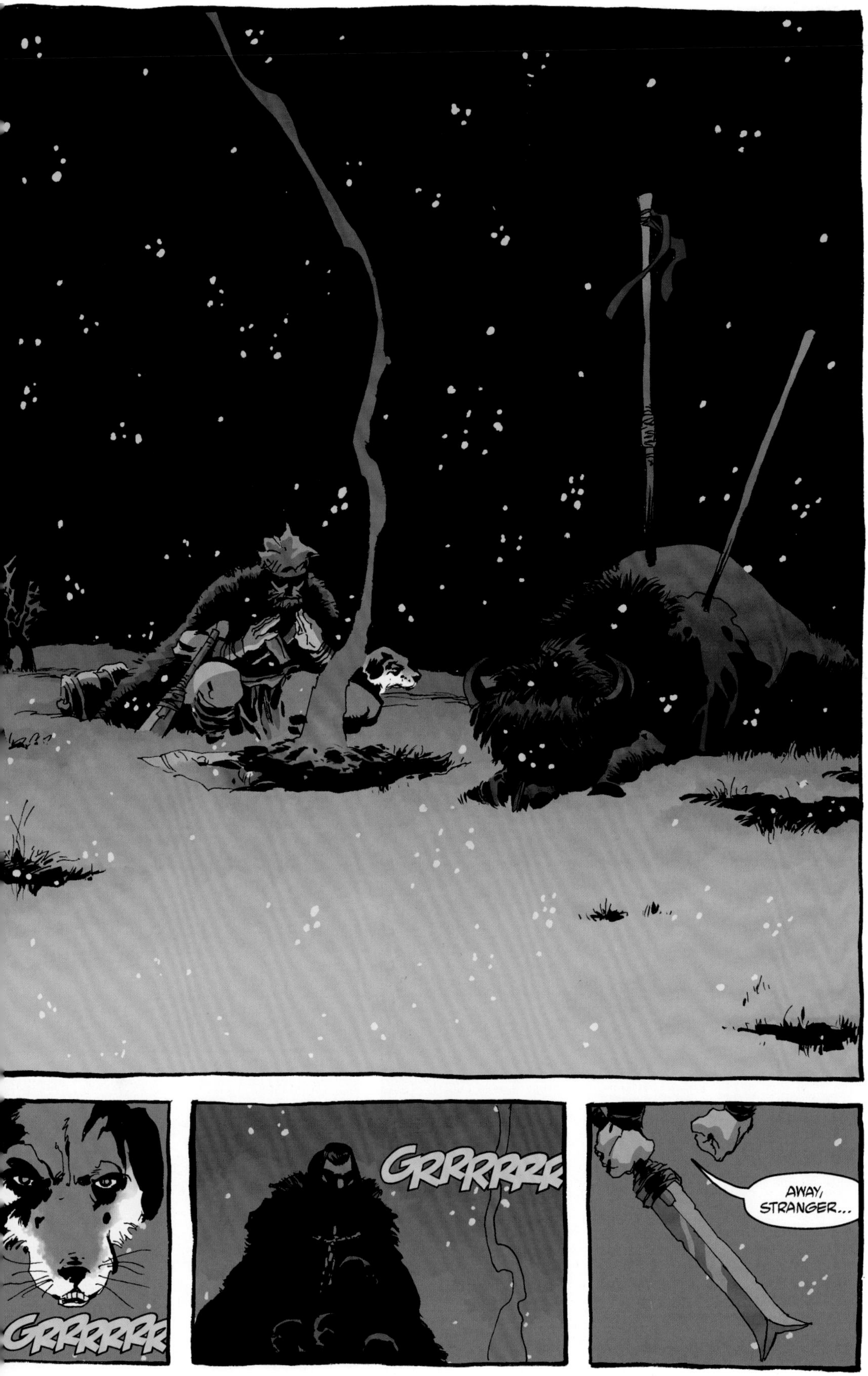
GRRRRRR
GRRRRRR
AWAY, STRANGER...

...THIS PLAIN'S BROAD ENOUGH FOR YOU TO GIVE ME A WIDE BERTH.

BUT TOO BARE FOR ME TO SCRAPE TOGETHER A FIRE OF MY OWN.

YOU'VE NOTHING TO FEAR FROM ME.

A COAT OF BONES CAN'T WARM A MAN?

HA. ONLY FIRE DOES THAT.

GRRRR

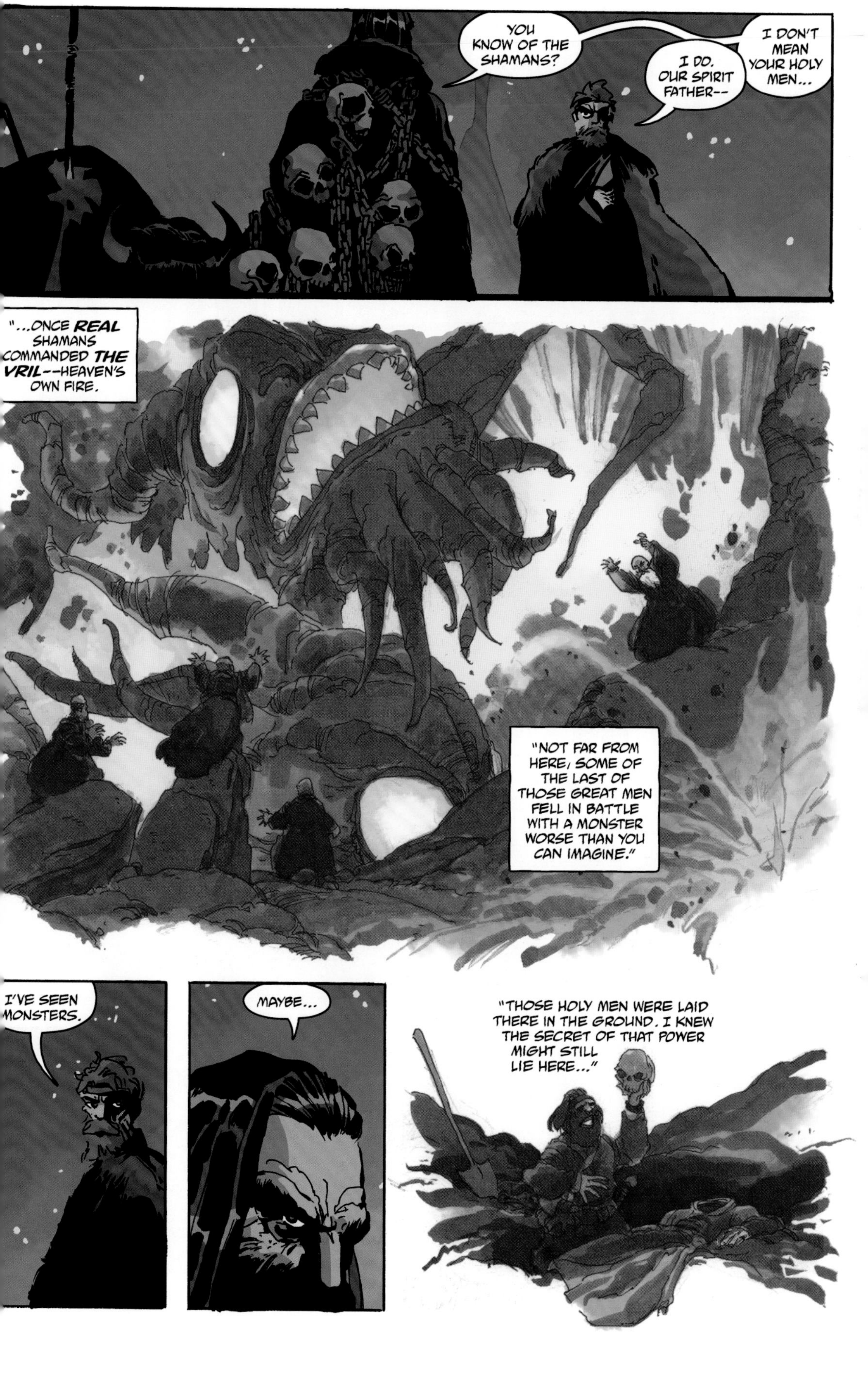

YOU KNOW OF THE SHAMANS?
I DO. OUR SPIRIT FATHER--
I DON'T MEAN YOUR HOLY MEN...
"...ONCE REAL SHAMANS COMMANDED THE VRIL--HEAVEN'S OWN FIRE.
"NOT FAR FROM HERE, SOME OF THE LAST OF THOSE GREAT MEN FELL IN BATTLE WITH A MONSTER WORSE THAN YOU CAN IMAGINE."
I'VE SEEN MONSTERS.
MAYBE...
"THOSE HOLY MEN WERE LAID THERE IN THE GROUND. I KNEW THE SECRET OF THAT POWER MIGHT STILL LIE HERE..."

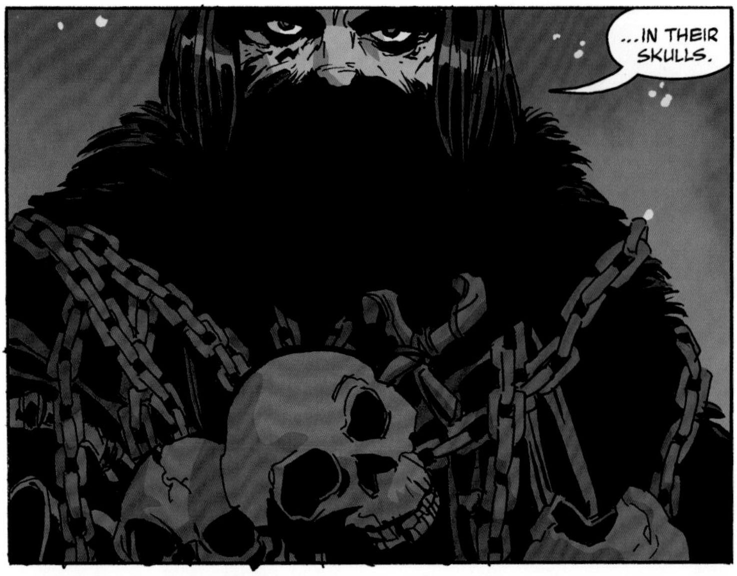
...IN THEIR SKULLS.

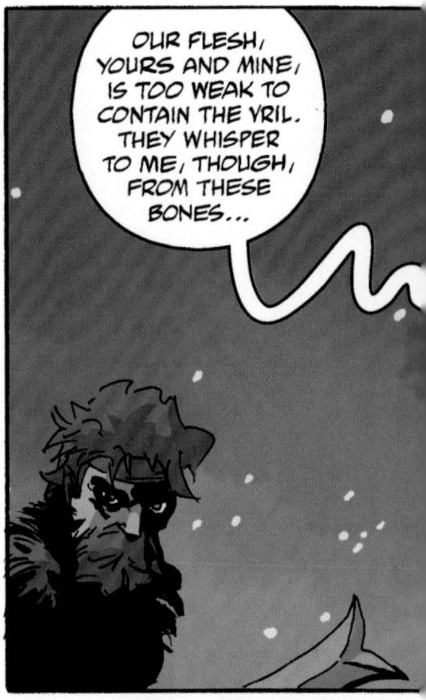
OUR FLESH, YOURS AND MINE, IS TOO WEAK TO CONTAIN THE VRIL. THEY WHISPER TO ME, THOUGH, FROM THESE BONES...

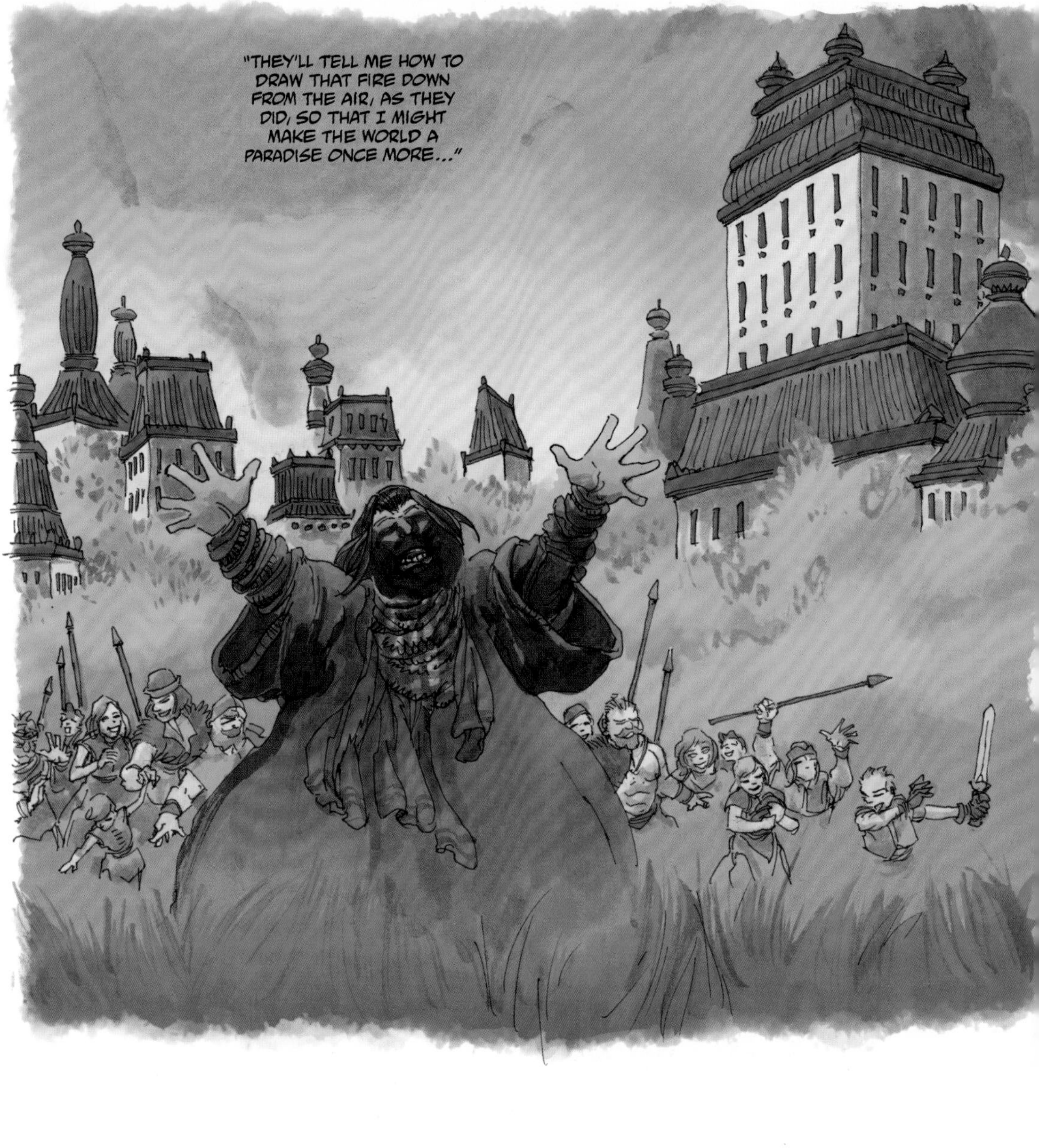
"THEY'LL TELL ME HOW TO DRAW THAT FIRE DOWN FROM THE AIR, AS THEY DID, SO THAT I MIGHT MAKE THE WORLD A PARADISE ONCE MORE..."

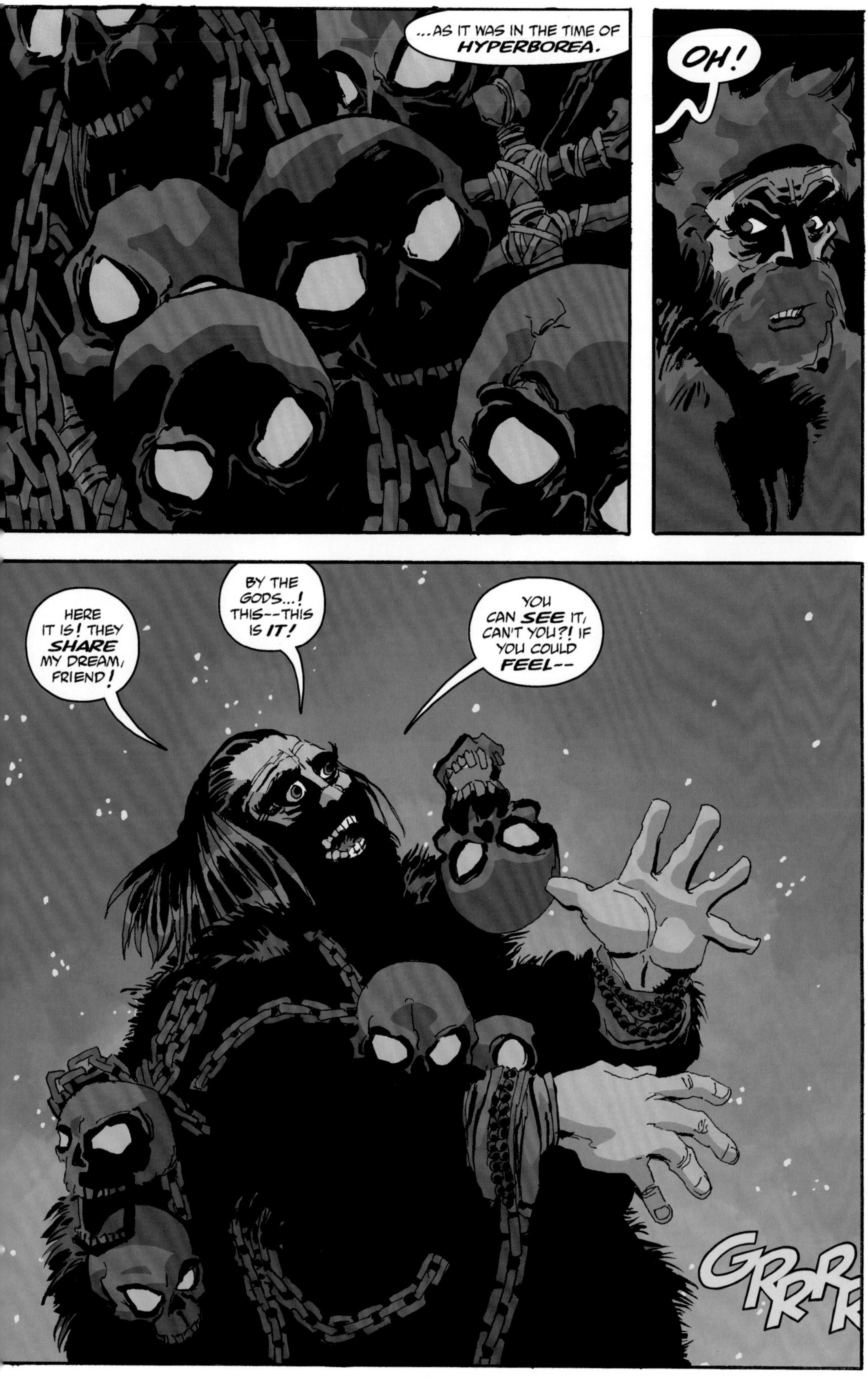
...AS IT WAS IN THE TIME OF HYPERBOREA.
OH!
HERE IT IS! THEY SHARE MY DREAM, FRIEND!
BY THE GODS...! THIS--THIS IS IT!
YOU CAN SEE IT, CAN'T YOU?! IF YOU COULD FEEL--
GRRRR

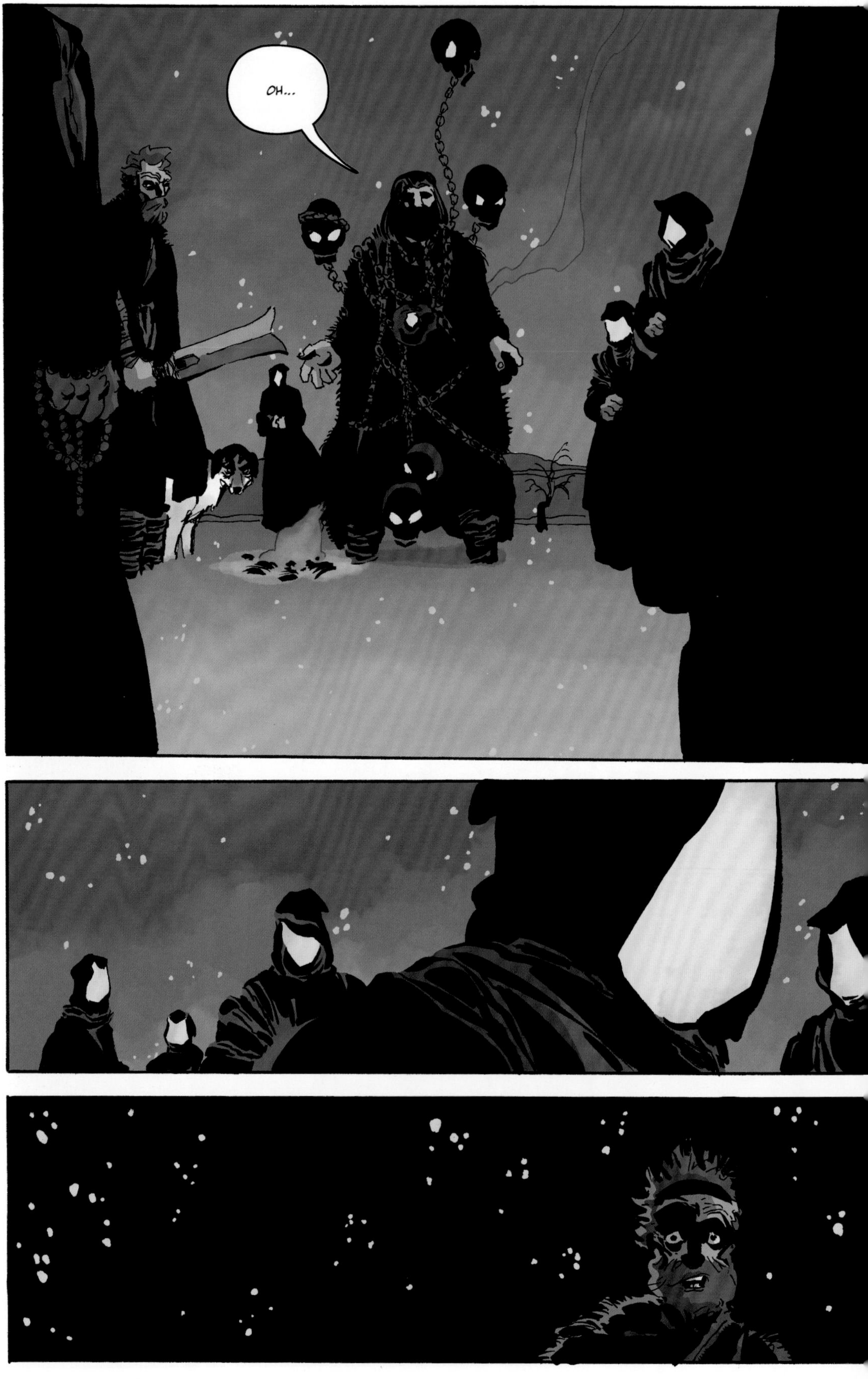
OH...

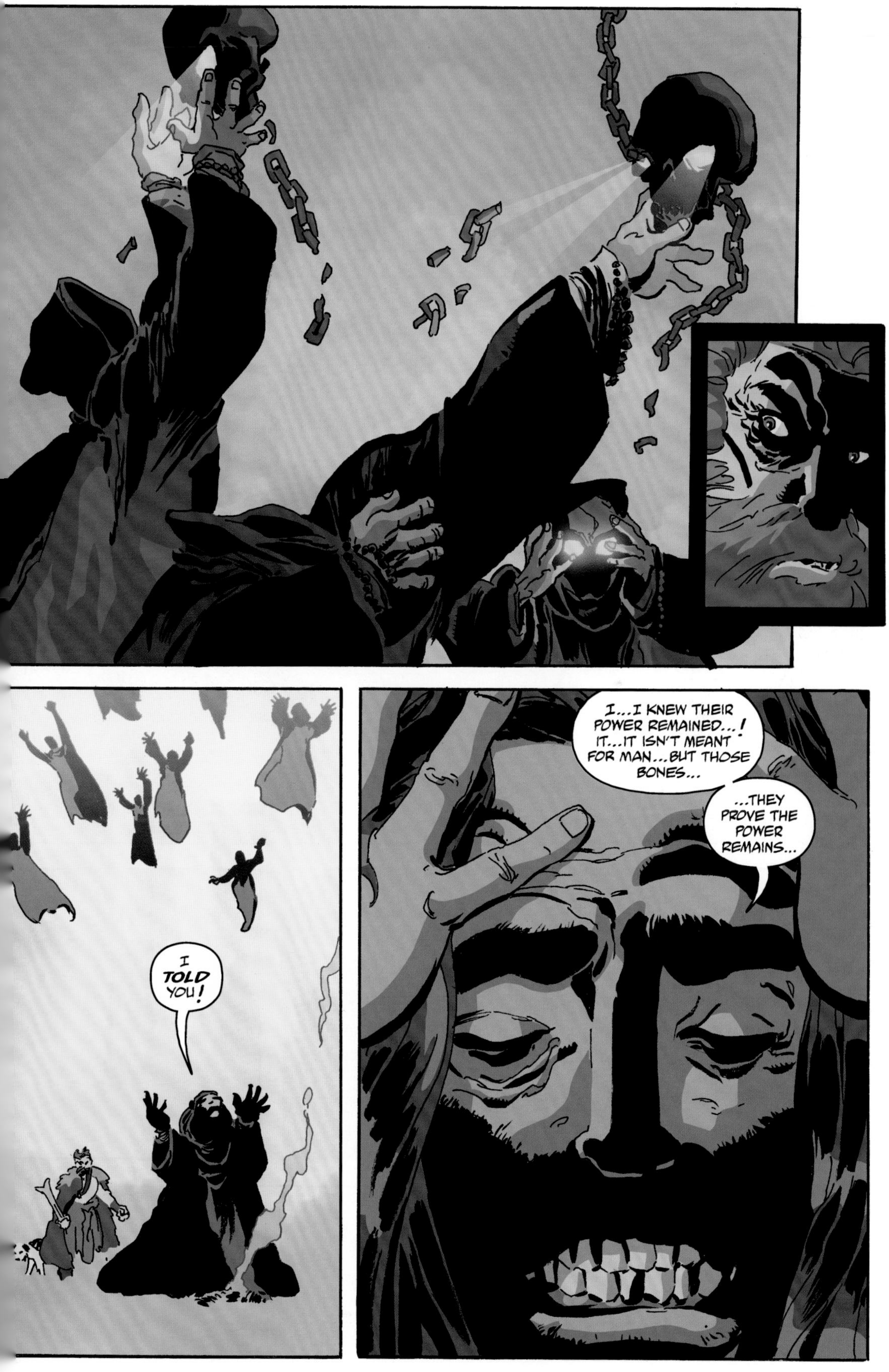
I TOLD YOU!
I...I KNEW THEIR POWER REMAINED...! IT...IT ISN'T MEANT FOR MAN...BUT THOSE BONES...
...THEY PROVE THE POWER REMAINS...

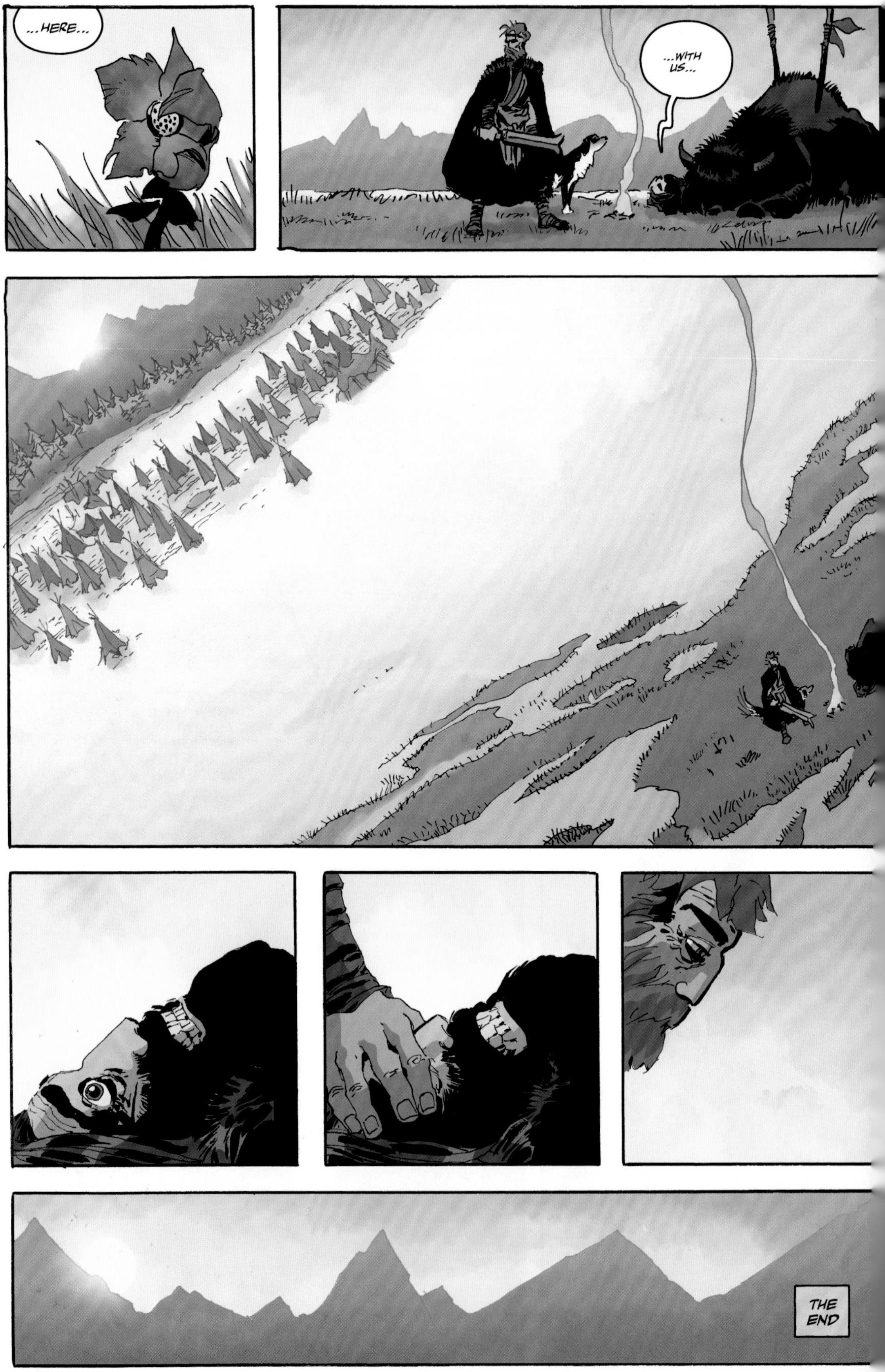
...HERE...
...WITH US...
THE END

Also by MIKE MIGNOLA

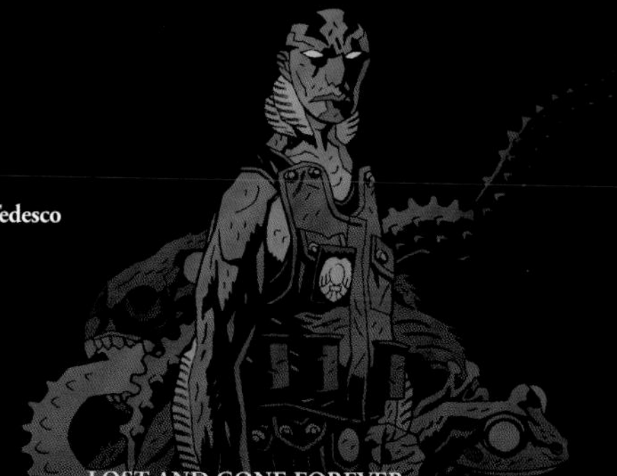

3.P.R.D.

PLAGUE OF FROGS
'olume 1
vith John Arcudi, Guy Davis, and others
TPB: ISBN 978-1-59582-675-6 | $19.99

'olume 2
SBN 978-1-59582-676-3 | $24.99

'olume 3
SBN 978-1-61655-622-8 | $24.99

'olume 4
SBN 978-1-61655-641-9 | $24.99

946–1948
ith Joshua Dysart, Paul Azaceta, Fábio Moon,
abriel Bá, Max Fiumara, and Arcudi
SBN 978-1-61655-646-4 | $34.99

EING HUMAN
ith Scott Allie, Arcudi, Davis, and others
SBN 978-1-59582-756-2 | $17.99

AMPIRE
ith Moon and Bá
SBN 978-1-61655-196-4 | $19.99

.P.R.D. HELL ON EARTH

EW WORLD
ith Arcudi and Davis
SBN 978-1-59582-707-4 | $19.99

ODS AND MONSTERS
ith Arcudi, Davis, and Tyler Crook
BN 978-1-59582-822-4 | $19.99

USSIA
ith Arcudi, Crook, and Duncan Fegredo
BN 978-1-59582-946-7 | $19.99

HE DEVIL'S ENGINE
ND THE LONG DEATH
ith Arcudi, Crook, and James Harren
BN 978-1-59582-981-8 | $19.99

HE PICKENS COUNTY
ORROR AND OTHERS
ith Allie, Jason Latour, Harren,
d Max Fiumara
BN 978-1-61655-140-7 | $19.99

HE RETURN OF THE MASTER
th Arcudi and Crook
BN 978-1-61655-193-3 | $19.99

COLD DAY IN HELL
th Arcudi, Peter Snejbjerg, and
urence Campbell
BN 978-1-61655-199-5 | $19.99

HE REIGN
F THE BLACK FLAME
th Arcudi and Harren
BN 978-1-61655-471-2 | $19.99

HE DEVIL'S WINGS
th Arcudi, Campbell,
e Querio, and Crook
BN 978-1-61655-617-4 | $19.99

AKE OF FIRE
th Arcudi and Crook
BN 978-1-61655-402-6 | $19.99

ESH AND STONE
th Arcudi and Harren
BN 978-1-61655-762-1 | $19.99

METAMORPHOSIS
with Arcudi, Snejbjerg, and Julián Totino Tedesco
ISBN 978-1-61655-794-2 | $19.99

END OF DAYS
with Arcudi and Campbell
ISBN 978-1-61655-910-6 | $19.99

THE EXORCIST
with Cameron Stewart, Chris Roberson, and Mike Norton
ISBN 978-1-50670-011-3 | $19.99

COMETH THE HOUR
with Arcudi and Campbell
ISBN 978-1-50670-131-8 | $19.99

ABE SAPIEN

THE DROWNING
with Jason Shawn Alexander
ISBN 978-1-59582-185-0 | $17.99

THE DEVIL DOES NOT JEST AND OTHER STORIES
with Arcudi, Harren, and others
ISBN 978-1-59582-925-2 | $17.99

DARK AND TERRIBLE
VOLUME 1
with Allie, S, Fiumara, and M. Fiumara
ISBN 978-1-50670-538-5 | $34.99

A DARKNESS SO GREAT
with Allie, S. Fiumara, and M. Fiumara
ISBN 978-1-61655-656-3 | $19.99

THE SECRET FIRE
with Allie, S. Fiumara, and M. Fiumara
ISBN 978-1-61655-891-8 | $19.99

THE DESOLATE SHORE
with Allie, S. Fiumara, and M. Fiumara
ISBN 978-1-50670-031-1 | $19.99

LOST LIVES AND OTHER STORIES
with Allie, Arcudi, Michael Avon Oeming, and others
ISBN 978-1-50670-220-9 | $19.99

LOBSTER JOHNSON

THE IRON PROMETHEUS
with Arcudi, Tonci Zonjic, and others
ISBN 978-1-59307-975-8 | $17.99

THE BURNING HAND
ISBN 978-1-61655-031-8 | $17.99

SATAN SMELLS A RAT
ISBN 978-1-61655-203-9 | $18.99

GET THE LOBSTER
ISBN 978-1-61655-505-4 | $19.99

THE PIRATE'S GHOST AND METAL MONSTERS OF MIDTOWN
ISBN 978-1-50670-206-3 | $19.99

A CHAIN FORGED IN LIFE
ISBN 978-1-50670-178-3 | $19.99

WITCHFINDER

IN THE SERVICE OF ANGELS
with Ben Stenbeck
ISBN 978-1-59582-483-7 | $17.99

LOST AND GONE FOREVER
with Arcudi and John Severin
ISBN 978-1-59582-794-4 | $17.99

THE MYSTERIES OF UNLAND
with Kim Newman, Maura McHugh, and Crook
ISBN 978-1-61655-630-3 | $19.99

CITY OF THE DEAD
with Roberson and Stenbeck
ISBN 978-1-50670-166-0 | $19.99

RISE OF THE BLACK FLAME

with Roberson and Christopher Mitten
ISBN 978-1-50670-155-4 | $19.99

FRANKENSTEIN UNDERGROUND

with Stenbeck
ISBN 978-1-61655-782-9 | $19.99

JOE GOLEM: OCCULT DETECTIVE—

THE RAT CATCHER & THE SUNKEN DEAD
with Christopher Golden and Patric Reynolds
ISBN 978-1-61655-964-9 | $24.99

BALTIMORE

THE PLAGUE SHIPS
with Golden, Stenbeck, and Peter Bergting
ISBN 978-1-59582-677-0 | $24.99

THE CURSE BELLS
ISBN 978-1-59582-674-9 | $24.99

A PASSING STRANGER AND OTHER STORIES
ISBN 978-1-61655-182-7 | $24.99

CHAPEL OF BONES
ISBN 978-1-61655-328-9 | $24.99

THE APOSTLE AND THE WITCH OF HARJU
ISBN 978-1-61655-618-1 | $24.99

THE CULT OF THE RED KING
ISBN 978-1-61655-821-5 | $24.99

EMPTY GRAVES
ISBN 978-1-50670-042-7 | $24.99

THE RED KINGDOM
ISBN 978-1-50670-197-4 | $24.99

NOVELS

LOBSTER JOHNSON: THE SATAN FACTORY
with Thomas E. Sniegoski
ISBN 978-1-59582-203-1 | $12.95

JOE GOLEM AND THE DROWNING CITY
with Golden
ISBN 978-1-59582-971-9 | $99.99

BALTIMORE; OR, THE STEADFAST TIN SOLDIER & THE VAMPIRE
with Golden
ISBN 978-1-61655-803-1 | $12.99

HELLBOY™

by MIKE MIGNOLA

HELLBOY LIBRARY EDITION VOLUME 1:
Seed of Destruction and Wake the Devil
ISBN 978-1-59307-910-9 | $49.99

HELLBOY LIBRARY EDITION VOLUME 2:
The Chained Coffin and The Right Hand of Doom
ISBN 978-1-59307-989-5 | $49.99

HELLBOY LIBRARY EDITION VOLUME 3:
Conqueror Worm and Strange Places
ISBN 978-1-59582-352-6 | $49.99

HELLBOY LIBRARY EDITION VOLUME 4:
The Crooked Man and the Troll Witch
with Richard Corben and others
ISBN 978-1-59582-658-9 | $49.99

HELLBOY LIBRARY EDITION VOLUME 5:
Darkness Calls and the Wild Hunt
with Duncan Fegredo
ISBN 978-1-59582-886-6 | $49.99

HELLBOY LIBRARY EDITION VOLUME 6:
The Storm and the Fury and The Bride of Hell
with Duncan Fegredo, Richard Corben, Kevin Nowlan, and Scott Hampton
ISBN 978-1-61655-133-9 | $49.99

SEED OF DESTRUCTION
with John Byrne
ISBN 978-1-59307-094-6 | $17.99

WAKE THE DEVIL
ISBN 978-1-59307-095-3 | $17.99

THE CHAINED COFFIN AND OTHERS
ISBN 978-1-59307-091-5 | $17.99

THE RIGHT HAND OF DOOM
ISBN 978-1-59307-093-9 | $17.99

CONQUEROR WORM
ISBN 978-1-59307-092-2 | $17.99

STRANGE PLACES
ISBN 978-1-59307-475-3 | $17.99

THE TROLL WITCH AND OTHERS
with Richard Corben and others
ISBN 978-1-59307-860-7 | $17.99

DARKNESS CALLS
with Duncan Fegredo
ISBN 978-1-59307-896-6 | $19.99

THE WILD HUNT
with Duncan Fegredo
ISBN 978-1-59582-431-8 | $19.99

THE CROOKED MAN AND OTHERS
with Richard Corben
ISBN 978-1-59582-477-6 | $17.99

THE BRIDE OF HELL AND OTHERS
with Richard Corben, Kevin Nowlan, and Scott Hampton
ISBN 978-1-59582-740-1 | $19.99

THE STORM AND THE FURY
with Duncan Fegredo
ISBN 978-1-59582-827-9 | $19.99

HOUSE OF THE LIVING DEAD
with Richard Corben
ISBN 978-1-59582-757-9 | $14.99

THE MIDNIGHT CIRCUS
with Duncan Fegredo
ISBN 978-1-61655-238-1 | $14.99

INTO THE SILENT SEA
with Gary Gianni
ISBN 978-1-50670-143-1 | $14.99

HELLBOY IN MEXICO
with Richard Corben, Fábio Moon, Gabriel Bá, and others
ISBN 978-1-61655-897-0 | $19.99

HELLBOY IN HELL VOLUME 1: THE DESCENT
ISBN 978-1-61655-444-6 | $17.99

HELLBOY IN HELL VOLUME 2: THE DEATH CARD
ISBN 978-1-50670-113-4 | $17.99

HELLBOY: THE FIRST 20 YEARS
ISBN 978-1-61655-353-1 | $19.99

THE ART OF HELLBOY
ISBN 978-1-59307-089-2 | $29.99

GARY GIANNI'S MONSTERMEN AND OTHER SCARY STORIES
By Gary Gianni
ISBN 978-1-59582-829-3 | $24.99

HELLBOY II: THE ART OF THE MOVIE
ISBN 978-1-59307-964-2 | $24.99

HELLBOY: THE COMPANION
ISBN 978-1-59307-655-9 | $14.99

HELLBOY: WEIRD TALES
ISBN 978-1-61655-510-8 | $24.99

HELLBOY: MASKS AND MONSTERS
with James Robinson and Scott Benefiel
ISBN 978-1-59582-567-4 | $17.99

HELLBOY AND THE B.P.R.D: 1952
with John Arcudi and Alex Maleev
ISBN 978-1-61655-660-0 | $19.99

HELLBOY AND THE B.P.R.D: 1953
with Chris Roberson, Ben Stenbeck, Paolo Rivera, and Joe Rivera
ISBN 978-1-61655-967-0 | $19.99

THE HELLBOY 100 PROJECT
TPB: ISBN 978-1-61655-932-8 | $12.99
HC: ISBN 978-1-61655-933-5 | $24.99

NOVELS

HELLBOY: EMERALD HELL
By Tom Piccirilli
ISBN 978-1-59582-141-6 | $12.99

HELLBOY: THE ALL-SEEING EYE
By Mark Morris
ISBN 978-1-59582-142-3 | $12.99

HELLBOY: THE FIRE WOLVES
By Tim Lebbon
ISBN 978-1-59582-204-8 | $12.99

HELLBOY: THE ICE WOLVES
By Mark Chadbourn
ISBN 978-1-59582-205-5 | $12.99

AVAILABLE AT YOUR LOCAL COMICS SHOP OR BOOKSTORE! • To find a comics shop in your area, visit comicshoplocator.com.
For more information or to order direct visit DarkHorse.com or call 1-800-862-0052 Mon.–Fri. 9 AM to 5 PM Pacific Time.
Prices and availability subject to change without notice.

DARK HORSE BOOKS
DarkHorse.com

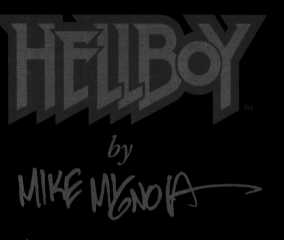

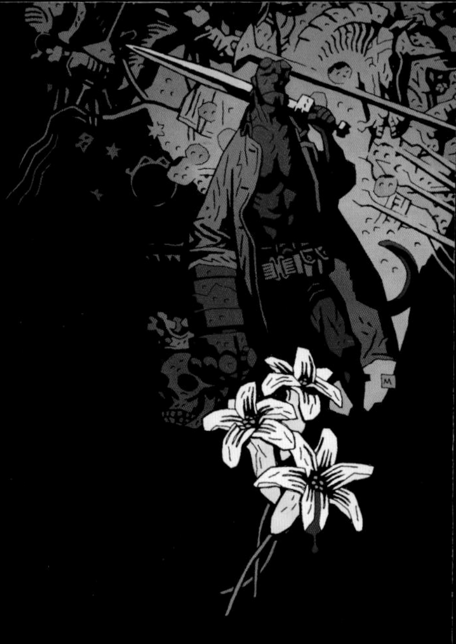